The Political Science Student Writer's Manual

Third Edition

Gregory M. Scott
Stephen M. Garrison
University of Central Oklahoma

Prentice Hall
Upper Saddle River, New Jersey 07458

Library of Congress Cataloging-in-Publication Data

Scott, Gregory M.
    The political science student writer's manual / Gregory M. Scott,
    Stephen M. Garrison.—3rd ed.
        p.   cm.
    Includes bibliographical references and index.
    ISBN 0-13-022558-4
    1. Political science—Authorship.   2. Political science—Research.
I. Garrison, Stephen M.   II. Title.
JA86.S39   2000
808'.06632—dc21   99-14484
                                                                CIP

Editorial Director: Charlyce Jones-Owen
Editor-in-Chief: Nancy Roberts
Senior Acquisitions Editor: Beth Ann Gillett
Editorial Assistant: Brian Prybella
Marketing Manager: Christopher DeJohn
Production Liaison: Fran Russello
Editorial/Production Supervision: Joseph Barron / P. M. Gordon Associates, Inc.
Copy Editor: Peter Reinhart

This book was set in 10/12 Baskerville by Stratford Publishing Services
and was printed and bound by R R Donnelly & Sons Company.
The cover was printed by Phoenix Color Corp.

Printed in the United States of America
10 9 8 7 6 5 4 3 2

ISBN 0-13-022558-4

Prentice-Hall International (UK) Limited, *London*
Prentice-Hall of Australia Pty. Limited, *Sydney*
Prentice-Hall of Canada, Inc., *Toronto*
Prentice-Hall Hispanoamericana, S.A., *Mexico*
Prentice-Hall of India Private Limited, *New Delhi*
Prentice-Hall of Japan, Inc., *Tokyo*
Pearson Education Asia Pte. Ltd., *Singapore*
Editora Prentice-Hall do Brasil, Ltda., *Rio de Janeiro*

To J. W. Peltason

Contents

PART TWO   Thinking Critically and Arguing Persuasively

PART THREE   Conducting Research in Political Science

PART FOUR   Writing Assignments for Students at All Levels

To the Student

This third edition of *The Political Science Student Writer's Manual* includes many additions and revisions that are necessary for keeping up to date in the constantly changing world of politics, political science, and information technology. Some things, however, never change. The basic goals we pursue as students of political science, for example, have remained constant since the days of Aristotle and Plato. Successful students, like successful political scientists, will always be competent writers. As students of politics we observe political institutions and behavior. We write to record what we observe, to explain what we record, and to defend what we explain. As citizens we write to take part in making decisions that direct our nation, our community, and our private lives. From the Declaration of Independence to the Emancipation Proclamation, from the United Nations Charter to President Kennedy's inaugural address, writing has brought us the freedom we enjoy today.

The Political Science Student Writer's Manual is designed to help you do two things: (1) improve your writing and (2) learn political science. These two objectives are addressed in the six major sections of this book. The Introduction tells you what political science is all about. Intended for both first-time and experienced political science students, the Introduction offers a basic historical orientation and a challenging account of current issues and analytical techniques.

Part One of the book addresses fundamental concerns of all writers. A vital concern throughout this part, and the rest of the book as well, is the three-way interrelationship among writer, topic, and audience. Our discussion of this relationship aims at building your self-confidence as you clarify your goals. Writing is not a magical process beyond the control of most people. It is instead a series of interconnected skills that any writer can improve with practice, and the end result of this practice is power. Part One of this manual treats the act of writing not as an empty exercise undertaken only to produce a grade but as a powerful learning tool, as well as the primary medium by which political scientists accomplish their goals. Chapter 1 explores the reasons why we write and examines the writing process itself. Chapter 2 examines those elements of grammar, punctuation, and style that cause the most confusion among writers. Chapter 3 explains the importance of formatting the research paper properly and supplies you with format models for title pages, tables of contents, and so on. Chapter 4 explains how to cite sources and discusses the crucial responsibility of every political science writer to use source material ethically.

Part Two of this manual is new to the third edition. Chapters 5 and 6 explain how to think critically about politics, construct an effective argument using valid logic, and avoid common fallacies.

Part Three of the manual focuses on research. Chapter 7, the first chapter in this part, describes the research process in detail, explaining how you can maintain self-confidence by establishing control over your project. Chapter 8 lists and describes major sources of information for political science researchers. The first section of this chapter provides examples of guides to information in your college library. The subsequent sections list Internet resources that will help you write well and also find immense amounts of information about politics, government, and political science.

The nine chapters in Parts Four, Five, and Six explain different types of papers common to political science classes. Each chapter begins by exploring the purposes and characteristics of the paper covered. Next, the steps for writing a successful paper are spelled out, and typical formats are provided. Each chapter encourages you to use your imagination and resourcefulness in confronting the paper's requirements. The chapters in Part Four explain writing assignments for students at all levels of college work; Parts Five and Six provide directions for papers for introductory and advanced students, respectively.

Your professor may give you a specific paper assignment from one of these chapters. If your professor does not make your assignment specific, you may want to select an assignment and discuss your selection with your instructor before proceeding.

This manual is a reference book. It has been written to help you become a better writer than you are now. We wish you all success as you accept a primary challenge of academic and professional life: to write, and write well.

Greg Scott and Steve Garrison

To the Teacher

This book has been updated and improved to help you deal with two problems commonly faced by teachers of political science. First, students often need substantial specific direction to produce a good paper. How many times have you assigned papers in your political science classes and found yourself teaching the class *how to write the paper*—not only content, but form and grammar as well? This text, which may accompany the primary text you assign in any political science class or may stand on its own, allows you to assign one of the papers explained in Parts Four, Five, and Six with the knowledge that virtually everything the student needs to know, from grammar to sources of information to citing sources, is here within one book. In addition to many updated examples throughout the text, the third edition features an entirely new Part Two—"Thinking Critically and Arguing Persuasively"—which contains the following chapters:

Chapter 5   Principles of Argument
Chapter 6   Avoiding Fallacies

Chapter 8 has been substantially revised to provide your students with lists of some of the best Internet resources for writing, politics, government, and political science. As in the second edition, you can direct your students, for example, to "write a position paper according to the directions in Chapter 12, and follow the instructions in Parts One and Two for formatting, grammar, and source citations." Almost every question a student could ask about the paper is answered in this book, but you will be able to supplement your assignment with special instructions.

This manual combines the latest political science research and writing techniques with a broad spectrum of writing activities, based on a total of twenty-seven years of experience teaching political science and English. Chapter 12, "Position Papers," provides directions for a writing assignment for beginning students that deserves special attention. Position papers are exercises in logic and problem solving. Whereas other writing assignments in this manual allow the student much flexibility in the writing process, position paper directions follow a precise formula that has proven to be successful in government, business, academic, and professional presentations throughout the United States. By completing a position paper, your students will learn to become competent problem solvers, thereby developing skills helpful in every profession. In addition, position papers require your students to actually visit government offices to experience firsthand the operations of government.

Some of the chapters are especially suited to specific upper-division courses:

Chapter 13   Political Analysis Papers
Chapter 14   Policy Analysis Papers
Chapter 15   Administrative Case Studies
Chapter 16   Case Briefs in Constitutional and International Law
Chapter 17   Public Opinion Survey Papers

As you know, writing skill is essential not only to becoming an effective citizen, but to becoming a success in any profession as well. This book was written to assist you in leading students toward that success. But gaining that success, as you probably know well, is not easy.

The second major problem faced by teachers who require written assignments is plagiarism. Although only the most exceptional diligence will eliminate plagiarism entirely, this book will help you to take one of the most effective preventive actions. In an age when whole papers can be downloaded from the Internet, one of the best ways to ensure an original paper is to make your assignment directions very specific. If your direction to students is "Write something on the First Amendment," it is relatively easy for a student to find a paper already prepared. If, however, you provide a very specific list of instructions, such as those in the chapters in this book, students who might otherwise be tempted to submit work that is not their own will find that it does not meet the requirements of the assignment.

We wish you the best in your endeavors and welcome your comments.

Greg Scott and Steve Garrison

Introduction:
The Discipline of Political Science

Is political science new to you?

If you are about to write your first paper in political science, this Introduction is for you. To write a political science paper, you need to know something about political science, and this section provides a brief overview of the discipline. Reading this Introduction will help you understand what political science is all about and what political scientists are trying to achieve when they write—knowledge that will save you time, effort, and confusion. You may want to read other books about political science before you begin to write, but some of the most important information you will need is right here.

Are you an experienced student of political science who needs to review trends in the discipline?

If you have already studied political science in some detail, you may want to skip this Introduction and read Chapters 1 through 10, which discuss writing and research in general, and then the chapter in Part Four, Five, or Six that provides the directions for the specific type of paper you have been assigned. You may find, however, that this Introduction helps to refresh your memory and establish your current writing efforts more firmly within the broader framework of the discipline. Wherever you may be in your progress toward mastering the methods and contributing to the rich tradition of political science, you are encouraged to read this section.

A Brief History

The story of politics and political science is the story of the human race. Politics began when the first people, experiencing themselves as different individuals, tried to find a way to get along. *Political science* began when these people, finding it difficult to live with one another, started to consider how they behaved when they acted together and how they might create a more satisfying and harmonious community. Many of the greatest documents in history have been written by political scientists, and the age in which we now live has been shaped by people in times, places, and cultures that seem, on the surface, very different from our own. A brief look at some of these writers and their achievements will help you see the vital social connections that link us to all times and cultures. It also will provide you with a sense of the depth and breadth of the study of politics so that, when you write about politics, you will do so creatively and knowledgeably.

Ancient Students of Politics

In 431 B.C., Pericles, Athenian democrat par excellence, general, orator, and primary catalyst of the explosion of creativity known as the Golden Age of Athens, stood thoughtfully before the tomb that had been prepared for the soldiers and sailors recently lost to the Spartans in the Peloponnesian War. Ascending from the tomb to a platform built on the burial ground, Pericles turned to address an expectant citizenry. He faced a dispirited crowd. Mourning those lost in battle against Sparta's fierce battalions, the Athenians were more anxious still about the plague that would soon claim even their courageous leader. Silently anticipating the words that would renew their vision of their historic destiny, they hoped to go forth refortified to face the perils yet to come. Meeting their gaze with words from the heart, Pericles engraved with a verbal chisel the indelible imprint of the Athenian mind on the pages of history. His description of democracy, spoken as part of a funeral oration twenty-four centuries ago, is remarkable because it sounds as if it could have been given by any British prime minister or U.S. president today:

> Let me say that our system of government does not copy the institutions of our neighbors. It is more the case of our being a model to others, than of our imitating anyone else. Our constitution is called a democracy because power is in the hands not of a minority but of the whole people. When it is a question of settling private disputes, everyone is equal before the law; when it is a question of putting one person before another in positions of public responsibility, what counts is not membership of a particular class, but the actual ability which the man possesses. No one, so long as he has it in him to be of service to the state, is kept in political obscurity because of poverty. And, just as our political life is free and open, so is our day-to-day life in our relations with each other. We do not get into a state with our next-door neighbor if he enjoys himself in his own way, nor do we give him the kind of black looks which, though they do no real harm, still do hurt people's feelings. We are free and tolerant in our private lives; but in public affairs we keep to the law. This is

because it commands our deepest respect. (Thucydides. 1986. *History of the Peloponnesian War.* Translated by Rex Warner. Harmondsworth: Penguin. 145.)

What does political science study?

From Pericles we learn *what* we experience as political beings and *what* we study as students of politics. He reminds us that the air we breathe is filled with the stuff of politics: influence, persuasion, coercion, debate, competition, cooperation, advantage, antagonism, altruism, generosity, and strife. Political science studies the ways in which these human behaviors create and are in turn shaped by individuals, groups, and the institutions of government. Pericles makes it clear that our innermost aspirations impel us, as students and participants, to grasp the fervor of political life with energy and enthusiasm, entering the world of politics with a natural affinity, or, as Aristotle would later say, like "political animals."

The greatest philosophical enemy of democracy who ever lived was probably listening to Pericles with the rest of the crowd. This short, balding gadfly named Socrates called himself a philosopher, literally a lover (*philo*) of wisdom (*sophia*). Mocking Pericles and other Athenian democrats, he told a story in which he compared them to hypothetical cave dwellers who were chained together by the neck so that they could see only what was in front of them. Behind these cave dwellers, hidden from their view, were people who manipulated marionettes in front of a fire, so that the shadows reflected on a wall in front of the chained people. To Socrates the democracy of Athens was like this cave—a world of illusions created by great manipulators (the democratic orators of Athens). The citizens of Athens knew no more of reality than the cave dwellers, who could see only the shadows dancing on the darkened wall. Socrates wanted to rescue these democrats from ignorance by providing them with a philosopher-king. This ruler would be a lover of wisdom who would have a superior understanding of the art of governing and would make wise decisions. As Americans, we would have counted ourselves among the democrats. We would have rejected Socrates' offer because, as Athenian democrats, we would have found it essential to our dignity as human beings to choose our own political fate. Even if someone wiser could make better choices for us, we would still have preferred to make mistakes of our own choosing than to walk a more assured path under the direction of someone else.

Why should we study politics?

Socrates did, nevertheless, give something to those of us who call ourselves political scientists by answering one of the fundamental questions of political science: *Why* should we study politics? Socrates enjoyed proclaiming that "the unexamined life is not worth living." This thought is the psychological engine that drives political science and indeed all science. For us as political scientists, the unexamined political life is certainly impoverished, if still worth living, so we examine politics in both large ways and small, from every conceivable angle.

How should we study politics?

We know of Socrates' ideas mainly because his student Plato formed them into dialogues in which Socrates is the main speaker. Plato also had a most famous student, Aristotle, who is called the father of political science because he provides, in the *Politics,* an answer to the question, *How* should we study politics?

As opposed to Plato, who searched for the ideal form of government through the use of reason, Aristotle based his research method on the observation of political life in all its varieties. He examined political behavior. He reviewed the constitutions and histories of about 350 of the Greek city-states (*polis*), grouped them into categories, and drew conclusions from his observations. He formulated the rudiments of the scientific method and applied them to the political institutions of his day. Aristotle considered political science to be the highest of all intellectual pursuits because its aim was to achieve life's highest goal: the virtuous society.

As we review the contributions of the greatest thinkers in the ancient tradition that has become the modern discipline of political science, we find many others who have sought answers to the fundamental questions of the field. Cicero, a Roman statesman who recorded political thought a century before the birth of Christ, might deserve to have his picture on our one-dollar bill because his ideas were so influential in shaping the government of the United States. Following a course set by Aristotle, Cicero compared governments ruled by one, by a few, and by many. When they operated in the interest of all the people, Aristotle called these governments, respectively, *monarchies, aristocracies,* and *polities.* He reserved the word democracy for regimes that ruled in the interest of the most numerous and lower classes only. Cicero found that none of these forms worked well by itself and preferred a combination of the three that he called *mixed government.*

If you read the Constitution of the United States of America, you will find that it creates a mixed government. It has elements of polity (democracy), in that citizens have many opportunities to participate, they vote to elect their representatives, and they enjoy a wide range of rights. There are also some elements of aristocracy in American government. Supreme Court justices, for example, are appointed by the president and serve life terms. The Senate was originally elected by the state legislatures. Other aspects of our government tend to make it look like a monarchy. The president receives ambassadors from other nations in elaborate formal ceremonies and has prerogatives, such as a private jumbo jet, that would be the envy of any king.

Revelation and Politics in the Medieval Period

During the centuries following Cicero, the teachings of Christ unsettled the political world. Periodic official persecution of Christians ended in 325, when the Emperor Constantine announced his conversion to Christianity. The conversion did not impede the fall of his empire, however, and in 410, when Alaric and his Goths stormed Rome, Christianity was blamed. It was said that Christians, who obeyed God rather than the state, were not good citizens and that the empire had been weakened by their focus on another world. In the midst of this chaos, a bishop in the city of Hippo in North Africa wrote a political defense of Christianity. In his lengthy work *The City of God,* Saint Augustine said that good Christians are citizens of the City of God and therefore participate in a rich spiritual life that frees them from the temptations of sin. They also, however, must live and work as responsible citizens of the City of This World. Christian citizens thus fulfill their lives here as well as in the spiritual realm. Making sense of politics in this world requires that we make practical use of what we learn about politics in everyday life.

Where should we look for answers to the problems of politics?

In exploring these issues, Saint Augustine helped to answer the question, *Where* should we look for answers to the problems of politics? He found the answer in the Bible. Today we find the answer in many places, such as in understanding the way people vote, in forming a picture of the whole political system, and in looking at how nations relate to one another.

At the turn of the year 1000, faced with despair over constant feudal wars and intermittent waves of plague, western Europeans turned hopefully to biblical revelation, which spoke of the passing of a millennium (one thousand years) before the return of Christ. Marching to the hilltops to await his return and leaving in disappointment when he did not appear, the faithful sought reasons to retain their faith. Saint Thomas Aquinas, in the thirteenth century, came up with some of them. He became the hero of the medieval church after writing in his voluminous *Summa Theologica* that God has given humanity two compatible sources of knowledge—reason and revelation—with reason helping us to know when to apply the varied particular elements of revelation. Using the newly rediscovered methods of Aristotle, Aquinas had developed a church doctrine that affirmed revelation and reason at the same time. Reason, he said, tells us that the church should exercise its proper authority over the population, an authority superior to that of secular governments.

When should different means of gaining knowledge be used in studying politics?

In attempting to answer the question, *When* should different means of gaining knowledge be used in studying politics? Saint Thomas Aquinas helped advance the progress of political science.

Political Science in the Modern Period

The beginning of modern political science is most often identified with the writings of Niccolò Machiavelli. Writing just after the voyages of Columbus, this exiled Florentine administrator produced his most famous work, *The Prince,* for Lorenzo de Medici in the hope that the ruler would restore him to his position of influence in Florence. Unlike political writers before him, Machiavelli was not interested in defining the best state. *The Prince* offered Lorenzo cold, hard, and practical advice on how to stay in power. Machiavelli marked an important turning point in the history of political science, as the study of politics began to turn from questions of What *ought* to be? to What *is?*

A century and a half later, looking out upon the bloody religious English Civil War of the 1640s, Thomas Hobbes wrote that human life is "solitary, poore, nasty, brutish, and short." (Thomas Hobbes, 1968. *Leviathan*. Edited and with an Introduction by C. B. Macpherson. Harmondsworth: Penguin. 186.) His response to this condition was the creation of an all-powerful ruler, a *Leviathan* (as he entitled his book of 1651), to whom all rights would be given by a populace in return for securing order in a chaotic world. Hobbes thus popularized the idea of social contract to a despondent English audience. Government, said Hobbes, derives its legitimate authority not from God, as the thinkers of the Middle Ages had argued, but from the consent of individuals who agree together to follow certain rules. They formulate these rules into a social contract, or a constitution, that provides the foundation for order in society.

John Locke took the social contract theory one step further. He wrote his second *Treatise on Government* to justify the peaceful English Revolution of 1688, in which the power of Parliament was increased at the cost of the power of the king, without the shedding of blood. Seeing more potential for human freedom in the social contract than had Hobbes, Locke advocated a constitution that would protect the natural right of every citizen to life, liberty, and property. Thomas Jefferson relied heavily on the writings of Locke, as a well-respected champion of democratic rights, to justify the American Revolution.

The founders of the United States also drew substantially from the thoughts of the French noble Montesquieu, whose writings epitomize the state of political science in the eighteenth century. In his *Spirit of the Laws* (1748), he examined governments, both ancient and modern, in an attempt to extract principles of good government. James Madison accepted Montesquieu's views on at least two important points. The first was that the structure of a government is important to its success. Others had believed that the form of a government did not matter as long as it was run by good people. Montesquieu and Madison resolutely rejected this idea. The second view was the necessity of a division of powers among different groups of people. The concentration of power in the hands of any particular group, thought Montesquieu and Madison, always leads to tyranny.

While political science in England and France focused on means of constructing viable democratic constitutions, political science in Germany was taking a different turn. Georg W. F. Hegel, teaching in the early nineteenth century in Berlin, developed the idea of the preeminence of the state in history. In his *Philosophy of*

Right, he argued that the state was the realization of the ethical idea in history. Hegel believed that a spiritual force, which manifests itself on earth most completely in the form of the state, is guiding history, particularly that of the German state. The aim of political science for Hegel was to understand this historical movement, which he said progressed in a dialectical pattern. By this he meant that the first regime that ruled any state would eventually, through its inability to overcome increasingly obvious deficiencies, be overcome by another regime that would in turn eventually be overcome by a third form of political rule. Eventually, through this process, the state would be perfected. Hegel believed he had discovered in his dialectic the key internal principle of political science. (Georg Wilhelm Friedrich Hegel. 1967. *Philosophy of Right.* Translated by J. M. Knox. Oxford: Clarendon Press. 155.)

Hegel's influence on history has been felt largely through someone who thoroughly studied and then altered his theories, Karl Marx, who transformed Hegel's spiritual dialectic into dialectical materialism. Marx believed that economics, not a spiritual force, is the key to history. The dialectical process of history, he asserted, is seen most clearly in the evolution of economic systems. Feudalism was rule by the aristocracy, the privileged few. It was overturned by the middle class (the bourgeoisie), which gained its strength through commerce and capitalism in the major trading cities of Europe at the end of the Middle Ages. Marx predicted that in time the lower classes (the proletariat) would naturally overthrow the middle class, just as the middle class had overthrown the upper class. He insisted that he was the first realist of history, claiming that he did not prescribe the way things should be but simply described the way things really are. In his *Manifesto of the Communist Party* (1848), however, Marx called upon the workers of the world to do what he expected would eventually happen: unite to throw off capitalist exploitation:

> A specter is haunting Europe—the specter of communism. All the powers of Old Europe have entered into a holy alliance to exorcise this specter: Pope and Czar, Metternich and Guizot, French Radicals and German police spies. . . . The history of all hitherto existing society is the history of class struggles. Free man and slave, patrician and plebeian, lord and serf, guild master and journeyman, in a word, oppressor and oppressed, stood in constant opposition to one another, carried on an uninterrupted, now hidden, now open fight, a fight that each time ended either in a revolutionary reconstitution of society at large or in the common ruin of the contending classes. . . . The modern bourgeois society that has sprouted from the ruins of feudal society has not done away with class antagonisms. It has but established new classes, new conditions of oppression, new forms of struggle in the place of old ones. . . . Society as a whole is more and more splitting into hostile camps, into two great classes directly facing each other: bourgeoisie and proletariat. . . . The bourgeoisie has stripped of its halo every occupation hitherto honored and looked up to with reverent awe. It has converted the physician, the lawyer, the priest, the poet, the man of science into its paid wage laborers. The bourgeoisie has torn away from the family its sentimental veil, and has reduced the family relation to a mere money relation. . . . The weapons with which the bourgeoisie felled feudalism to the ground are now

turned against the bourgeoisie itself. . . . It has also called into existence the men who are to wield those weapons—the modern working class—the proletarians. . . . These laborers, who must sell themselves piecemeal, are a commodity, like every other article of commerce, and are consequently exposed to all the vicissitudes of competition, to all the fluctuations of the market. . . . The distinguishing feature of communism is not the abolition of property generally, but the abolition of bourgeois property. . . . You are horrified at our intending to do away with private property. But in your existing society private property is already done away with for nine tenths of the population; its existence for the few is solely due to its nonexistence in the hands of the nine tenths. Communism deprives no man of the power to appropriate the products of society; all that it does is to deprive him of the power to subjugate the labor of others by means of such appropriation. . . . In short, the communists everywhere support every revolutionary movement against the existing social and political order of things. . . . They openly declare that their ends can be attained only by the forcible overthrow of all existing social conditions. Let the ruling classes tremble at a communistic revolution. The proletarians have nothing to lose but their chains. They have a world to win.
     WORKINGMEN OF ALL COUNTRIES, UNITE!
(Karl Marx and Friedrich Engels. 1965. "Manifesto of the Communist Party." In *Marx & Engels: Basic Writings on Politics and Philosophy*. Edited by Lewis S. Feuer. New York: Anchor. 6–29.)

Meanwhile, back in Great Britain and France, political science was taking another turn. In Britain, utilitarians built a "calculus" of utility in which the policies of government were formulated in such a way as to create the greatest good for the greatest number. John Stuart Mill, whose father James Mill had been a founder of the utilitarian movement, established the study of political economy, which adopted principles known today as traditional liberalism. Traditional liberalism is only partly similar to what is now called "liberal." In the nineteenth century it held that political liberty, especially freedom of speech, should be combined with economic freedom, meaning a lack of government control over business and industry. The only basis for restricting freedom, according to John Stuart Mill, was the likelihood of harm to others. According to the liberal tradition, political science had as its purpose the development of knowledge that would help perfect government under utilitarian principles.

A Century of American Political Science, 1880–1980

Before 1880, the academic study of politics was carried on mainly in Europe, within the disciplines of history and economics. In 1876 a graduate program in social sciences was formed at Johns Hopkins University, and in 1880, John Burgess, professor of political science and law, established the first American graduate program in political science at Columbia College. Before this time, Americans had had to travel to Europe, especially to Germany, to earn graduate degrees. From their earliest days, American political science programs, following the German model, have placed strong emphasis on faculty research and publication. Advancement in the profession, at least in the leading universities in the

United States, is still tied more to scholarship than to the quality of teaching. The *Political Science Quarterly,* the first American academic journal in political science, issued its first edition in 1888 to provide political scientists with an opportunity to publish their research and to comment on public events of the day. The American Political Science Association (APSA) was organized at Tulane University in New Orleans in 1903 to promote the study of politics in the United States and to provide a forum for the exchange of ideas. The creation of the APSA helped to establish political science as a discipline independent of history and economics. *The American Political Science Review (APSR),* its official journal, began publication in November 1906. From these origins the field has grown to the point that there are 117 political science departments in the United States that grant a Ph.D. Dozens of journals now publish articles written by political scientists in the hundreds of undergraduate and graduate departments across the country.

During the twentieth century, the discipline has perceived itself as having three major roles in society: (1) providing information about politics through research; (2) educating the citizenry on the practices and principles of government; and (3) helping to develop sound public policies. However, two major interwoven controversies have divided the profession from its inception. The first is the division between traditionalism (normative, historical, or institutional) on one side and scientific (empirical or behavioral) studies on the other. The second controversy is between idealism and realism.

Traditionalism versus Behavioralism

As mentioned earlier, the first political science programs in the United States were heavily influenced by the German model, which emphasized comparative studies, history, economics, and law. Following this German model, the traditional approach to political science is grounded on describing institutions of government and evaluating their effects on the political process. The goal is to understand the way government works in order to improve it. Traditionalism therefore combines an interest in description with a desire to prescribe changes in government and administration.

In the last two decades of the nineteenth century, this approach was increasingly challenged by scientism, which looked for ways to use the methods of the natural sciences to study politics. Scientism was based on the philosophy of science known as positivism, whose basic premise is that scientific knowledge should be derived solely from positive data—that is, from information gained by observing phenomena with our senses. Positive data in political science include such items as the physical boundaries of a country, the number of registered voters, and the party identification of the members of the legislature. Although positivism traces its roots to the nineteenth-century French philosopher Auguste Comte, A. J. Ayer is a more contemporary proponent. Ayer said that value-oriented statements are not verifiable and that statements that express values, such as "Developing nations ought to adopt democratic procedures" or "Dictators are evil," tell us nothing and therefore are nonsense. Statements that purport to describe reality, however, are positive and may be verified or refuted by observation.

Examples of positive statements are "A majority of voters in New York are Democrats" and "Candidates who spend more money than their opponents are more likely to win."

Much controversy developed over the application of traditional versus scientific methods to politics. In the early twentieth century, Woodrow Wilson, who would become president of the American Political Science Association as well as president of the United States, argued that the fundamentals of political science must be based on actual observations of political processes rather than on deductively devised philosophies of good government. Many other political scientists, following Wilson's lead, have attempted to move the discipline away from the traditional approach in favor of scientific methods. One of the first of these scientific innovators was Charles Merriam, who in the 1920s started a movement for a New Science of Politics, which advocated the use of statistical and psychological methods to search systematically for solutions to social problems. Another important researcher of the 1920s, G. E. G. Catlin, used economics as his model to assert that political science observes political phenomena scientifically and is therefore necessarily value-free.

A Noted Traditionalist: Edwin S. Corwin

One of the most famous examples of traditional political science is Edwin S. Corwin's *The Constitution and What It Means Today* (1920). Corwin was troubled by the ethical neutrality of behavioral studies and believed that political science must always provide information that society can use to improve government policies and services. His treatment of the Constitution is typically traditional in that it focuses on the history, politics, and policies of a government institution (in this case, the Supreme Court) and evaluates the trends it finds in that institution's development in terms of its influence on society. In his preface to his book's eleventh edition, published in 1954, Corwin defends his findings in spite of behavioral criticisms of his methods:

> Although *The Constitution and What It Means Today* utilizes now and then other materials . . . [the] general design and method of treatment which were adopted early in the evolution of *The Constitution and What It Means Today* are, nevertheless, still adhered to. I have endeavored, especially in connection with such important subjects as judicial review, the commerce clause, executive power, the war power, national supremacy, freedom of speech, press and religion, etc., to accompany explanation of currently prevailing doctrine and practice with a brief summation of the historical development thereof. The serviceability of history to make the present more understandable has been remarked upon by writers from Aristotle to the late Samuel Butler, famed author of *Erewhon* and *The Way of All Flesh;* and the idea is particularly pertinent to legal ideas and institutions. (Edwin S. Corwin. 1954. *The Constitution and What It Means Today*. Princeton, N.J.: Princeton University Press. v.)

After World War II, the scientific movement emerged as behavioralism, which is based on the belief that political science may be constructed as an empirical, value-free social science. According to behavioralists, instead of describing what government *should* do, political science ought to seek to predict political phenomena by making quantifiable observations in studies that test hypotheses according to methods developed in political science and other social sciences. David Truman's *The Governmental Process* (1951) exemplified the behavioral approach by using empirical methods and focusing on the behavior of individuals and groups in the political process. Throughout the 1950s and 1960s, behaviorists gained many leadership positions in the profession. In 1961 one of the leaders, Robert A. Dahl, said that he believed that behavioralism as a movement would fade away not because it had failed but because it would be so successful that it would soon be integrated into the discipline as a normally accepted approach:

> The empirical political scientist is concerned with what is, as he says, not with what ought to be. Hence, he finds it difficult and uncongenial to assume the historic burden of the political philosopher who attempted to determine, prescribe, elaborate and employ ethical standards—values, to use the fashionable term—in appraising political acts and political systems. The behaviorally minded student is prepared to describe values as empirical data; but, qua "scientist" he seeks to avoid prescription or inquiry into the grounds on which judgments of value can properly be made. (Robert A. Dahl. 1961. "The Behavioral Approach in Political Science: Epitaph for a Monument to a Successful Protest." *American Political Science Review* 55:771.)

Some traditionalists have reacted against the scientific approach. In 1928, William Elliot, for example, claimed that, because politics is infinitely complex, is composed of many variables, and is based on the independent actions of individuals, a "science" of politics that copies the physical sciences is impossible. He applauded the practitioners of the scientific approach for their attempt to develop objective criteria by which to measure political phenomena but believed the results of their studies fell far short of their intentions. His sharpest criticism of the scientific movement was his belief that political science should never give up its traditional concern for developing public policy and for trying to find the true and beneficial goals of government.

The next generation of critics of the scientific approach attacked behavioralism. A leading example is University of Chicago professor of political science Hans J. Morgenthau. In *Scientific Man versus Power Politics,* he discussed the failure of the scientific approach to solve the problems of American foreign policy. Other critics, such as Christian Bay, declared that behavioralism asks the wrong questions. Because politics is about power, rule, and authority, political science should address conceptions of human welfare and the common good.

Idealism versus Realism

The second major division within political science has been between idealists and realists. Disturbed by the horrifying destructiveness of the machine gun, tanks, submarines, and artillery in World War I, idealists such as Woodrow Wilson believed that improvements in military technology would soon result in global

destruction if an alternative to wars were not found. Through international organizations like the League of Nations, the idealists hoped to find new ways to promote global cooperation. These efforts between the two world wars were not
successful, however, and immediately after World War II, the realists emerged to
place new emphasis on the idea that power politics is an intrinsic part of relations
among nations and that idealism is harmful because it leads to faulty judgments
about what action should be taken to maintain peace in the world.

In his widely read *Politics among Nations,* the political realist Hans Morgenthau defined the idealist-realist controversy:

> The history of modern political thought is the story of a contest between two
> schools that differ fundamentally in their conceptions of the nature of man,
> society, and politics. One [the idealist school] believes that a rational and
> moral political order, derived from universally valid abstract principles, can
> be achieved here and now. It assumes the essential goodness and infinite mal-
> leability of human nature, and blames the failure of the social order to mea-
> sure up to the rational standards on lack of knowledge and understanding,
> obsolescent social institutions, or the depravity of certain isolated individuals
> or groups. It trusts in education, reform, and the sporadic use of force to rem-
> edy these defects.
>
>   The other [realist] school believes that the world, imperfect as it is
> from the rational point of view, is the result of forces inherent in human
> nature. To improve the world one must work with those forces, not against
> them. This being inherently a world of opposing interests and of conflict
> among them, moral principles can never be fully realized, but must be at least
> approximated through the ever temporary balancing of interests and the ever
> precarious settlement of conflicts. This school, then, sees in a system of
> checks and balances a universal principle for all pluralist societies. It appeals
> to historic precedent rather than to abstract principles, and aims at the real-
> ization of the lesser evil rather than the absolute good. (Hans J. Morgenthau
> and Kenneth W. Thompson. 1985. *Politics among Nations: The Struggle for Power
> and Peace.* 6th ed. New York: Knopf. 3–4.)

Morgenthau stressed that nation-states act as autonomous units in ways designed
to promote their own national interests. He argued that the United States should
actively further its own interest by building a strong military capable of fending
off the aggressions of the Soviet Union.

Since the 1970s, critics of realism have affected the thought of its foremost
proponents. For example, the neorealism advocated by Joseph Nye at Harvard
University proposes modifying the realist paradigm by integrating new developments in international economics, such as the spread of multinational corporations, into the framework of sovereign nation-states. These developments have
resulted in political scientists' viewing the international system as more complex
and interdependent than Morgenthau's model indicates.

The controversies between behavioralism versus traditionalism and realism
versus idealism continue today. Realists and behavioralists have dominated international political science since 1950, but both continue to change and respond
to the renewed vitality of their academic opponents.

Marxism

Before ending this overview of the first century of American political science, more needs to be said about Marxism. Since the fall of the Berlin Wall and the collapse of the Soviet empire in the late 1980s and 1990s, Marxism has been viewed as a much less formidable political force than it was once thought to be. It has always been, and continues to be, however, more than the discarded ideology of a block of nations. Marxism is not only a social and economic philosophy, but also a school of political science. Marxist interpretations of political events have been discussed across continents because Marxists consider political phenomena in categories of thought that are of perennial interest.

Marxism, as political science, sees all political action as occurring within the context of class conflict. Marxists view politics as a continuous struggle of the wealthy against the poor. Political science is not neutral. It exists for the purpose of understanding the class struggle so that it may be won by the oppressed lower classes. Although American traditionalists find Marxist predictions of the eventual triumph of the working class to be false, Marxism may continue to have influential support if it finds new ways to continue to focus on inequality in society and abandons the rigidity of some of its outmoded economic concepts. In fact, the person who had the greatest influence on the American Constitution, James Madison, also believed that class antagonism was of primary concern to those who build new nations.

Class Conflict in James Madison's Federalist No. 10

The conflict between rich and poor in the struggle for wealth has always been a primary concern for political writers. James Madison, who became the fourth president of the United States, is often credited with having had more influence on the content of the U.S. Constitution than any other individual. Along with Alexander Hamilton and John Jay, in 1787–1788 Madison wrote a series of newspaper articles intended to persuade the electorate in the thirteen states to ratify the newly written Constitution. These articles, which together became known as *The Federalist Papers,* are regarded by some as the most important documents in the history of American political thought. In the following excerpt, Madison explains that the ability to avoid violent conflict between rich and poor is one of the most important benefits that a constitution can provide. A fierce and bloody revolution like the one then beginning in France was exactly what Madison hoped to avoid.

> Among the advantages promised by a well-constructed Union, none deserves to be more accurately developed than its tendency to break and control the violence of faction. . . . By faction I understand a number of citizens, whether amounting to a majority or a minority of the whole who are united and actuated by some common impulse of passion, or of interest, adverse to the rights of other citizens, or to the permanent and aggregate interest of the community. . . . The latent causes of faction are thus sown in the nature of man. . . . But the most common and durable source of factions has been the various

and unequal distribution of property. . . . Those who hold and those who are without property have ever formed distinct interests in society. (James Madison, Alexander Hamilton, and John Jay. 1961. *The Federalist Papers.* Introduction by Clinton Rossiter. New York: New American Library/Mentor. 77–84.)

In *Federalist 10,* Madison writes that one of the greatest benefits of a constitution is its ability to "break and control the violence of faction" that arises from the two constantly competing classes of rich and poor. Marxism, again, may continue to have a place in international discussions of politics if it finds new ways to understand and address class struggle and to unfold a vision of a better life for the millions who are deprived and oppressed.

The Power of Language

The great political thinkers of the past are read today not only because of the quality of their ideas but also because of their ability to communicate *clearly* and *powerfully.* As you read the other chapters in this manual, keep in mind that historians regard Abraham Lincoln as the greatest American president at least in part because his words are both compassionate and compelling. On page 15, note the tribute paid by the English to Lincoln's command of the language in the letter that hangs on the walls of Brasenose College, Oxford University.

An Eclectic Discipline: Political Science Today

The greatest failure of political science in the twentieth century is its inability to identify a common methodology, a common approach to the study of politics. Economics, history, and psychology all contain many schools of thought, yet there is far greater agreement on the value and proper use of basic methodological tools within these disciplines than in political science. Although many political scientists have attempted to reach such an agreement, thus far they have failed. In his *Invisible Government* of 1927, William Munro proposed that the discipline direct itself to the discovery of the "fundamental laws" of political behavior, which then could be applied to solve problems of government and administration. (William Munro. 1928. *The Invisible Government.* New York: Macmillan.) Finding such laws has become so difficult, however, that the search is no longer the central concern of the discipline. If there is any accepted approach to the study of politics today, it is best called "eclectic." That is, political scientists use a variety of tools and methods, and borrow insights from many approaches and disciplines in order to carry on their studies.

Subfields and Recent Developments in the Study of Politics

Political science today hosts many specialties. Political scientists study different nations of the world and many aspects of the American political system; they borrow techniques from the other social sciences. Political science in the United

Executive Mansion
Washington, Nov 21. 1864

To Mrs Bixby,   Boston,   Mass,

      Dear Madam.

             I have been shown in the files of the War Department a statement of the Adjutant General of Massachusetts that you are the mother of five sons who have died gloriously on the field of battle I feel how weak and fruitless must 'be any word of mine which should attempt to beguile you from the grief of a loss so overwhelming But I cannot refrain from tendering you the consolation that may be found in the thanks of the republic they died to save I pray that our Heavenly Father may assuage the anguish of your bereavement, and leave you only the cherished memory of the loved and lost, and the solemn pride that must be yours to have laid so costly a sacrifice upon the altar of freedom

             Yours very sincerely and respectfully

                    A. Lincoln

On the walls of Brasenose College, Oxford University, England, this letter of the "rail-splitter" president hangs as a model of purest English, rarely, if ever, surpassed.

States is organized by the American Political Science Association, which encompasses a number of regional and state associations that hold annual meetings at which papers are presented and discussions are held. In this subsection we present a list of "sections" of the American Political Science Association. Sections are groups within the association organized to study a specific topic such as the American presidency or religion and politics. Looking at the list of sections you can get an idea of the diversity of topics studied within the discipline of political science.

Broadly speaking, the study of political science in the United States is divided into four major areas:

- Political theory and methodology
- American government, political behavior, public policy, and administration
- Comparative politics and area studies
- International relations

Many scholars of international relations present their research at the meetings of the International Studies Association as well as at the meetings of the American Political Science Association. The ninety-fifth annual meeting of the American Political Science Association, held in Atlanta, Georgia, on September 2 to 5, 1999, focused on the theme "Political Science and the World of Politics and Policy: Contribution and Impact." The meeting featured more than seven hundred panel sessions in which hundreds of papers were discussed by more than 6,500 members, exhibitors, and guests. Panels are arranged by people in forty-three formal program divisions, which are presented in the following list to give you an idea of the range and breadth of contemporary political science:

1. Political Thought and Philosophy: Historical Approaches
2. Foundations of Political Theory
3. Normative Political Theory
4. Formal Political Theory
5. Political Psychology
6. Political Economy
7. Politics and History
8. Political Methodology
9. Teaching and Learning in Political Science
10. Undergraduate Education
11. Comparative Politics
12. Comparative Politics of Developing Nations
13. Politics of Communist and Post-Communist Countries
14. Comparative Politics of Advanced Industrial Societies
15. Politics and Society in Western Europe
16. International Political Economy
17. International Collaboration
18. International Security
19. International Security and Arms
20. Domestic Sources of Foreign Policy/Foreign Policy Analysis

21. Conflict Processes
22. Legislative Studies
23. Presidency Research
24. Public Administration
25. Public Policy
26. Law and Courts
27. Constitutional Law and Jurisprudence
28. Federalism and Intergovernmental Relations
29. State Politics and Policy
30. Urban Politics
31. Women and Politics
32. Race, Ethnicity, and Politics
33. Religion and Politics
34. Representative and Electoral Systems
35. Political Organizations and Parties
36. Elections and Voting Behavior
37. Public Opinion and Participation
38. Political Communication
39. Science, Technology, and Environmental Politics
40. Computers and Multimedia
41. Politics and Literature
42. New Political Science
43. Ecological and Transformational Politics

Testing Hypotheses: The Basics of Political Analysis

Political analysis is the systematic attempt to explain political events. To do so, we must be able to (1) define the subject of our study—that is, politics; and (2) explain our method of study—that is, political science.

Defining Politics

The subject of thoughtful study for more than twenty-five centuries, politics has been defined in many ways. Examining ancient conceptions of politics, we become aware that in the most general sense politics is the substance of self-interested human interaction. This does not mean that all human interaction is political, or that self-interest necessarily excludes the interests of others. Every definition of politics, however, addresses *interests* of human beings. As human beings, we emerge from the womb preoccupied with having our own basic needs met. At least two of these needs are relevant to politics. The first is the need for some form of unity with others, which, according to Freudian psychologists, comes from a desire to overcome the separation from our mothers that we encountered upon emergence from the warmth of our prenatal world. Aristotle said that "man is a political animal." The word *politics* is derived from the Greek word πολισ (*polis*), the name given to the city-states of ancient Greece, such as Athens and Sparta. Aristotle believed that the highest purpose of human life is participation in the political community (*polis*). This participation means helping to make the fundamental decisions that guide society and carrying out our responsibility to serve the common interest.

The second basic human political need is individuality. Although we want to feel that we belong to a family, a religious group, a school, a city, or a country, we also want to be recognized as unique and special. We want our own distinctive talents, contributions, opinions, and aspirations to be seen as having value. It may well be said that the history of politics and political thought is the story of our continuous struggle to attain a sense of unity with others while at the same time actualizing our potential as respected and valued individuals.

Most contemporary definitions of politics focus on the competition of interests in society. For example, politics is described by David Easton as the "authoritative allocation of values" and by Harold Laswell as "who gets what, when, and how." In order to study politics, then, we must find a way to study the process by which a society allocates values and interests. In other words, our task becomes at least in part to find answers to such questions as, How are political decisions made? and What motivates political action?

The concept of influence is central to our efforts to answer these questions. Because political analysis is the systematic attempt to describe political events, and political events are the result of influence, political analysis is largely the science of describing how political influence operates within a particular situation. Political analysis therefore is the study of the varieties, causes, and manifestations of influence.

The Scientific Method

The goal of science is to explain reality. Scientists develop theories, which are general explanations for the existence or causes of certain classes of phenomena. Two centuries after Christ, for example, Ptolemy constructed a theory to explain the movement of the stars in the sky. His theory, which stated that the sun and planets revolve around the earth, described much of what could be observed in the sky at night. More precise observations, however, would later cast doubt on Ptolemy's theory.

Once they have been developed, theories must be tested to see if they actually explain the phenomena they are intended to explain. We test theories by first creating specific statements that should be true if the theory is correct and then devising tests of these statements, known as hypotheses. A substantial part of the work of political science is to test research hypotheses.

Formulating and Testing Hypotheses

A hypothesis is an educated guess. It is a declarative sentence that states that a specific relationship exists between two or more phenomena. Consider the following example: "When a candidate's ratings in the polls rise, contributions to that person's campaign increase." This hypothesis states that there is a specific relationship between two variables: (1) a candidate's ratings in the polls, and (2) the number of campaign contributions that the candidate receives. In addition, the hypothesis describes the nature of that relationship: an increase in the first is associated with an increase in the second. This hypothesis can be tested by collecting and examining data on poll ratings and campaign finances to see if indeed such a relationship exists.

A hypothesis is a statement that is constructed for the sole purpose of testing whether or not it is "true"—that is, whether or not a certain relationship exists between two phenomena that the writer of the hypothesis is interested in investigating. Hypotheses help define the question that our research is trying to answer. Suppose that we want to know if presidential elections are affected by economic conditions. We would like eventually to develop a theory of how various economic conditions would lead to different results in voting patterns. Before we can understand the general patterns of the relationship between these variables and create a theory to explain them, we must become much more specific. Hypotheses can help us to identify specific aspects of a problem and then explore them one at a time. In our example of the economy and presidential elections, we might propose the following hypothesis: "When the economy is strong, incumbents are elected, and when the economy is weak, challengers are elected." We notice, however, that there will be difficulties in testing this hypothesis. What, for example, are "strong" and "weak" economies? Our hypothesis will need to be more specific. We will perhaps find that a combination of selected economic indicators, such as the rate of unemployment or the amount of manufacturing production, will help us to define "strong" and "weak" in economic terms. The problem has now become more rather than less complicated, however. How will we know if elections are influenced by only one of these factors and not others? What if only certain combinations of these factors, and not others, have an effect on elections? The answer to these questions is that we need to start with one simple hypothesis which we test in a careful, systematic way. Our first hypothesis might be "When the national unemployment rate is greater than 7 percent at the time of the election, presidential incumbents are not reelected."

Two types of hypotheses are commonly used in political science: *causal* and *relational* hypotheses. Causal hypotheses attempt to show that one phenomenon causes another. Relational hypotheses, on the other hand, are statements that indicate whether two phenomena are related in a specific way, without demonstrating that one causes the other. Testing the hypothesis about the national unemployment rate and the reelection of presidential incumbents will only indicate if a relationship exists between the two factors, not that unemployment causes incumbents not to be reelected. Relations between hypotheses may be either positive or negative. A positive relation exists when an increase in one variable is associated with an increase in another. A negative relation exists when the presence of one variable coincides with the absence of another.

Once hypotheses have been constructed, we test them by observing the behavior of the phenomena, or *variables,* that they contain. For example, let our hypothesis be "Extended registration periods increase voter turnout." The *dependent variable* is the phenomenon that is in some way affected by other variables. In our example, voter turnout is the dependent variable:

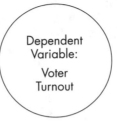

The *independent variable* is the phenomenon that may have some effect on the dependent variable that we are most interested in examining. In our example, the time period allowed for voter registration is the independent variable:

```
Independent Variable:
Time for Registration
```

Antecedent variables are phenomena that act upon or relate to independent variables. In our example, if we said that "Extended registration occurs in states with smaller proportions of independent voters," the proportion of independent voters would be the antecedent variable:

```
Antecedent Variable:
Percentage of
Independent Voters
```

Intervening variables are variables other than the independent variable which affect the dependent variable directly. In our example, if we said that "Voter turnout decreases when it rains," then rain would be an intervening variable.

A diagram that represents the relationships among the variables in our example hypothesis would look like this:

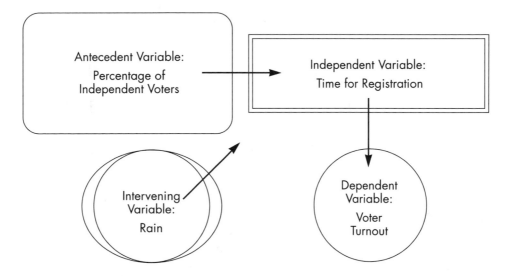

In research, the identification of the dependent, independent, antecedent, and intervening variables is very important, because it helps to define carefully the relationships that are being examined.

Because hypotheses are constructed to find out what relationship, if any, exists between the independent and dependent variables, in order to test a hypothesis you need to measure the amount of change that occurs in the dependent variable as you observe change in the independent variable. To do so, you must complete two tasks:

1. Accurately measure the dependent and independent variables as they vary over time or circumstances. For measurements to be accurate, they must be both valid and reliable. A *valid* measurement is one that measures the intended effect instead of something else. A *reliable* measurement is one that can be made under different conditions and still yield the same result.
2. Determine the effects of the antecedent and intervening variables on the dependent variable in order to measure the effect of the independent

variable. If the voter turnout is greater in one community than another, and the communities have different registration time periods, you must determine how much of the difference in turnout was due to the registration periods as opposed to the percentage of independent voters or the occurrence of rain.

Conducting a study that is reliable and valid requires an analysis that utilizes accepted statistical methods. The instructor in your course in political science research methods will help you determine the correct methods for your analysis.

Problems for the Scientific Study of Politics

Hypotheses are not easy to test. When attempting to test hypotheses in political science, we often encounter three general problems:

1. Data insufficiency or incongruity
2. Multiplicity and ambiguity of variables
3. Methodological uncertainty

Data Insufficiency or Incongruity.   Once we have stated our hypothesis, we may find that sufficient data are not available to test it. Sometimes the records that we need have not been kept consistently or accurately, or have been compiled according to different systems or categories. If we want to compare the funds contributed to political campaigns in the United States and Italy, for example, we may find that the two governments have different reporting requirements and that the procedures used to validate data may be much more reliable in one country than in another.

Multiplicity and Ambiguity of Variables.   Sometimes it is difficult to determine which variables are causing the phenomenon we are studying. If we want to find out what factors increase voter turnout, for example, we may need to try to sort out the competing effects of local customs, political efficacy, transportation systems, physical access to registration, and ease of registration procedures, as well as weather and political party loyalty.

Methodological Uncertainty.   The third problem with the scientific study of politics originates in epistemology, or the study of the nature of knowledge itself. The testing of hypotheses, which is fundamental to the scientific method, is an inductive process. This means that the scientific method examines numerous specific cases in hopes of finding general principles that help explain or predict behavior. For example, some may conclude that, if all known oak trees have acorns, then all oak trees have acorns. However, in *The Logic of Discovery* (1934), Karl Popper pointed out that to show that some examples of a certain phenomenon behave in a certain manner is not to demonstrate that others will also. Even if all known examples of a certain phenomenon behave in a certain way, other examples that deviate from the pattern may be found in the future. Thus even if all known oak trees have acorns, it is possible that an oak tree without acorns will be found.

Further, said Popper, scientific observation is always selective. That is, we have made the decision to observe before the actual observation takes place, and that observation will always take place within a particular context. Hypotheses are thus observations not of reality but merely of one context, and therefore are not genuine observations but only bold guesses. Since we can never be sure that a hypothesis is true, we can refute it only when it is proven to be in error. Scientific progress is made not by verifying hypotheses, but instead by refuting them. If a statement is refutable, it is scientific. If it is not refutable, it is something else. Science therefore ought to proceed not by attempting to prove hypotheses but rather by trying to refute them. A hypothesis established precisely for the purpose of being refuted is called a *null hypothesis*. Returning to our previous example, if we wanted to try to prove that extended registration periods increase voter turnout, we would begin by testing the null hypothesis "Extended registration periods do not increase voter turnout." If we can find a case in which an extended registration period does increase voter turnout, we will have disproven that null hypothesis. We will not have proven that extended registration periods *always* increase voter turnout, but we will have taken the first step by showing that extended registration periods *sometimes* increase voter turnout. Science thus proceeds by disproving successively specific null hypotheses.

Even the process of invalidating null hypotheses, however, may not lead to scientific breakthroughs. According to Thomas Kuhn, the refutation of null hypotheses is not a viable strategy if one wants to achieve the occasional new perspective that revolutionizes science. When Copernicus proposed his heliocentric theory of astronomy, the Ptolemaic approach was well entrenched in the scientific community. Kuhn calls such established patterns of scientific inquiry paradigms. Discrepancies in the Ptolemaic paradigm were met by increasingly complicated explanations devised to make observation conform to the theory. Copernicus's system was so different from Ptolemy's that it became a new scientific paradigm, but at first it had little evidence from observation to support it. Kuhn argues that Copernicus did not come up with his new theory by refuting the Ptolemaic system, but instead by having a flash of intuition. A paradigm, for Kuhn, is never refuted by evidence; it can be overturned only when another one takes its place. Social science, to Kuhn, needs a paradigm. Paradigms are essential to scientific progress. Because it has no paradigm, political science winds its way endlessly through a series of disagreements over methods and goals. The scientific method therefore is the normal way of adding to our common store of knowledge about politics. The great breakthroughs of the future, however, may well come from exceptional moments of human creativity as well as from the steady testing of statements within our normal range of exploration.

1

Writing as Communication

1.1 Writing to Learn

Writing is a way of ordering your experience. Think about it. No matter what you are writing—it may be a paper for your American government class, a short story, a limerick, a grocery list—you are putting pieces of your world together in new ways and making yourself freshly conscious of those pieces. This is one of the reasons writing is so hard. From the infinite welter of data that your mind continually processes and locks in your memory, you are selecting only certain items significant to the task at hand, relating them to other items, and phrasing them in a new coherence. You are mapping a part of your universe that has hitherto been unknown territory. You are gaining a little more control over the processes by which you interact with the world around you.

This is why the act of writing, no matter what its result, is never insignificant. It is always *communication*—if not with another human being, then with yourself. It is a way of making a fresh connection with your world.

Writing therefore is also one of the best ways to learn. This statement may sound odd at first. If you are an unpracticed writer, you may share a common notion that the only purpose of writing is to express what you already know or think. According to this view, any learning that you as a writer might have experienced has already occurred by the time your pen meets the paper; your task is thus to inform and even surprise the reader. But, if you are a practiced writer, you know that at any moment as you write, you are capable of surprising *yourself*. And it is surprise that you look for: the shock of seeing what happens in your own mind when you drop an old, established opinion into a batch of new facts or bump into a cherished belief from a different angle. Writing synthesizes new understanding for the writer. E. M. Forester's famous question "How do I know what I think until I see what I say?" is one that all of us could ask. We make meaning as we write, jolting ourselves by little, surprising discoveries into a larger and more interesting universe.

The Irony of Writing

Good writing, especially good writing about politics, helps the reader become aware of the ironies and paradoxes of human existence. One such paradox is that good writing expresses both that which is unique about the writer and that which the writer shares with every human being. Many of our most famous political statements share this double attribute of mirroring the singular and the ordinary simultaneously. For example, read the following excerpt from President Franklin Roosevelt's first inaugural address, spoken on March 4, 1933, in the middle of the Great Depression, then answer this question: Is Roosevelt's speech famous because its expression is extraordinary or because it appeals to something that is basic to every human being?

This is pre-eminently the time to speak the truth, the whole truth, frankly and boldly. Nor need we shrink from honestly facing conditions in our country today. This great nation will endure as it has endured, will revive and will prosper.

So first of all let me assert my firm belief that the only thing we have to fear is fear itself—nameless, unreasoning, unjustified terror which paralyzes needed efforts to convert retreat into advance.

In every dark hour of our national life a leadership of frankness and vigor has met with that understanding and support of the people themselves which is essential to victory. I am convinced that you will again give that support to leadership in these critical days.

In such a spirit on my part and on yours we face our common difficulties. They concern, thank God, only material things. Values have shrunken to fantastic levels; taxes have risen; our ability to pay has fallen; government of all kinds is faced by serious curtailment of income; the means of exchange are frozen in the currents of trade; the withered leaves of industrial enterprise lie on every side; farmers find no markets for their produce; the savings of many years in thousands of families are gone.

More important, a host of unemployed citizens face the grim problem of existence, and an equally great number toil with little return. Only a foolish optimist can deny the dark realities of the moment.

Yet our distress comes from no failure of substance. We are stricken by no plague of locusts. Compared with the perils which our forefathers conquered because they believed and were not afraid, we have still much to be thankful for. Nature still offers her bounty and human efforts have multiplied it. Plenty is at our doorstep, but a generous use of it languishes in the very sight of the supply. . . .

The measure of the restoration lies in the extent to which we apply social values more noble than mere monetary profit.

Happiness lies not in the mere possession of money; it lies in the joy of achievement, in the thrill of creative effort.

The joy and moral stimulation of work no longer must be forgotten in the mad chase of evanescent profits. These dark days will be worth all they cost us if they teach us that our true destiny is not to be ministered unto but to minister to ourselves and to our fellow-men. (Henry Steele Commager, ed. 1963. *Documents of American History.* 7th ed. New York: Appleton-Century-Crofts. 240.)

The help that writing gives us with learning and with controlling what we learn is one of the major reasons why your political science instructors will require a great deal of writing from you. Learning the complex and diverse world of the political scientist takes more than a passive ingestion of facts. You have to understand the processes of government, come to grips with social issues and with your own attitudes toward them. When you write in a class on American government or public policy, you are entering into the world of political scientists in the same way they do—by testing theory against fact and fact against belief.

Writing is the means of entering political life. Virtually everything that happens in politics happens first on paper. Documents are wrestled into shape before their contents can affect the public. Great speeches are written before they are spoken. The written word has helped bring slaves to freedom, end wars, and shape the values of nations. Often, in politics as elsewhere, gaining recognition for ourselves and our ideas depends less on what we say than on how we say it. Accurate and persuasive writing is absolutely vital to the political scientist.

EXERCISE   *Learning by Writing*

One way of testing the notion that writing is a powerful learning tool is rewriting your notes from a recent class lecture. The type of class does not matter; it can be history, chemistry, advertising, whatever. If possible, choose a difficult class, one in which you are feeling somewhat unsure of the material and for which you have taken copious notes.

As you rewrite, provide the transitional elements (connecting phrases such as *in order to, because of, and, but, however*) that you were unable to supply in class because of the press of time. Furnish your own examples or illustrations of the ideas expressed in the lecture.

This experiment will force you to supply necessary coherence to your own thought processes. See if the time it takes you to rewrite the notes is not more than compensated for by your increased understanding of the lecture material.

Challenge Yourself

There is no way around it: writing is a struggle. Did you think you were the only one to feel this way? Take heart! Writing is hard for everybody, great writers included. Bringing order to the world is never easy. Isaac Bashevis Singer, winner of the 1978 Nobel Prize in literature, once wrote, "I believe in miracles in every area of life *except* writing. Experience has shown me that there are no miracles in writing. The only thing that produces good writing is hard work." (Quoted in Andrea Lunsford and Robert Connors. 1992. *The St. Martin's Handbook.* 2nd ed. Annotated Instructor's Edition. New York: St. Martin's. 2.)

Hard work was evident in the words of John F. Kennedy's inaugural address. Each word was crafted to embed an image in the listener's mind. As you read the following excerpt from Kennedy's speech, what images does it evoke? Historians tend to consider a president "great" when his words live longer than his deeds in the minds of the people. Do you think this will be—or has been—true of Kennedy?

We observe today not a victory of party but a celebration of freedom—symbol-izing an end as well as a beginning—signifying renewal as well as change. For I have sworn before you and Almighty God the same solemn oath our fore-bears prescribed nearly a century and three-quarters ago.

The world is very different now. For man holds in his mortal hands the power to abolish all forms of human poverty and all forms of human life. And yet the same revolutionary beliefs for which our forebears fought are still at issue around the globe—the belief that the rights of man come not from the generosity of the state but from the hand of God.

We dare not forget today that we are the heirs of that first revolution. Let the word go forth from this time and place, to friend and foe alike, that the torch has been passed to a new generation of Americans—born in this century, tempered by war, disciplined by a hard and bitter peace, proud of our ancient heritage—and unwilling to witness or permit the slow undoing of those human rights to which this nation has always been committed, and to which we are committed today at home and around the world. . . .

In the long history of the world, only a few generations have been granted the role of defending freedom in its hours of maximum danger. I do not shrink from this responsibility—I welcome it. I do not believe that any of us would exchange places with any other people or any other generation. The energy, the faith, the devotion which we bring to this endeavor will light our country and all who serve it—and the glow from that fire can truly light the world.

And so, my fellow Americans: ask not what your country can do for you—ask what you can do for your country.

My fellow citizens of the world: ask not what America will do for you, but what together we can do for the freedom of man. (Henry Steele Com-mager, ed. 1963. *Documents of American History.* 7th ed. New York: Appleton-Century-Crofts. 688, 689.)

One reason that writing is difficult is that it is not actually a single activity at all but a process consisting of several activities that can overlap, with two or more sometimes operating *simultaneously* as you labor to organize and phrase your thoughts. (We will discuss these activities later in this chapter.) The writing process tends to be sloppy for everyone, an often-frustrating search for meaning and for the best way to articulate that meaning.

Frustrating though that search may sometimes be, it need not be futile. Remember this: The writing process uses skills that we all have. The ability to write, in other words, is not some magical competence bestowed on the rare, for-tunate individual. Although few of us may achieve the proficiency of Isaac Bashe-vis Singer or John F. Kennedy, we are all capable of phrasing thoughts clearly and in a well-organized fashion. But learning how to do so takes *practice.*

The one sure way to improve your writing is to write.

One of the toughest but most important jobs in writing is to maintain enthusiasm for your writing project. Such commitment may sometimes be hard to achieve, given the difficulties that are inherent in the writing process and that can be made worse when the project is unappealing at first glance. How, for example, can you be enthusiastic about having to write a paper analyzing cam-paign financing for the 1998 congressional elections when you have never once thought about campaign finances and can see no use in doing so now?

One of the worst mistakes that unpracticed student writers make is to fail to assume responsibility for keeping themselves interested in their writing. No matter how hard it may seem at first to drum up interest in your topic, *you have to do it*—that is, if you want to write a paper you can be proud of, one that contributes useful material and a fresh point of view to the topic. One thing is guaranteed: If you are bored with your writing, your reader will be, too. So what can you do to keep your interest and energy level high?

Challenge yourself. Think of the paper not as an assignment but as a piece of writing that has a point to make. To get this point across persuasively is the real reason why you are writing, *not* the simple fact that a teacher has assigned you a project. If someone were to ask you why you are writing your paper and your immediate, unthinking response is "Because I've been given a writing assignment" or "Because I want a good grade," or some other nonanswer along these lines, your paper may be in trouble.

If, on the other hand, your first impulse is to explain the challenge of your main point—"I'm writing to show how campaign finance reform will benefit every taxpayer in America"—then you are thinking usefully about your topic.

Maintain Self-Confidence

Having confidence in your ability to write well about your topic is essential for good writing. This does not mean that you will always know what the result of a particular writing activity will be. In fact, you have to cultivate your ability to tolerate a high degree of uncertainty while weighing evidence, testing hypotheses, and experimenting with organizational strategies and wording. Be ready for temporary confusion and for seeming dead ends, and remember that every writer faces these obstacles. It is from your struggle to combine fact with fact, to buttress conjecture with evidence, that order arises.

Do not be intimidated by the amount and quality of work that others have already done in your field of inquiry. The array of opinion and evidence that confronts you in the literature can be confusing. But remember that no important topic is ever exhausted. *There are always gaps*—questions that have not been satisfactorily explored in either the published research or the prevailing popular opinion. It is in these gaps that you establish your own authority, your own sense of control.

Remember that the various stages of the writing process reinforce each other. Establishing a solid motivation strengthens your sense of confidence about the project, which in turn influences how successfully you organize and write. If you start out well, use good work habits, and give yourself ample time for the various activities to coalesce, you should produce a paper that will reflect your best work, one that your audience will find both readable and useful.

1.2 The Writing Process

The Nature of the Process

As you engage in the writing process, you are doing many things at once. While planning, you are no doubt defining the audience for your paper at the same time that you are thinking about its purpose. As you draft the paper, you may organize your next sentence while revising the one you have just written. Different parts of the writing process overlap, and much of the difficulty of writing occurs because so many things happen at once. Through practice—in other words, through *writing*—it is possible to learn how to control those parts of the process that can in fact be controlled and to encourage those mysterious, less controllable activities.

No two people go about writing in exactly the same way. It is important to recognize the routines—modes of thought as well as individual exercises—that help you negotiate the process successfully. It is also important to give yourself as much time as possible to complete the process. Procrastination is one of the writer's greatest enemies. It saps confidence, undermines energy, destroys concentration. Writing regularly and following a well-planned schedule as closely as possible often make the difference between a successful paper and an embarrassment.

Although the various parts of the writing process are interwoven, there is naturally a general order to the work of writing. You have to start somewhere! What follows is a description of the various stages of the writing process—planning, drafting, revising, editing, and proofreading—along with suggestions on how to approach each most successfully.

Planning

Planning includes all activities that lead to the writing of the first draft of a paper. The particular activities in this stage differ from person to person. Some writers, for instance, prefer to compile a formal outline before writing the draft. Others perform brief writing exercises to jump-start their imaginations. Some draw diagrams; some doodle. Later we will look at a few starting strategies, and you can determine which may help you.

Now, however, let us discuss certain early choices that all writers must make during the planning stage. These choices concern *topic, purpose,* and *audience,* elements that make up the writing context, or the terms under which we all write. Every time you write, even if you are only writing a diary entry or a note to the milkman, these elements are present. You may not give conscious consideration to all of them in each piece of writing that you do, but it is extremely important to think carefully about them when writing a political science paper. Some or all of these defining elements may be dictated by your assignment, yet you will always have a degree of control over them.

Selecting a Topic

No matter how restrictive an assignment may seem, there is no reason to feel trapped by it. Within any assigned subject you can find a range of topics to explore. What you are looking for is a topic that engages your own interest. Let your curiosity be your guide. If, for example, you have been assigned the subject of campaign finances, then guide yourself to find some issue concerning campaign finances that interests you. (How influential are they in the average state senate race? What would be the repercussions of limiting financial contributions from special interest groups?) Any good topic comes with a set of questions; you may well find that your interest increases if you simply begin asking questions. One strong recommendation: Ask your questions *on paper*. Like most mental activities, the process of exploring your way through a topic is transformed when you write down your thoughts as they come, instead of letting them fly through your mind unrecorded. Remember the words of Louis Agassiz: "A pen is often the best of eyes." (*A Scientist of Two Worlds: Louis Agassiz*. Edited by Catherine Owens Pearce. Philadelphia: Lippincott, 1958. 106.)

Although it is vital to be interested in your topic, you do not have to know much about it at the outset of your investigation. In fact, having too heartfelt a commitment to a topic can be an impediment to writing about it; emotions can get in the way of objectivity. Better often to choose a topic that has piqued your interest yet remained something of a mystery to you: a topic discussed in one of your classes, perhaps, or mentioned on television or in a conversation with friends.

Narrowing the Topic

The task of narrowing your topic offers you a tremendous opportunity to establish a measure of control over the writing project. It is up to you to hone your topic to just the right shape and size to suit both your own interests and the requirements of the assignment. Do a good job of it, and you will go a long way toward guaranteeing yourself sufficient motivation and confidence for the tasks ahead. If you do not do this well, somewhere along the way you may find yourself directionless and out of energy.

Generally, the first topics that come to your mind will be too large for you to handle in your research paper. For example, the subject of a national health policy has recently generated a tremendous number of news reports. Despite all the attention, there is still plenty of room for you to investigate the topic on a level that has real meaning for you and that does not merely recapitulate the published research. What about an analysis of how one of the proposed U.S. health policies might affect insurance costs in a locally owned company?

The problem with most topics is not that they are too narrow or have been too completely explored, but rather that they are so rich that it is often difficult to choose the most useful way to address them. Take some time to narrow your topic. Think through the possibilities that occur to you and, as always, jot down your thoughts.

Students in an undergraduate course on political theory were told to write an essay of 2,500 words on one of the following topics. Next to each general topic is an example of how students narrowed it into a manageable paper topic.

GENERAL TOPIC	NARROWED TOPIC
Plato	Plato's philosophy of the role of women in politics
Freedom	A comparison of Jean Jacques Rousseau's concept of freedom with John Locke's
Revolution	Thomas Paine's arguments for the legitimacy of revolution
Thomas Hobbes	Hobbes's definition of the state in *Leviathan*

EXERCISE   *Narrowing Topics*

Without doing research, see how you can narrow the following general topics:

EXAMPLE

General topic	The United Nations
Narrowed topic	The United Nations' intervention in civil wars
	The United Nations' attempts to end starvation
	The role of the United Nations in stopping nuclear proliferation

GENERAL TOPICS

crime in America	political corruption
international terrorism	military spending
education	affirmative action hiring policies
freedom of speech	freedom of religion
gun control	abortion rights

Finding a Thesis

As you plan your writing, be on the lookout for an idea that can serve as your thesis. A *thesis* is not a fact, which can be immediately verified by data, but an assertion worth discussing, an argument with more than one possible conclusion. Your thesis sentence will reveal to your reader not only the argument you have chosen, but also your orientation toward it and the conclusion that your paper will attempt to prove.

In looking for a thesis, you are doing many jobs at once:

1. You are limiting the amount and kind of material that you must cover, thus making it manageable.
2. You are increasing your own interest in the narrowing field of study.

3. You are working to establish your paper's purpose, the *reason* why you are writing about your topic. (If the only reason you can see for writing is to earn a good grade, then you probably won't!)
4. You are establishing your notion of who your audience is and what sort of approach to the subject might best catch its interest.

In short, you are gaining control over your writing context. For this reason, it is a good idea to come up with a thesis early on, a *working thesis,* which will very probably change as your thinking deepens but which will allow you to establish a measure of order in the planning stage.

The Thesis Sentence.   The introduction of your paper will contain a sentence that expresses the task that you intend to accomplish. This *thesis sentence* communicates your main idea, the one you are going to prove, defend, or illustrate. It sets up an expectation in the reader's mind which it is your job to satisfy. But, in the planning stage, a thesis sentence is more than just the statement that informs your reader of your goal: It is a valuable tool to help you narrow your focus and confirm in your own mind your paper's purpose.

Developing a Thesis

Students in a class on public policy analysis were assigned a twenty-page paper on a problem currently being faced by the municipal authorities in their own city. The choice of the problem was left to the students. One, Richard Cory, decided to investigate the problem posed by the large number of abandoned buildings in a downtown neighborhood through which he drove on his way to the university. His first working thesis was as follows:

Abandoned houses result in negative social effects to the city.

The problem with this thesis, as Richard found out, was that it was not an idea that could be argued, but rather a fact that could be easily corroborated by the sources Richard began to consult. As he read reports from such groups as the Urban Land Institute and the City Planning Commission and talked with representatives from the Community Planning Department, he began to get interested in the dilemma his city faced in responding to the problem of abandoned buildings. Richard's second working thesis was as follows:

Removal of abandoned buildings is a major problem facing the city.

His second thesis narrowed the topic somewhat and gave Richard an opportunity to use material from his research, but there was still no real comment attached to it. It still stated a bare fact, easily proved. At this point, Richard became interested in the even narrower topic of how building removal should best be handled. He found that the major issue was funding and that different civic groups favored different methods of accomplishing this. As Richard explored the arguments for and against funding plans, he began to feel that one of them might be best for the city.

Richard's third working thesis:

Assessing a demolition fee on each property offers a viable solution to the city's building removal problem.

Note how this thesis narrows the focus of Richard's paper even further than the other two, while also presenting an arguable hypothesis. It tells Richard what he has to do in his paper, just as it tells his readers what to expect.

At some time during your preliminary thinking on a topic, you should consult the library to see how much published work on your issue exists. This search has at least two benefits:

1. It acquaints you with a body of writing that will become very important in the research phase of your paper.
2. It gives you a sense of how your topic is generally addressed by the community of scholars you are joining. Is the topic as important as you think it is? Has there been so much research on the subject as to make your inquiry, in its present formulation, irrelevant?

As you go about determining your topic, remember that one goal of political science writing in college is always to enhance your own understanding of the political process, to build an accurate model of the way politics works. Let this goal help you to aim your research into those areas that you know are important to your knowledge of the discipline.

Defining a Purpose

There are many ways to classify the purposes of writing, but in general most writing is undertaken either to inform or to persuade an audience. The goal of informative, or expository, writing is, simply, to impart information about a particular subject, whereas the aim of *persuasive* writing is to convince your reader of your point of view on an issue. The distinction between expository and persuasive writing is not hard and fast, and most writing in political science has elements of both types. Most effective writing, however, is clearly focused on either exposition or persuasion. Position papers (Chapter 12), for example, are designed to persuade, whereas policy analysis papers (Chapter 14) are meant to inform. When you begin writing, consciously select a primary approach of exposition or persuasion, and then set out to achieve that goal.

EXERCISE   *To Explain or to Persuade*

Can you tell from the titles of these two papers, both on the same topic, which is an expository paper and which is a persuasive paper?

1. Social Services Funding in the Reagan Administration
2. How the Reagan Administration Shifted Shares of Wealth in America

---

Again taking up the subject of campaign finances, let us assume that you must write a paper explaining how finances were managed in the 1972 Republican presidential campaign. If you are writing an expository paper, your task could be to describe as coherently and impartially as possible the methods by which the Republicans administered their campaign funds. If, however, you are attempting to convince your readers that the 1972 Republican campaign finances were criminally mismanaged by an elected official, you are writing to persuade, and your strategy will be radically different. Persuasive writing seeks to influence the opinions of its audience toward its subject.

Learn what you want to say. By the time you write your final draft, you must have a very sound notion of the point you wish to argue. If, as you write that final draft, someone were to ask you to state your thesis, you should be able to give a satisfactory answer with a minimum of delay and no prompting. If, on the other hand, you have to hedge your answer because you cannot easily express your thesis, you may not yet be ready to write a final draft. You may have to write a draft or two or engage in various prewriting activities in order to arrive at a secure understanding of your task.

EXERCISE   *Knowing What You Want to Say*

Two writers have been asked to state the thesis of their papers. Which one better understands the writing task?

Writer 1:   "My paper is about tax reform for the middle class."
Writer 2:   "My paper argues that tax reform for the middle class would be unfair to the upper and lower classes, who would then have to share more responsibility for the cost of government."

Watch out for bias! There is no such thing as pure objectivity. You are not a machine. No matter how hard you may try to produce an objective paper, the fact is that every choice you make as you write is influenced to some extent by your personal beliefs and opinions. What you tell your readers is truth. In other words, it is influenced, sometimes without your knowing, by a multitude of factors: your environment, upbringing, and education; your attitude toward your audience;

your political affiliation; your race and gender; your career goals; and your ambitions for the paper you are writing. The influence of such factors can be very subtle, and it is something you must work to identify in your own writing as well as in the writing of others in order not to mislead or to be misled. Remember that one of the reasons for writing is *self-discovery*. The writing you will do in political science classes—as well as the writing you will do for the rest of your life—will give you a chance to discover and confront honestly your own views on your subjects. Responsible writers keep an eye on their own biases and are honest about them with their readers.

Defining Your Audience

In any class that requires you to write, it may sometimes be difficult to remember that the point of your writing is not simply to jump through the technical hoops imposed by the assignment. The point is *communication*—the transmission of your knowledge and your conclusions to readers in a way that suits you. Your task is to pass on to your readers the spark of your own enthusiasm for your topic. Readers who were indifferent to your topic before reading your paper should look at it in a new way after finishing the paper. This is the great challenge of writing: to enter into a reader's mind and leave behind both new knowledge *and* new questions.

It is tempting to think that most writing problems would be solved if the writer could view the writing as if it had been produced by another person. The discrepancy between the understanding of the writer and that of the audience is the single greatest impediment to accurate communication. To overcome this barrier you must consider your audience's needs. By the time you begin drafting, most if not all of your ideas will have begun to attain coherent shape in your mind, so that virtually any words with which you try to express those ideas will reflect your thought accurately—*to you*. Your readers, however, do not already hold the conclusions that you have so painstakingly achieved. If you omit from your writing the material that is necessary to complete your readers' understanding of your argument, they may well be unable to supply that information themselves.

The potential for misunderstanding is present for any audience, whether it is made up of general readers, experts in the field, or your professor, who is reading in part to see how well you have mastered the constraints that govern the relationship between writer and reader. Make your presentation as complete as possible, bearing in mind your audience's knowledge of your topic.

Invention Strategies

We have discussed various methods of selecting and narrowing the topic of a paper. As your focus on a specific topic sharpens, you will naturally begin to think about the kinds of information that will go into the paper. In the case of papers not requiring formal research, that material will come largely from your own recollections. Indeed, one of the reasons instructors assign such papers is to convince you of the incredible richness of your memory, the vastness and variety of the "database" you have accumulated and which, moment by moment, you continue to build.

So vast is your hoard of information that it can sometimes be difficult to find within it the material that would best suit your paper. In other words, finding out what you already know about a topic is not always easy. *Invention,* a term borrowed from classical rhetoric, refers to the task of discovering, or recovering from memory, such information. As we write, we go through some sort of invention procedure that helps us explore our topic. Some writers seem to have little problem coming up with material; others need more help. Over the centuries, writers have devised different exercises that can help locate useful material housed in memory. We will look at a few of these briefly.

Freewriting

Freewriting is an activity that forces you to get something down on paper. There is no waiting around for inspiration. Instead, you set a time limit—perhaps three minutes or five minutes—and write for that length of time without stopping, not even to lift the pen from the paper or your hands from the keyboard. Focus on the topic, and do not let the difficulty of finding relevant material stop you from writing. If necessary, you may begin by writing, over and over, some seemingly useless phrase, such as "I cannot think of anything to write" or perhaps the name of your topic. Eventually, something else will occur to you. (It is surprising how long a three-minute period of freewriting can seem to last!) At the end of the freewriting, look over what you have produced for anything you might be able to use. Much of the writing will be unusable, but there might be an insight or two that you did not know you had.

In addition to its ability to help you recover from your memory usable material for your paper, freewriting has certain other benefits. First, it takes little time, and therefore you may repeat the exercise as often as you like. Second, it breaks down some of the resistance that stands between you and the act of writing. There is no initial struggle to find something to say; you just write.

Freewriting

For his second-year American government class, John Alexander had to write a paper on some aspect of local government. John, who felt his understanding of local government was slight, began the job of finding a topic that interested him with two minutes of freewriting. Thinking about local government, John wrote steadily for this period without lifting his pen from the paper. Here is the result of his freewriting:

Okay okay local government. Local, what does that mean? Like police? Chamber of Commerce? the mayor——whoever that is? judges? I got that parking ticket last year, went to *court, had to pay it anyway, bummer. Maybe trace what happens to a single parking ticket—and my money. Find out the public officials who deal with it, from the traffic cop who gives it out to wherever it ends up. Point would be, what? Point point point. To find out how much the local government spends to give out and process a $35 parking ticket—how much do they really make after expenses, and where does that money go? Have to include cop's salary? judge's? Printing costs for ticket? Salary for clerk or whoever deals only with ticket. Is there somebody who lives whole life only processing traffic tickets? Are traffic tickets and parking tickets handled differently? Assuming the guy fights it. Maybe find out the difference in revenue between a contested and an uncontested ticket? Lots of phone calls to make. Who? Where to start?*

Brainstorming

Brainstorming is simply making a list of ideas about a topic. It can be done quickly and at first without any need to order items in a coherent pattern. The point is to write down everything that occurs to you as quickly and briefly as possible, using individual words or short phrases. Once you have a good-sized list of items, you can then group them according to relationships that you see among them. Brainstorming thus allows you to uncover both ideas stored in your memory and useful associations among those ideas.

Brainstorming

A professor in an international politics class asked his students to write a 700-word paper, in the form of a letter to be translated and published in a Warsaw newspaper, giving Polish readers useful advice about living in a democracy. One student, Melissa Jessup, started thinking about the assignment by brainstorming. First, she simply wrote down anything about life in a democracy that occurred to her:

voting rights	*welfare*	*freedom of press*
protest movements	*everybody equal*	*minorities*
racial prejudice	*American Dream*	*injustice*
the individual	*no job security*	*lobbyists and PACs*
justice takes time	*psychological factors*	*aristocracy of wealth*
size of bureaucracy		

Thinking through her list, Melissa decided to rearrange it into two lists: one devoted to positive aspects of life in a democracy; the other, to negative aspects. At this point she decided to discard some items that were redundant or did not seem to have much potential. As you can see, Melissa had some questions about where some of her items would fit.

POSITIVE	NEGATIVE
voting rights	aristocracy of wealth
freedom of the press	justice takes time
everybody equal	racial prejudice
American Dream	welfare
psychological factors	lobbyists and PACs
protest movements (positive?)	size of bureaucracy

At this point, Melissa decided that her topic would be the ways in which money and special interests affect a democratically elected government. Which items on her lists would be relevant to Melissa's paper?

Asking Questions

It is always possible to ask most or all of the following questions about any topic: *Who? What? When? Where? Why? How?* They force you to approach the topic as a journalist does, setting it within different perspectives that can then be compared.

Asking Questions

A professor asked her class on the judicial process to write a paper describing the impact of Supreme Court clerks on the decision-making process. One student developed the following questions as he began to think about a thesis:

Who are the Supreme Court's clerks? (How old? What is their racial and gender mix? What are their politics?)

What are their qualifications for the job?

What exactly is their job?

When during the court term are they most influential?

Where do they come from? (Is there any geographical or religious pattern in the way they are chosen? Do certain law schools contribute a significantly greater number of clerks than others?)

How are they chosen? (Are they appointed? elected?)

When in their careers do they serve?

Why are they chosen as they are?

Who have been some influential court clerks? (Have any gone on to sit on the bench themselves?)

Can you think of other questions that would make for useful inquiry?

Maintaining Flexibility

As you engage in invention strategies, you are also performing other writing tasks. You are still narrowing your topic, for example, as well as making decisions that will affect your choice of tone or audience. You are moving forward on all fronts, with each decision you make affecting the others. You must be flexible enough to allow for slight adjustments in your understanding of the paper's development and of your goal. Never be so determined to prove a particular theory that you fail to notice when your own understanding of it changes. *Stay objective.*

Organizing Your Writing

A paper that contains all the necessary facts but presents them in an ineffective order will confuse rather than inform or persuade. Although there are various methods of grouping ideas, none is potentially more effective than outlining. Unfortunately, no organizing process is more often misunderstood.

Outlining for Yourself

Outlining can do two jobs. First, it can force you, the writer, to gain a better understanding of your ideas by arranging them according to their interrelationships. There is one primary rule of outlining: Ideas of equal weight are placed on the same level within the outline. This rule requires you to determine the relative importance of your ideas. You have to decide which ideas are of the same type or order, and into which subtopic each idea best fits.

If, in the planning stage, you carefully arrange your ideas in a coherent outline, your grasp of your topic will be greatly enhanced. You will have linked your ideas logically together and given a basic structure to the body of the paper. This sort of subordinating and coordinating activity is difficult, however, and as a result, inexperienced writers sometimes begin to write their first draft without an effective outline, hoping for the best. This hope is usually unfulfilled, especially in complex papers involving research.

EXERCISE   *Organizing Thoughts*

Rodrigo, a student in a second-year class in government management, researched the impact of a worker-retraining program in his state and came up with the following facts and theories. Number them in logical order:

___ A growing number of workers in the state do not possess the basic skills and education demanded by employers.

___ The number of dislocated workers in the state increased from 21,000 in 1987 to 32,000 in 1997.

___ A public policy to retrain uneducated workers would allow them to move into new and expanding sectors of the state economy.

___ Investment in high technology would allow the state's employers to remain competitive in the production of goods and services in both domestic and foreign markets.
___ The state's economy is becoming more global and more competitive.

Outlining for Your Reader

The second job an outline can perform is to serve as a reader's blueprint to the paper, summarizing its points and their interrelationships. By consulting your outline, a busy policy maker can quickly get a sense of your paper's goal and the argument you have used to promote it. The clarity and coherence of the outline helps determine how much attention your audience will give to your ideas.

As political science students, you will be given a great deal of help with the arrangement of your material into an outline to accompany your paper. A look at the models presented in Chapter 3 of this manual will show you how strictly these formal outlines are structured. But, although you must pay close attention to these requirements, do not forget how powerful a tool an outline can be in the early planning stages of your paper.

The Formal Outline Pattern

Following this pattern accurately during the planning stage of your paper helps to guarantee that your ideas are placed logically:

Thesis sentence (precedes the formal outline)
    I. First main idea
        A. First subordinate idea
            1. Reason, example, or illustration
                a. Supporting detail
                b. Supporting detail
                c. Supporting detail
            2. Reason, example, or illustration
                a. Supporting detail
                b. Supporting detail
                c. Supporting detail
        B. Second subordinate idea
    II. Second main idea

Notice that each level of the paper must have more than one entry; for every A there must be at least a B (and, if required, a C, a D, and so on), and for every 1 there must be a 2. This arrangement forces you to *compare ideas,* looking carefully at each one to determine its place among the others. The insistence on assigning relative values to your ideas is what makes an outline an effective organizing tool.

The Patterns of Political Science Papers

The structure of any particular type of political science paper is governed by a formal pattern. When rigid external controls are placed on their writing, some writers feel that their creativity is hampered by a kind of "paint-by-numbers" approach to structure. It is vital to the success of your paper that you never allow yourself to be overwhelmed by the pattern rules for any type of paper. Remember that such controls exist not to limit your creativity but to make the paper immediately and easily useful to its intended audience. It is as necessary to write clearly and confidently in a position paper or a policy analysis paper as in a term paper for English literature, a résumé, a short story, or a job application letter.

Drafting

The Rough Draft

The planning stage of the writing process is followed by the writing of the first draft. Using your thesis and outline as direction markers, you must now weave your amalgam of ideas, data, and persuasion strategies into logically ordered sentences and paragraphs. Although adequate prewriting may facilitate drafting, it still will not be easy. Writers establish their own individual methods of encouraging themselves to forge ahead with the draft, but here are some tips.

1. Remember that this is a rough draft, not the final paper. At this stage, it is not necessary that every word be the best possible choice. Do not put that sort of pressure on yourself. You must not allow anything to slow you down now. Writing is not like sculpting in stone, where every chip is permanent; you can always go back to your draft and add, delete, reword, and rearrange. *No matter how much effort you have put into planning, you cannot be sure how much of this first draft you will eventually keep.* It may take several drafts to get one that you find satisfactory.

2. Give yourself sufficient time to write. Do not delay the first draft by telling yourself there is still more research to do. You cannot uncover all the material there is to know on a particular subject, so do not fool yourself into trying. Remember that writing is a process of discovery. You may have to begin writing before you can see exactly what sort of research you need to do. Keep in mind that there are other tasks waiting for you after the first draft is finished, so allow for them as you determine your writing schedule.

It is also very important to give yourself time to write, because the more time that passes after you have written a draft, the better your ability to view it with objectivity. It is very difficult to evaluate your writing accurately soon after you complete it. You need to cool down, to recover from the effort of putting all those words together. The "colder" you get on your writing, the better you are able to read it as if it were written by someone else and thus acknowledge the changes you will need to make to strengthen the paper.

3. Stay sharp. Keep in mind the plan you created as you narrowed your topic, composed a thesis sentence, and outlined the material. But, if you begin to

feel a strong need to change the plan a bit, do not be afraid to do so. Be ready for surprises dealt you by your own growing understanding of your topic. Your goal is to record your best thinking on the subject as accurately as possible.

Language Choices

To be convincing, your writing has to be *authoritative*; that is, you have to sound as if you have complete confidence in your ability to convey your ideas in words. Sentences that sound stilted, or that suffer from weak phrasing or the use of clichés, are not going to win supporters for the positions that you express in your paper. So a major question becomes, How can I sound confident?

Here are some points to consider as you work to convey to your reader that necessary sense of authority:

Level of Formality. Tone is one of the primary methods by which you signal to the reader who you are and what your attitude is toward him or her and toward your topic. Your major decision is which level of language formality is most appropriate to your audience. The informal tone you would use in a letter to a friend might well be out of place in a paper titled "Waste in Military Spending" written for your government professor. Remember that tone is only part of the overall decision that you make about how to present your information. Formality is, to some extent, a function of individual word choices and phrasing. For example, is it appropriate to use contractions such as *isn't* or *they'll*? Would the strategic use of a sentence fragment for effect be out of place? The use of informal language, the personal *I*, and the second person *you* is traditionally forbidden— for better or worse—in certain kinds of writing. Often, part of the challenge of writing a formal paper is simply finding ways to give your prose impact while staying within the conventions.

Jargon. One way to lose readers quickly is to overwhelm them with jargon—phrases that have a special, usually technical meaning within your discipline but that are unfamiliar to the average reader. The very occasional use of jargon may add an effective touch of atmosphere, but anything more than that will severely dampen a reader's enthusiasm for the paper. Often the writer uses jargon in an effort to impress the reader by sounding lofty or knowledgeable. Unfortunately, all jargon usually does is cause confusion. In fact, the use of jargon indicates a writer's lack of connection to the audience.

Political science writing is a haven for jargon. Perhaps writers of policy analyses and position papers believe their readers are all completely attuned to their terminology. Or some may hope to obscure damaging information or potentially unpopular ideas in confusing language. In other cases the problem could simply be unclear thinking by the writer. Whatever the reason, the fact is that political science papers too often sound like prose made by machines to be read by machines.

Students may feel that, in order to be accepted as political scientists, their papers should conform to the practices of their published peers. *This is a mistake.* Remember that it is *never* better to write a cluttered or confusing sentence than a clear one and that burying your ideas in jargon defeats the effort that you went through to form them.

EXERCISE   *Revising Jargon*

What words in the following sentence, from a published article in a political science journal, are jargon? Can you rewrite it to clarify its meaning?

> The implementation of statute-mandated regulated inputs exceeds the conceptualization of the administrative technicians.

Clichés.   In the heat of composition, as you are looking for words to help you form your ideas, it is sometimes easy to plug in a *cliché*—a phrase that has attained universal recognition by overuse. (*Note:* Clichés differ from jargon in that clichés are part of the general public's everyday language, whereas jargon is specific to the language of experts in a field.) Our vocabularies are brimming with clichés:

It's *raining cats and dogs.*
That issue is *dead as a doornail.*
It's time for the governor to *face the music.*
Angry voters *made a beeline* for the ballot box.

The problem with clichés is that they are virtually meaningless. Once colorful means of expression, they have lost their color through overuse, and they tend to bleed energy and color from the surrounding words. When revising, replace clichés with fresh wording that more accurately conveys your point.

Descriptive Language.   Language that appeals to readers' senses will always engage their interest more fully than language that is abstract. This is especially important for writing in disciplines that tend to deal in abstracts, such as political science. The typical political science paper, with its discussions of principles, demographics, or points of law, is usually in danger of floating off into abstraction, with each paragraph drifting further away from the felt life of the readers. Whenever appropriate, appeal to your readers' sense of sight, hearing, taste, touch, or smell.

EXERCISE   *Using Descriptive Language*

Which of these two sentences is more effective?

1. The housing project had deteriorated badly since the last inspection.
2. The housing project had deteriorated badly since the last inspection; stench rose from the plumbing, grime coated the walls and floors, and rats scurried through the hallways.

Sexist Language.   Language can be a very powerful method of either rein-
forcing or destroying cultural stereotypes. By treating the sexes in subtly different
ways in your language, you may unknowingly be committing an act of discrimination. A common example is the use of the pronoun *he* to refer to a person whose
gender has not been identified.

Some writers, faced with this problem, alternate the use of male and female
personal pronouns; others use the plural to avoid the need to use a pronoun of
either gender:

SEXIST	NONSEXIST
A lawyer should always treat his client with respect.	A lawyer should always treat his or her client with respect.
	Lawyers should always treat their clients with respect.
Man is a political animal.	People are political animals.

Remember that language is more than the mere vehicle of your thought.
Your words shape perceptions for your readers. How well you say something will
profoundly affect your readers' response to what you say. Sexist language denies
to a large number of your readers the basic right to fair and equal treatment.
Make sure your writing is not guilty of this form of discrimination.

Revising

Revising is one of the most important steps in assuring the success of your
essay. Although unpracticed writers often think of revision as little more than making sure all the *i*'s are dotted and *t*'s are crossed, it is much more than that. Revising
is *reseeing* the essay, looking at it from other perspectives, trying always to align
your view with the one that will be held by your audience. Research indicates that
we are actually revising all the time, in every phase of the writing process, as we
reread phrases, rethink the placement of an item in an outline, or test a new
topic sentence for a paragraph. Subjecting your entire hard-fought draft to cold,
objective scrutiny is one of the toughest activities to master, but it is absolutely
necessary. You have to make sure that you have said everything that needs to be
said clearly and logically. One confusing passage can deflect the reader's attention from where you want it to be. Suddenly the reader has to become a detective,
trying to figure out why you wrote what you did and what you meant by it. You do
not want to throw such obstacles in the path of understanding.

Here are some tips to help you with revision:

1. *Give yourself adequate time for revision.* As discussed previously, you need
time to become "cold" on your paper in order to analyze it objectively. After you
have written your draft, spend some time away from it. Then try to reread it as if it
had been written by someone else.

2. *Read the paper carefully.* This task is tougher than it sounds. One good
strategy is to read it aloud yourself or to have a friend read it aloud while you listen. (Note, however, that friends are usually not the best critics. They are rarely

trained in revision techniques and are often unwilling to risk disappointing you
by giving your paper a really thorough examination.)

3. *Have a list of specific items to check.* It is important to revise in an orderly
fashion, in stages, looking first at large concerns, such as the overall organization,
and then rereading the paper for problems with smaller elements, such as paragraph or sentence structure.

4. *Check for unity*—the clear and logical relation of all parts of the essay to
its thesis. Make sure that every paragraph relates well to the whole of the paper
and is in the right place.

5. *Check for coherence.* Make sure there are no gaps between the various parts
of the argument. Look to see that you have adequate *transition* everywhere it is
needed. Transitional elements are markers indicating places where the paper's
focus or attitude changes. Transitional elements can be one word long—*however,
although, unfortunately, luckily*—or as long as a sentence or a paragraph: *In order to
fully appreciate the importance of democracy as a shaping presence in post–cold war Polish
politics, it is necessary to examine briefly the Poles' last historical attempt to implement
democratic government.*

Transitional elements rarely introduce new material. Instead, they are
direction pointers, either indicating a shift to new subject matter or signaling
how the writer wishes certain material to be interpreted by the reader. Because
you, the writer, already know where and why your paper changes direction and
how you want particular passages to be received, it can be very difficult for you to
catch those places where transition is needed.

6. *Avoid unnecessary repetition.* Two types of repetition can annoy a reader:
repetition of content and repetition of wording.

Repetition of content occurs when you return to a subject you have already discussed. Ideally, you should deal with a topic once, memorably, and then move on
to your next subject. Organizing a paper is a difficult task, however, which usually
occurs through a process of enlightenment in terms of purposes and strategies,
and repetition of content can happen even if you have used prewriting strategies.
What is worse, it can be difficult for you to be aware of the repetition in your own
writing. As you write and revise, remember that any unnecessary repetition of
content in your final draft is potentially annoying to your readers, who are working to make sense of the argument they are reading and do not want to be distracted by a passage repeating material they have already encountered. You must
train yourself, through practice, to look for material that you have repeated
unnecessarily.

Repetition of wording occurs when you overuse certain phrases or words. This
can make your prose sound choppy and uninspired, as the following examples
demonstrate:

> The subcommittee's report on education reform will surprise a number of
> people. A number of people will want copies of the report.

> The chairman said at a press conference that he is happy with the report.
> He will circulate it to the local news agencies in the morning. He will also
> make sure that the city council has copies.

I became upset when I heard how the committee had voted. I called the chairman and expressed my reservations about the committee's decision. I told him I felt that he had let the teachers and students of the state down. I also issued a press statement.

The last passage illustrates a condition known by composition teachers as the *I-syndrome*. Can you hear how such duplicated phrasing can hurt a paper? Your language should sound fresh and energetic. Make sure, before you submit your final draft, to read through your paper carefully, looking for such repetition. However, not all repetition is bad. You may wish to repeat a phrase for rhetorical effect or special emphasis: *I came. I saw. I conquered.* Just make sure that any repetition in your paper is intentional, placed there to produce a specific effect.

Editing

Editing is sometimes confused with the more involved process of revising. But editing is done later in the writing process, after you have wrestled through your first draft—and maybe your second and third—and arrived at the final draft. Even though your draft now contains all the information you want to impart, and you have arranged the information to your satisfaction, there are still many factors to check, such as sentence structure, spelling, and punctuation.

It is at this point that an unpracticed writer might be less than vigilant. After all, most of the work on the paper is finished, as the "big jobs" of discovering, organizing, and drafting information have been completed. *But watch out!* Editing is as important as any other part of the writing process. Any error that you allow in the final draft will count against you in the mind of the reader. This may not seem fair, but even a minor error—a misspelling or confusing placement of a comma—will make a much greater impression on your reader than perhaps it should. Remember that everything about your paper is your responsibility, including performing even the supposedly little jobs correctly. Careless editing undermines the effectiveness of your paper. It would be a shame if all the hard work you put into prewriting, drafting, and revising were to be damaged because you carelessly allowed a comma splice!

Most of the tips given above for revising hold for editing as well. It is best to edit in stages, looking for only one or two kinds of errors each time you reread the paper. Focus especially on errors that you remember committing in the past. If, for instance, you know that you have a tendency to misplace commas, go through your paper looking at each comma carefully. If you have a weakness for writing unintentional sentence fragments, read each sentence aloud to make sure that it is indeed a complete sentence. Have you accidentally shifted verb tenses anywhere, moving from past to present tense for no reason? Do all the subjects in your sentences agree in number with their verbs? *Now is the time to find out.*

Watch out for *miscues*—problems with a sentence that the writer simply does not see. Remember that your search for errors is hampered in two ways:

1. As the writer, you hope not to find any errors in your work. This desire can cause you to miss mistakes when they do occur.

2. Because you know your material so well, it is easy, as you read, to unconsciously supply missing material—a word, a piece of punctuation—as if it were present.

How difficult is it to see that something is missing in the following sentence?

Unfortunately, legislators often have too little regard their constituents.

We can guess that the missing word is probably *for,* which should be inserted after *regard.* It is quite possible, however, that the writer of the sentence would automatically supply the missing for, as if it were on the page. This is a miscue, which can be hard for writers to spot because they are so close to their material.

One tactic for catching mistakes in sentence structure is to read the sentences aloud, starting with the last one in the paper and then moving to the next-to-last, then the previous sentence, thus going backward through the paper (reading each sentence in the normal, left-to-right manner, of course) until you reach the first sentence of the introduction. This backward progression strips each sentence of its rhetorical context and helps you to focus on its internal structure.

Editing is the stage where you finally answer those minor questions that you had put off when you were wrestling with wording and organization. Any ambiguities regarding the use of abbreviations, italics, numerals, capital letters, titles (When do you capitalize the title "president," for example?), hyphens, dashes (usually created on a typewriter or computer by striking the hyphen key twice), apostrophes, and quotation marks have to be cleared up now. You must also check to see that you have used the required formats for footnotes, endnotes, margins, and page numbers.

Guessing is not allowed. Sometimes unpracticed writers who realize that they do not quite understand a particular rule of grammar, punctuation, or format do nothing to fill that knowledge gap. Instead they rely on guesswork and their own logic—which is not always up to the task of dealing with so contrary a language as English—to get them through problems that they could solve if they referred to a writing manual. Remember that it does not matter to the reader why or how an error shows up in your writing. It only matters that you have dropped your guard. You must not allow a careless error to undo all the good work that you have done.

Proofreading

Before you hand in the final version of your paper, it is vital that you check it one more time to make sure there are no errors of any sort. This job is called *proofreading,* or *proofing.* In essence, you are looking for many of the same things you had checked for during editing, but now you are doing it on the last draft, which is about to be submitted to your audience. Proofreading is as important as editing; you may have missed an error that you still have time to find, or an error may have been introduced when the draft was recopied or typed for the last time. Like every other stage of the writing process, proofreading is your responsibility.

At this point, you must check for typing mistakes: transposed or deleted letters, words, phrases, or punctuation. If you have had the paper professionally typed, you still must check it carefully. Do not rely solely on the typist's proofreading. If you are creating your paper on a computer or a word processor, it is possible for you to unintentionally insert a command that alters your document drastically by slicing out a word, line, or sentence at the touch of a key. Make sure such accidental deletions have not occurred.

Above all else, remember that your paper represents *you*. It is a product of your best thinking, your most energetic and imaginative response to a writing challenge. If you have maintained your enthusiasm for the project and worked through the stages of the writing process honestly and carefully, you should produce a paper you can be proud of, one that will serve its readers well.

2

Writing Competently

2.1 Composition

The Competent Writer

Good writing places your thoughts in your readers' minds in exactly the way you want them to be there. Good writing tells your readers just what you want them to know without telling them anything you do not want them to know. This statement may sound odd, but the fact is that writers have to be careful not to let unwanted messages slip into their writing. Look, for example, at the following passage, taken from a paper analyzing the impact of a worker-retraining program. Hidden within the prose is a message that jeopardizes the paper's success. Can you detect the message?

> Recent articles written on the subject of dislocated workers have had little to say about the particular problems dealt with in this paper. Because few of these articles focus on the problem at the state level.

Chances are, when you reached the end of the second "sentence," you felt that something was missing and perceived a gap in logic or coherence, so you went back through both sentences to find the place where things had gone wrong. The second sentence is actually not a sentence at all. It does have certain features of a sentence—for example, a subject (*few*) and a verb (*focus*)—but its first word (*Because*) subordinates the entire clause that follows, taking away its ability to stand on its own as a complete idea. The second "sentence," which is properly called a *subordinate clause,* merely fills in some information about the first sentence, telling us why recent articles about dislocated workers fail to deal with problems discussed in the present paper.

The sort of error represented by the second "sentence" is commonly called a *sentence fragment,* and it conveys to the reader a message that no writer wants to send: that the writer either is careless or, worse, has not mastered the language. Language errors such as fragments, misplaced commas, or shifts in verb tense send out warnings in readers' minds. As a result, readers lose some of their concentration on the issue being discussed; they become distracted and begin to wonder about the language competency of the writer. The writing loses effectiveness.

NOTE. Whatever goal you set for your paper—be it to persuade, describe, analyze, or speculate—you must also set one other goal: *to display language competence.* If your paper does not meet this goal, it will not completely achieve its other aims. Language errors spread doubt like a virus; they jeopardize all the hard work you have done on your paper.

Language competence is especially important in political science, for credibility in politics depends on such skill. Anyone who doubts this should remember the beating that Vice President Dan Quayle took in the press for misspelling the word *potato* at a 1992 spelling bee. His error caused a storm of humiliating publicity for the hapless Quayle, adding to an impression of his general incompetence.

Correctness Is Relative

Although they may seem minor, the sort of language errors we are discussing—often called *surface errors*—can be extremely damaging in certain kinds of writing. Surface errors come in a variety of types, including misspellings, punctuation problems, grammar errors, and the inconsistent use of abbreviations, capitalization, and numerals. These errors are an affront to your readers' notion of correctness, and therein lies one of the biggest problems with surface errors. Different audiences tolerate different levels of correctness. You know that you can get away with surface errors in, say, a letter to a friend, who will probably not judge you harshly for them, whereas those same errors in a job application letter might eliminate you from consideration for the position. Correctness depends to an extent on context.

Another problem is that the rules governing correctness shift over time. What would have been an error to your grandmother's generation—the splitting of an infinitive, for example, or the ending of a sentence with a preposition—is taken in stride by most readers today.

So how do you write correctly when the rules shift from person to person and over time? Here are some tips:

Consider Your Audience

One of the great risks of writing is that even the simplest of choices regarding wording or punctuation can sometimes prejudice your audience against you in ways that may seem unfair. For example, look again at the old grammar rule forbidding the splitting of infinitives. After decades of telling students to never split an infinitive (something just done in this sentence), composition experts now concede that a split infinitive is *not* a grammar crime. But suppose you have written a position paper trying to convince your city council of the need to hire security personnel for the library, and half of the council members—the people you wish to convince—remember their eighth-grade grammar teacher's warning about splitting infinitives. How will they respond when you tell them, in your introduction, that librarians are compelled "to always accompany" visitors to the rare book room because of the threat of vandalism? How much of their attention have you suddenly lost because of their automatic recollection of what is now a nonrule? It is possible, in other words, to write correctly and still offend your readers' notions of language competence.

Make sure that you tailor the surface features and the degree of formality of your writing to the level of competency that your readers require. When in doubt, take a conservative approach. Your audience might be just as distracted by contractions as by a split infinitive.

Aim for Consistency

When dealing with a language question for which there are different answers—such as whether to use a comma before the conjunction in a series of three ("The mayor's speech addressed taxes, housing for the poor, and the job situation")—always use the same strategy throughout your paper. If, for example, you avoid splitting one infinitive, avoid splitting *all* infinitives.

Have Confidence in What You Know about Writing!

It is easy for unpracticed writers to allow their occasional mistakes to shake their confidence in their writing ability. The fact is, however, that most of what we know about writing is correct. We are all capable, for example, of writing grammatically sound phrases, even if we cannot list the rules by which we achieve coherence. Most writers who worry about their chronic errors make fewer mistakes than they think. Becoming distressed about errors makes writing even more difficult.

Grammar

As various composition theorists have pointed out, the word *grammar* has several definitions. One meaning is "the formal patterns in which words must be arranged in order to convey meaning." We learn these patterns very early in life and use them spontaneously, without thinking. Our understanding of grammatical patterns is extremely sophisticated, despite the fact that few of us can actually cite the rules by which the patterns work. Patrick Hartwell tested grammar learning by asking native English speakers of different ages and levels of education, including high school teachers, to arrange these words in natural order:

French   the   young   girls   four

Everyone could produce the natural order for this phrase: "the four young French girls." Yet none of Hartwell's respondents said they knew the rule that governs the order of the words. (Patrick Hartwell. 1985. "Grammar, Grammars, and the Teaching of Grammar." *College English* 47:111.)

Eliminate Chronic Errors

But if just thinking about our errors has a negative effect on our writing, how do we learn to write more correctly? Perhaps the best answer is simply to write as often as possible. Give yourself lots of practice in putting your thoughts into written shape—and then in revising and proofing your work. As you write and revise, be honest with yourself—and patient. Chronic errors are like bad habits; getting rid of them takes time.

You probably know of one or two problem areas in your writing that you could have eliminated but have not. Instead, you may have "fudged" your writing at the critical points, relying on half-remembered formulas from past English classes or trying to come up with logical solutions to your writing problems. (*Warning:* The English language does not always work in a way that seems logical.) You may have simply decided that comma rules are unlearnable or that you will never understand the difference between the verbs *lay* and *lie*. And so you guess, and you come up with the wrong answer a good part of the time. What a shame, when just a little extra work would give you mastery over those few gaps in your understanding and boost your confidence as well.

Instead of continuing with this sort of guesswork and living with the gaps in your knowledge, why not face the problem areas now and learn the rules that have heretofore escaped you? What follows is a discussion of those surface features of writing where errors most commonly occur. You will probably be familiar with most if not all of the rules discussed, but there may well be a few you have not yet mastered. Now is the time to do so.

2.2 Grammar and Punctuation

Apostrophes

An apostrophe is used to show possession. When you wish to say that something belongs to someone or something, you add either an apostrophe and an *s* or an apostrophe alone to the word that represents the owner.

When the owner is *singular* (a single person or thing), the apostrophe precedes an added *s*:

> According to Mayor Anderson's secretary, the news broadcast has been canceled.
>
> The union's lawyers challenged the government's policy in court.
>
> Somebody's briefcase was left in the auditorium.

The same rule applies if the word showing possession is a plural that does not end in *s*:

> The women's club sponsored several debates during the last presidential campaign.

> Governor Smith has proven himself a tireless worker for children's rights.

When the word expressing ownership is a plural ending in *s*, the apostrophe follows the *s*:

> The new legislation was discussed at the secretaries' conference.

There are two ways to form the possessive for two or more nouns:

1. To show joint possession (both nouns owning the same thing or things), the last noun in the series is possessive:

   The president and first lady's invitations were sent out yesterday.
2. To indicate that each noun owns an item or items individually, each noun must show possession:

   Mayor Scott's and Mayor MacKay's speeches took different approaches to the same problem.

The importance of the apostrophe is obvious when you consider the difference in meaning between the following two sentences:

> Be sure to pick up the senator's bags on your way to the airport.

> Be sure to pick up the senators' bags on your way to the airport.

In the first sentence, you have only one senator to worry about, whereas in the second, you have at least two!

A Prepostrophe?

James Swanson, political commentator and editor of the *Gesundheit Gazette*, occasionally encounters political statements that he finds to be preposterous. He believes that journalists should warn us when they print one of these statements by placing a "prepostrophe" (∧) at the end of a preposterous sentence. Consider, for example, how a prepostrophe might assist the reader in the following statement: "We can cut taxes without reducing services∧" For even more preposterous statements, we add more prepostrophes, as in "I never had sex with that woman, Miss Lewinsky∧∧"

Capitalization

Here is a brief summary of some hard-to-remember capitalization rules:

1. You may, if you choose, capitalize the first letter of the first word in a sentence that follows a colon. However, make sure you use one pattern consistently throughout your paper:

   Our instructions are explicit: *Do not* allow anyone into the conference without an identification badge.

   Our instructions are explicit: *do not* allow anyone into the conference without an identification badge.

2. Capitalize *proper nouns* (names of specific people, places, or things) and *proper adjectives* (adjectives made from proper nouns). A common noun following a proper adjective is usually not capitalized, nor is a common adjective preceding a proper adjective (such as *a, an,* or *the*):

PROPER NOUNS	PROPER ADJECTIVES
Poland	Polish officials
Iraq	the Iraqi ambassador
Shakespeare	a Shakespearean tragedy

Proper nouns include

- *Names of monuments and buildings:* the Washington Monument, the Empire State Building, the Library of Congress
- *Historical events, eras, and certain terms concerning calendar dates:* the Civil War, the Dark Ages, Monday, December, Columbus Day
- *Parts of the country:* the North, the Southwest, the Eastern Seaboard, the West Coast, New England

NOTE. *When words like north, south, east, west, northwest are used to designate direction rather than geographical region, they are not capitalized:* "We drove *east* to Boston and then made a tour of the East Coast."

- *Words referring to race, religion, and nationality:* Islam, Muslim, Caucasian, White (*or* white), Asian, Negro, Black (*or* black), Slavic, Arab, Jewish, Hebrew, Buddhism, Buddhists, Southern Baptists, the Bible, the Koran, American
- *Names of languages:* English, Chinese, Latin, Sanskrit
- *Titles of corporations, institutions, universities, and organizations:* Dow Chemical, General Motors, the National Endowment for the Humanities, University of Tennessee, Colby College, Kiwanis Club, American Association of Retired Persons, Oklahoma State Senate

NOTE. Some words once considered proper nouns or adjectives have, over time, become common, such as *french fries, pasteurized milk, arabic numerals,* and *italics.*

3. Titles of individuals may be capitalized if they precede a proper name; otherwise, titles are usually not capitalized:

The committee honored Senator Jones.

The committee honored the senator from Kansas.

We phoned Doctor Jessup, who arrived shortly afterward.

We phoned the doctor, who arrived shortly afterward.

A story on Queen Elizabeth's health appeared in yesterday's paper.

A story on the queen's health appeared in yesterday's paper.

Pope John Paul's visit to Colorado was a public relations success.

The pope's visit to Colorado was a public relations success.

When Not to Capitalize

In general, you do not capitalize nouns when your reference is nonspecific. For example, you would not capitalize *the senator,* but you would capitalize *Senator Smith.* The second reference is as much a title as it is a term of identification, whereas the first reference is a mere identifier. Likewise, there is a difference in degree of specificity between *the state treasury* and *the Texas State Treasury.*

NOTE. The meaning of a term may change somewhat depending on its capitalization. What, for example, might be the difference between a *Democrat* and a *democrat?* When capitalized, the word refers to a member of a specific political party; when not capitalized, it refers to someone who believes in the democratic form of government.

Capitalization depends to some extent on the context of your writing. For example, if you are writing a policy analysis for a specific corporation, you may capitalize words and phrases that refer to that corporation—such as *Board of Directors, Chairman of the Board,* and *the Institute*—that would not be capitalized in a paper written for a more general audience. Likewise, in some contexts it is not unusual to see the titles of certain powerful officials capitalized even when not accompanying a proper noun:

The President took few members of his staff to Camp David with him.

Colons

We all know certain uses for the colon. A colon can, for example, separate the parts of a statement of time (4:25 A.M.), separate chapter and verse in a biblical quotation (John 3:16), and close the salutation of a business letter (*Dear Senator Keaton:*). But the colon has other, less well known uses that can add extra flexibility to sentence structure.

The colon can introduce into a sentence certain kinds of material, such as a list, a quotation, or a restatement or description of material mentioned earlier:

LIST

The committee's research proposal promised to do three things: (1) establish the extent of the problem; (2) examine several possible solutions; and (3) estimate the cost of each solution.

QUOTATION

In his speech, the mayor challenged us with these words: "How will your council's work make a difference in the life of our city?"

RESTATEMENT OR DESCRIPTION

Ahead of us, according to the senator's chief of staff, lay the biggest job of all: convincing our constituents of the plan's benefits.

Commas

The comma is perhaps the most troublesome of all marks of punctuation, no doubt because its use is governed by so many variables, such as sentence length, rhetorical emphasis, and changing notions of style. The most common problems are outlined in the following subsections.

The Comma Splice

A *comma splice* is the joining of two complete sentences with only a comma:

An impeachment is merely an indictment of a government official, actual removal usually requires a vote by a legislative body.

An unemployed worker who has been effectively retrained is no longer an economic problem for the community, he has become an asset.

It might be possible for the city to assess fees on the sale of real estate, however, such a move would be criticized by the community of real estate developers.

In each of these passages, two complete sentences (also called independent clauses) have been spliced together by a comma, which is an inadequate break between the two sentences.

One foolproof way to check your paper for comma splices is to read the structures on both sides of each comma carefully. If you find a complete sentence on each side, and if the sentence following the comma does not begin with a coordinating conjunction (*and, but, for, nor, or, so, yet*), then you have found a comma splice.

Simply reading the draft to try to "hear" the comma splices may not work, because the rhetorical features of your prose—its "movement"—may make it hard to detect this kind of error in sentence completeness. There are five commonly used ways to correct comma splices:

1. Place a period between the two independent clauses:

   INCORRECT   A political candidate receives many benefits from his or her affiliation with a political party, there are liabilities as well.

   CORRECT   A political candidate receives many benefits from his or her affiliation with a political party. There are liabilities as well.

2. Place a comma and a coordinating conjunction (*and, but, for, or, nor, so, yet*) between the sentences:

   INCORRECT   The councilman's speech described the major differences of opinion over the economic situation, it also suggested a possible course of action.

   CORRECT   The councilman's speech described the major differences of opinion over the economic situation, *and* it also suggested a possible course of action.

3. Place a semicolon between the independent clauses:

   INCORRECT   Some people feel that the federal government should play a large role in establishing a housing policy for the homeless, many others disagree.

   CORRECT   Some people feel that the federal government should play a large role in establishing a housing policy for the homeless; many others disagree.

4. Rewrite the two clauses as one independent clause:

   INCORRECT   Television ads played a big part in the campaign, however they were not the deciding factor in the challenger's victory over the incumbent.

   CORRECT   Television ads played a large but not a decisive role in the challenger's victory over the incumbent.

5. Change one of the independent clauses into a dependent clause by beginning it with a *subordinating word* (for example, *although, after, as, because, before, if, though, unless, when, which, where*), which prevents the clause from being able to stand on its own as a complete sentence.

   INCORRECT   The election was held last Tuesday, there was a poor voter turnout.

   CORRECT   When the election was held last Tuesday, there was a poor voter turnout.

Commas in a Compound Sentence

A *compound sentence* is composed of two or more independent clauses—two complete sentences. When these two clauses are joined by a coordinating conjunction, the conjunction should be preceded by a comma to signal the reader that another independent clause follows. (This is method number 2 for fixing a comma splice.) When the comma is missing, the reader is not expecting to find the second half of a compound sentence and may be distracted from the text.

As the following examples indicate, the missing comma is especially a problem in longer sentences or in sentences in which other coordinating conjunctions appear. Notice how the comma sorts out the two main parts of the compound sentence, eliminating confusion:

INCORRECT	The senator promised to visit the hospital and investigate the problem and then he called the press conference to a close.
CORRECT	The senator promised to visit the hospital and investigate the problem, and then he called the press conference to a close.
INCORRECT	The water board can neither make policy nor enforce it nor can its members serve on auxiliary water committees.
CORRECT	The water board can neither make policy nor enforce it, nor can its members serve on auxiliary water committees.

An exception to this rule arises in shorter sentences, where the comma may not be necessary to make the meaning clear:

The mayor phoned and we thanked him for his support.

However, it is never wrong to place a comma after the conjunction between independent clauses. If you are the least bit unsure of your audience's notion of "proper" grammar, it is a good idea to take the conservative approach and use the comma:

The mayor phoned, and we thanked him for his support.

Commas with Restrictive and Nonrestrictive Elements

A *nonrestrictive element* is a part of a sentence—a word, phrase, or clause—that adds information about another element in the sentence without restricting or limiting its meaning. Although this information may be useful, the nonrestrictive element is not needed for the sentence to make sense. To signal its inessential nature, the nonrestrictive element is set off from the rest of the sentence with commas.

The failure to use commas to indicate the nonrestrictive nature of a sentence element can cause confusion. See, for example, how the presence or absence of commas affects our understanding of the following sentence:

The mayor was talking with the policeman, who won the outstanding service award last year.

The mayor was talking with the policeman who won the outstanding service award last year.

Can you see that the comma changes the meaning of the sentence? In the first version of the sentence, the comma makes the information that follows it incidental: *The mayor was talking with the policeman, who happens to have won the service award last year.* In the second version of the sentence, the information following the word policeman is vital to the sense of the sentence; it tells us specifically which *policeman*—presumably there are more than one—the mayor was addressing. Here the lack of a comma has transformed the material following the word *policeman* into a *restrictive element,* which means that it is necessary to our understanding of the sentence.

Be sure that you make a clear distinction in your paper between nonrestrictive and restrictive elements by setting off the nonrestrictive elements with commas.

Commas in a Series

A series is any two or more items of a similar nature that appear consecutively in a sentence. These items may be individual words, phrases, or clauses. In a series of three or more items, the items are separated by commas:

The senator, the mayor, and the police chief all attended the ceremony.

Because of the new zoning regulations, *all trailer parks must be moved out of the neighborhood, all small businesses must apply for recertification and tax status, and the two local churches must repave their parking lots.*

The final comma in the series, the one before *and,* is sometimes left out, especially in newspaper writing. This practice, however, can make for confusion, especially in longer, complicated sentences like the second example preceding this paragraph. Here is the way this sentence would read without the final, or *serial,* comma:

Because of the new zoning regulations, all trailer parks must be moved out of the neighborhood, all small businesses must apply for recertification and tax status and the two local churches must repave their parking lots.

Notice that, without a comma, the division between the second and third items in the series is not clear. This is the sort of ambiguous structure that can cause a reader to backtrack and lose concentration. You can avoid such confusion by always using that final comma. Remember, however, that if you do decide to include it, you should do so consistently; make sure it appears in every series in your paper.

Dangling Modifiers

A *modifier* is a word or group of words used to describe, or modify, another word in the sentence. A *dangling modifier* appears at either the beginning or the end of a sentence and seems to be describing some word other than the one the writer obviously intended. The modifier therefore "dangles," disconnected from its correct meaning. It is often hard for the writer to spot a dangling modifier, but readers can—and will—find them, and the result can be disastrous for the sentence, as the following examples demonstrate:

INCORRECT	Flying low over Washington, the White House was seen.
CORRECT	Flying low over Washington, we saw the White House.
INCORRECT	Worried at the cost of the program, sections of the bill were trimmed in committee.
CORRECT	Worried at the cost of the program, the committee trimmed sections of the bill.
INCORRECT	To lobby for prison reform, a lot of effort went into the television ads.
CORRECT	The lobby group put a lot of effort into the television ads advocating prison reform.
INCORRECT	Stunned, the television broadcast the defeated senator's concession speech.
CORRECT	The television broadcast the stunned senator's concession speech.

Note that, in the first two incorrect sentences, the confusion is largely due to the use of *passive-voice* verbs: "the White House *was seen*," "sections of the bill *were trimmed*." Often, although not always, a dangling modifier results because the actor in the sentence—we in the first sentence, *the committee* in the second—is either distanced from the modifier or obliterated by the passive-voice verb. It is a good idea to avoid using the passive voice unless you have a specific reason for doing so.

One way to check for dangling modifiers is to examine all modifiers at the beginning or end of your sentences. Look especially for *to be* phrases or for words ending in *-ing* or *-ed* at the start of the modifier. Then see if the modified word is close enough to the phrase to be properly connected.

Parallelism

Series of two or more words, phrases, or clauses within a sentence should have the same grammatical structure, called *parallelism*. Parallel structures can add power and balance to your writing by creating a strong rhetorical rhythm. Here is a famous example of parallelism from the Preamble to the U.S. Constitution. (The capitalization follows that of the original eighteenth-century document. Parallel structures have been italicized.)

We the People of the United States, in Order to *form a more perfect Union, Establish justice, insure Domestic Tranquillity, provide for the common defense, promote the general Welfare, and secure the Blessings of Liberty* to ourselves and our Posterity, do *ordain* and *establish* this Constitution for the United States of America.

There are actually two series in this sentence: the first, composed of six phrases, each of which completes the infinitive phrase beginning with the word *to* (*to form, [to] Establish, [to] insure, [to] provide, [to] promote,* and *[to] secure);* the second, consisting of two verbs (*ordain* and *establish*). These parallel series appeal to our love of balance and pattern, and give an authoritative tone to the sentence. The writer, we feel, has thought long and carefully about the matter at hand and has taken firm control of it.

Because we find a special satisfaction in balanced structures, we are more likely to remember ideas phrased in parallelisms than in less highly ordered language. For this reason, as well as for the sense of authority and control that they suggest, parallel structures are common in political utterances:

> We hold these truths to be self-evident, that all men are created equal, that they are endowed by their Creator with certain unalienable rights, that among these are life, liberty, and the pursuit of happiness.
>
> The Declaration of Independence, 1776

> But in a larger sense, we cannot dedicate, we can not consecrate, we cannot hallow this ground. The brave men, living and dead, who struggled here, have consecrated it far above our poor power to add or detract. The world will little note, nor long remember what we say here; but it can never forget what they did here.
>
> Abraham Lincoln, Gettysburg Address, 1863

> Ask not what your country can do for you, ask what you can do for your country.
>
> John F. Kennedy, Inaugural Address, 1961

Faulty Parallelism

If the parallelism of a passage is not carefully maintained, the writing can seem sloppy and out of balance. Scan your writing to make sure that all series and lists have parallel structure. The following examples show how to correct faulty parallelism:

INCORRECT	The mayor promises not only *to reform* the police department but also *the giving of raises* to all city employees. [Connective structures such as *not only . . . but also,* and *both . . . and* introduce elements that should be parallel.]
CORRECT	The mayor promises not only *to reform* the police department but also *to give* raises to all city employees.
INCORRECT	The cost *of doing nothing* is greater than the cost *to renovate* the apartment block.
CORRECT	The cost *of doing nothing* is greater than the cost *of renovating* the apartment block.
INCORRECT	Here are the items on the committee's agenda: (1) *to discuss* the new property tax; (2) *to revise* the wording of the city charter; (3) *a vote* on the city manager's request for an assistant.

CORRECT   Here are the items on the committee's agenda: (1) *to discuss* the new property tax; (2) *to revise* the wording of the city charter; (3) *to vote* on the city manager's request for an assistant.

Fused (Run-on) Sentences

A *fused sentence* is one in which two or more independent clauses (passages that can stand as complete sentences) have been run together without the aid of any suitable connecting word, phrase, or punctuation. There are several ways to correct a fused sentence:

INCORRECT   The council members were exhausted they had debated for two hours.

CORRECT   The council members were exhausted. They had debated for two hours. [The clauses have been separated into two sentences.]

CORRECT   The council members were exhausted; they had debated for two hours. [The clauses have been separated by a semicolon.]

CORRECT   The council members were exhausted, having debated for two hours. [The second clause has been rephrased as a dependent clause.]

INCORRECT   Our policy analysis impressed the committee it also convinced them to reconsider their action.

CORRECT   Our policy analysis impressed the committee and also convinced them to reconsider their action. [The second clause has been rephrased as part of the first clause.]

CORRECT   Our policy analysis impressed the committee, and it also convinced them to reconsider their action. [The clauses have been separated by a comma and a coordinating word.]

Although a fused sentence is easily noticeable to the reader, it can be maddeningly difficult for the writer to catch. Unpracticed writers tend to read through the fused spots, sometimes supplying the break that is usually heard when sentences are spoken. To check for fused sentences, read the independent clauses in your paper *carefully,* making sure that there are adequate breaks among all of them.

Pronoun Errors

Its Versus It's

Do not make the mistake of trying to form the possessive of *it* in the same way that you form the possessive of most nouns. The pronoun *it* shows possession by simply adding an *s.*

The prosecuting attorney argued the case on *its* merits.

The word *it's* is a contraction of *it is*:

It's the most expensive program ever launched by the council.

What makes the *its/it's* rule so confusing is that most nouns form the singular possessive by adding an apostrophe and an *s*:

The *jury's* verdict startled the crowd.

When proofreading, any time you come to the word *it's,* substitute the phrase *it is* while you read. If the phrase makes sense, you have used the correct form. If you have used the word *it's,*

The newspaper article was misleading in *it's* analysis of the election.

then read it as *it is*:

The newspaper article was misleading in *it is* analysis of the election.

If the phrase makes no sense, substitute *its* for *it's*:

The newspaper article was misleading in *its* analysis of the election.

Vague Pronoun References

Pronouns are words that take the place of nouns or other pronouns that have already been mentioned in your writing. The most common pronouns include *he, she, it, they, them, those, which,* and *who.* You must make sure there is no confusion about the word to which each pronoun refers:

The mayor said that *he* would support our bill if the city council would also back it.

The word that the pronoun replaces is called its *antecedent.* To check the accuracy of your pronoun references, ask yourself, *To what does the pronoun refer?* Then answer the question carefully, making sure that there is not more than one possible antecedent.

Consider the following example:

Several special interest groups decided to defeat the new health care bill. *This* became the turning point of the government's reform campaign.

To what does the word *This* refer? The immediate answer seems to be the word *bill* at the end of the previous sentence. It is more likely that the writer was referring to the attempt of the special interest groups to defeat the bill, but there is no word in the first sentence that refers specifically to this action. The pronoun reference is thus unclear. One way to clarify the reference is to change the beginning of the second sentence:

Several special interest groups decided to defeat the new health care bill. *Their attack on the bill* became the turning point of the government's reform campaign.

This point is further demonstrated by following sentence:

When John F. Kennedy appointed his brother Robert to the position of U.S. attorney general, *he* had little idea how widespread the corruption in the Teamsters Union was.

To whom does the word *he* refer? It is unclear whether the writer is referring to John or *Robert* Kennedy. One way to clarify the reference is simply to repeat the antecedent instead of using a pronoun:

When John F. Kennedy appointed his brother Robert to the position of U.S. attorney general, Robert had little idea how widespread the corruption in the Teamsters Union was.

Pronoun Agreement

A pronoun must agree with its antecedent in both gender and number, as the following examples demonstrate:

Mayor Smith said that *he* appreciated our club's support in the election.

One reporter asked the senator what *she* would do if the president offered *her* a cabinet post.

Having listened to our case, the judge decided to rule on *it* within the week.

Engineers working on the housing project said *they* were pleased with the renovation so far.

Certain words, however, can be troublesome antecedents, because they may look like plural pronouns but are actually singular:

anyone   each   either   everybody   everyone
nobody   no one   somebody   someone

A pronoun referring to one of these words in a sentence must be singular too.

INCORRECT	*Each* of the women in the support group brought *their* children.
CORRECT	*Each* of the women in the support group brought *her* children.
INCORRECT	Has *everybody* received *their* ballot?
CORRECT	Has *everybody* received *his or her* ballot? [The two gender-specific pronouns are used to avoid sexist language.]
CORRECT	Have *all the delegates* received *their* ballots? [The singular antecedent has been changed to a plural one.]

A Shift in Person

It is important to avoid shifting unnecessarily among first person (*I, we*), second person (*you*), and third person (*she, he, it, one, they*). Such shifts can cause confusion.

INCORRECT	*Most people* [third person] who run for office find that if *you* [second person] tell the truth during your campaign, *you* will gain the voters' respect.
CORRECT	*Most people* who run for office find that if *they* tell the truth during their campaigns, *they* will gain the voters' respect.
INCORRECT	*One* [first person] cannot tell whether *they* [third person] are suited for public office until *they* decide to run.
CORRECT	*One* cannot tell whether *one* is suited for public office until *one* decides to run.

Quotation Marks

It can be difficult to remember when to use quotation marks and where they go in relation to other punctuation. When faced with these questions, unpracticed writers often try to rely on logic rather than on a rulebook, but the rules do not always seem to rely on logic. The only way to make sure of your use of quotation marks is to memorize the rules. Luckily, there are not many.

The Use of Quotation Marks

Use quotation marks to enclose direct quotations that are not longer than four typed lines:

> In his farewell address to the American people, George Washington warned, "The great rule of conduct for us, in regard to foreign nations, is, in extending our commercial relations, to have with them as little political connection as possible." (U.S. Congress, Senate, *Washington's Farewell Address to the People of the United States,* 102d Cong., Ist sess., 1991, S. Doc. 3.)

Longer quotes are placed in a double-spaced block, *without* quotation marks:

> Lincoln clearly explained his motive for continuing the Civil War in his response to Horace Greeley's open letter:

I would save the Union. I would *save* it the shortest way under the Constitution. The sooner the National authority can be restored, the nearer the Union will be the Union as it was. If there be those who would not save the Union unless they could at the same time save Slavery, I do not agree with them. If there be those who would not save the Union unless they could at the same time *destroy* Slavery, I do not agree with them. (Letter to Horace Greeley. August 22, 1862, in *Abraham Lincoln: His Speeches and Writings.* 1946. Edited by Roy Basler. Cleveland: World, 652.)

Use single quotation marks to set off quotations within quotations:

> "I intend," said the senator, "to use in my speech a line from Frost's poem 'The Road Not Taken.'"

NOTE. When the quote occurs at the end of the sentence, both the single and double quotation marks are placed outside the period.

Use quotation marks to set off titles of the following:

short poems (those not printed as a separate volume)
short stories
articles or essays
songs
episodes of television or radio shows

Use quotation marks to set off words or phrases used in special ways:

1. To convey irony:

   The "liberal" administration has done nothing but cater to big business.

2. To indicate a technical term:

   To "filibuster" is to delay legislation, usually through prolonged speech-making. The last notable filibuster occurred just last week in the Senate. [Once the term has been defined, it is not placed in quotation marks again.]

Quotation Marks in Relation to Other Punctuation

Place commas and periods *inside* closing quotation marks:

"My fellow Americans," said the president, "there are tough times ahead of us."

Place colons and semicolons *outside* closing quotation marks:

In his speech on voting, the governor warned against "an encroaching indolence"; he was referring to the middle class.

There are several victims of the government's campaign, "Turn Back the Clock": the homeless, the elderly, the mentally impaired.

Use the context to determine whether to place question marks, exclamation points, and dashes inside or outside closing quotation marks. If the punctuation is part of the quotation, place it inside the quotation mark:

"When will Congress make up its mind?" asked the ambassador.

The demonstrators shouted, "Free the hostages!" and "No more slavery!"

If the punctuation is not part of the quotation, place it outside the quotation mark:

> Which president said, "We have nothing to fear but fear itself"? [Although the quote is a complete sentence, you do not place a period after it. There can only be one piece of terminal punctuation, or punctuation that ends a sentence.]

Semicolons

The semicolon is a little-used punctuation mark that you should learn to incorporate into your writing strategy because of its many potential applications. For example, a semicolon can be used to correct a comma splice:

INCORRECT	The union representatives left the meeting in good spirits, their demands were met.
CORRECT	The union representatives left the meeting in good spirits; their demands were met.
INCORRECT	Several guests at the fundraiser had lost their invitations, however, we were able to seat them anyway.
CORRECT	Several guests at the fundraiser had lost their invitations; however, we were able to seat them anyway. [Conjunctive adverbs such as *however, therefore,* and *thus* are not coordinating words (such as *and, but, or, for, so, yet*) and cannot be used with a comma to link independent clauses. If the second independent clause begins with *however,* it must be preceded by either a period or a semicolon.]

As you can see from the second example, connecting two independent clauses with a semicolon instead of a period strengthens their relationship.

Semicolons can also separate items in a series when the series items themselves contain commas:

> The newspaper account of the rally stressed the march, which drew the biggest crowd; the mayor's speech, which drew tremendous applause; and the party in the park, which lasted for hours.

Avoid misusing semicolons. For example, use a comma, not a semicolon, to separate an independent clause from a dependent clause:

INCORRECT	Students from the college volunteered to answer phones during the pledge drive; which was set up to generate money for the new arts center.
CORRECT	Students from the college volunteered to answer phones during the pledge drive, which was set up to generate money for the new arts center.

Do not overuse semicolons. Although they are useful, too many semicolons in your writing can distract your readers' attention. Avoid monotony by using semicolons sparingly.

Sentence Fragments

A fragment is an incomplete part of a sentence that is punctuated and capitalized as if it were an entire sentence. It is an especially disruptive error, because it obscures the connections that the words of a sentence must make in order to complete the reader's understanding.

Students sometimes write fragments because they are concerned that a sentence needs to be shortened. Remember that cutting the length of a sentence merely by adding a period somewhere often creates a fragment. When you check writing for fragments, it is essential that you read each sentence carefully to determine whether it has (1) a complete subject and a verb, and (2) a subordinating word before the subject and verb, which makes the construction a subordinate clause rather than a complete sentence.

Types of Sentence Fragments

Some fragments lack a verb:

INCORRECT
The chairperson of our committee, having received a letter from the mayor. [The word *having*, which can be used as a verb, is here being used as a gerund introducing a participial phrase. *Watch out* for words that look like verbs but are being used in another way.]

CORRECT
The chairperson of our committee received a letter from the mayor.

Some fragments lack a subject:

INCORRECT
Our study shows that there is broad support for improvement in the health care system. And in the unemployment system.

CORRECT
Our study shows that there is broad support for improvement in the health care system and in the unemployment system.

Some fragments are subordinate clauses:

INCORRECT
After the latest edition of the newspaper came out. [This clause has the two major components of a complete sentence: a subject (*edition*) and a verb (*came*). Indeed, if the first word (*After*) were deleted, the clause would be a complete sentence. But that first word is a *subordinating word*, which prevents the following clause from standing on its

own as a complete sentence. *Watch out* for this kind of construction. It is called a *subordinate clause,* and it is *not a sentence.*]

CORRECT   After the latest edition of the newspaper came out, the mayor's press secretary was overwhelmed with phone calls. [A common method of correcting a subordinate clause that has been punctuated as a complete sentence is to connect it to the complete sentence to which it is closest in meaning.]

INCORRECT   Several representatives asked for copies of the vice president's position paper. Which called for reform of the Environmental Protection Agency.

CORRECT   Several representatives asked for copies of the vice president's position paper, which called for reform of the Environmental Protection Agency.

Spelling

All of us have problems spelling certain words that we have not yet committed to memory. But most writers are not as bad at spelling as they believe they are. Usually an individual finds only a handful of words troubling. It is important to be as sensitive as possible to your own particular spelling problems—and to keep a dictionary handy. There is no excuse for failing to check spelling.

What follows are a list of commonly confused words and a list of commonly misspelled words. Read through the lists, looking for those words that tend to give you trouble. If you have any questions, *consult your dictionary*.

COMMONLY CONFUSED WORDS

accept/except	council/counsel	human/humane
advice/advise	dairy/diary	its/it's
affect/effect	descent/dissent	know/no
aisle/isle	desert/dessert	later/latter
allusion/illusion	device/devise	lay/lie
an/and	die/dye	lead/led
angel/angle	dominant/dominate	lessen/lesson
ascent/assent	elicit/illicit	loose/lose
bare/bear	eminent/immanent/	may be/maybe
brake/break	imminent	miner/minor
breath/breathe	envelop/envelope	moral/morale
buy/by	every day/everyday	of/off
capital/capitol	fair/fare	passed/past
choose/chose	formally/formerly	patience/patients
cite/sight/site	forth/fourth	peace/piece
complement/compliment	hear/here	personal/personnel
conscience/conscious	heard/herd	plain/plane
corps/corpse	hole/whole	precede/proceed

presence/presents   scene/seen   waist/waste
principal/principle   sense/since   waive/wave
quiet/quite   stationary/stationery   weak/week
rain/reign/rein   straight/strait   weather/whether
raise/raze   taught/taut   were/where
reality/realty   than/then   which/witch
respectfully/respectively   their/there/they're   whose/who's
reverend/reverent   threw/through   your/you're
right/rite/write   too/to/two
road/rode   track/tract

COMMONLY MISSPELLED WORDS

a lot	easily	irritate	professor
acceptable	efficient	knowledge	prominent
accessible	environment	license	pronunciation
accommodate	equipped	likelihood	psychology
accompany	exceed	maintenance	publicly
accustomed	exercise	manageable	pursue
acquire	existence	meanness	pursuing
against	experience	mischievous	questionnaire
annihilate	fascinate	missile	realize
apparent	finally	necessary	receipt
arguing	foresee	nevertheless	received
argument	forty	no one	recession
authentic	fulfill	noticeable	recommend
before	gauge	noticing	referring
begin	guaranteed	nuisance	religious
beginning	guard	occasion	remembrance
believe	harass	occasionally	reminisce
benefited	hero	occurred	repetition
bulletin	heroes	occurrences	representative
business	humorous	omission	rhythm
cannot	hurried	omit	ridiculous
category	hurriedly	opinion	roommate
committee	hypocrite	opponent	satellite
condemn	ideally	parallel	scarcity
courteous	immediately	parole	scenery
definitely	immense	peaceable	science
dependent	incredible	performance	secede
desperate	innocuous	pertain	secession
develop	intercede	practical	secretary
different	interrupt	preparation	senseless
disappear	irrelevant	probably	separate
disappoint	irresistible	process	sergeant

shining
significant
sincerely
skiing
stubbornness
studying
succeed
success

successfully
susceptible
suspicious
technical
temporary
tendency
therefore
tragedy

truly
tyranny
unanimous
unconscious
undoubtedly
until
vacuum
valuable

various
vegetable
visible
without
women
writing

3
Paper Formats

Your format makes your paper's first impression. Justly or not, accurately or not, it announces your professional competence—or lack of competence. A well-executed format implies that your paper is worth reading. More importantly, however, a proper format brings information to your readers in a familiar form that has the effect of setting their minds at ease. Your paper's format should therefore impress your readers with your academic competence as a political scientist by following accepted professional standards. Like the style and clarity of your writing, your format communicates messages that are often more readily and profoundly received than the content of the document itself.

The format described in this chapter is in conformance with generally accepted standards in the discipline of political science, including instructions for the following elements:

General page format	Table of contents
Title page	List of tables and figures
Abstract	Text
Executive summary	Reference page
Outline page	Appendixes

Except for special instructions from your instructor, follow the directions in this manual exactly.

3.1 General Page Format

Political science assignments should be typed or printed on 8½-by-11-inch premium white bond paper, 20 pound or heavier. Do not use any other color or size except to comply with special instructions from your instructor, and do not use off-white or poor quality (draft) paper. Political science that is worth the time to write and read is worth good paper.

Always submit to your instructor an original typed or computer- (preferably laser-) printed manuscript. Do not submit a photocopy! Always make a second copy for your own files in case the original is lost.

Margins, except for theses and dissertations, should be one inch on all sides of the paper. Unless otherwise instructed, all papers should be *double-spaced* in a 12–point word processing font or typewriter pica type. Typewriter elite type may be used if another is not available. Select a font that is plain and easy to read, such as Helvetica, Courier, Garamond, or Times Roman. Do not use script, stylized, or elaborate fonts.

Page numbers should appear in the upper-right-hand corner of each page, starting immediately after the title page. No page number should appear on the title page or on the first page of the text. Page numbers should appear one inch from the right side and one-half inch from the top of the page. They should proceed consecutively beginning with the title page (although the first number is not actually printed on the title page). You may use lowercase roman numerals (i, ii, iii, iv, v, vi, vii, viii, ix, x, and so on) for the pages, such as the title page, table of contents, and table of figures, that precede the first page of text, but if you use them, the numbers must be placed at the center of the bottom of the page.

Ask your instructor about bindings. In the absence of further directions, *do not bind* your paper or enclose it within a plastic cover sheet. Place one staple in the upper-left-hand corner, or use a paper clip at the top of the paper. Note that a paper to be submitted to a journal for publication should not be clipped, stapled, or bound in any form.

3.2 Title Page

The following information will be centered on the title page:

Title of the paper
Name of writer
Course name, section number, and instructor
College or university
Date

```
                 The Impeachment of Bill Clinton

                             by

                 Ambrose Percival Bierce



                 The American Presidency

                           POL213

                    Dr. Marion Swanson

                  St. Johnswort College

                     January 1, 2000
```

As the sample title page shows, the title should clearly describe the problem addressed in the paper. If the paper discusses juvenile recidivism in Albemarle County jails, for example, the title "Recidivism in the Albemarle County Criminal Justice System" is professional, clear, and helpful to the reader. "Albemarle County," "Juvenile Justice," and "County Jails" are all too vague to be effective. Also, the title should not be "cute." A cute title may attract attention for a play on Broadway, but it will detract from the credibility of a paper in political science. "Inadequate Solid Waste Disposal Facilities in Denver" is professional. "Down in the Dumps" is not.

In addition, title pages for position papers and policy analysis papers must include the name, title, and organization of the public official who has the authority and responsibility to implement the recommendation of your paper. The person to whom you address the paper should be the person who has the responsibility and the authority to make the decision that is called for in your paper. The "address" should include the person's name, title, and organization. An example of a title page for a position paper that includes an address follows this paragraph. To identify the appropriate official, first carefully define the problem and the best solution. Then ascertain the person or persons who have the authority to solve the problem. If you recommend installation of a traffic signal at a particular intersection, for example, find out who makes the decisions regarding such actions in your community. It may be the public safety director, a transportation planning commission, or a town council.

```
            Oak City Police Department Personnel Policy Revisions


                               submitted to


                              Alice Davison
                          Director of Personnel
                            Police Department
                            Oak City, Arkansas


                                   by


                               Joan Smith
                       American National Government
                               GOV 1001
                            Dr. Alan McCann
                          Midwestern University
                            January 1, 2000
```

3.3 Abstract

An abstract is a brief summary of a paper written primarily to allow potential readers to see if the paper contains information of sufficient interest for them to read. People conducting research want specific kinds of information, and they often read dozens of abstracts looking for papers that contain relevant data. Abstracts have the designation "Abstract" centered near the top of the page. Next is the title, also centered, followed by a paragraph that precisely states the paper's topic, research and analysis methods, and results and conclusions. The abstract should be written in one paragraph of no more than 150 words. Remember, an abstract is not an introduction; instead, it is a summary, as demonstrated in the following sample.

Abstract

Bertrand Russell's View of Mysticism

This paper reviews Bertrand Russell's writings on religion, mysticism, and science, and defines his perspective of the contribution of mysticism to scientific knowledge. Russell drew a sharp distinction between what he considered to be (1) the essence of religion, and (2) dogma or assertions attached to religion by theologians and religious leaders. Although some of his writings, including *Why I Am Not a Christian*, appear hostile to all aspects of religion, Russell actually asserts that religion, freed from doctrinal encumbrances, not only fulfills certain psychological needs but also evokes many of the most beneficial human impulses. He believes that religious mysticism generates an intellectual disinterestedness that may be useful to science, but that it is not a source of a special type of knowledge beyond investigation by science.

3.4 Executive Summary

An executive summary, like an abstract, summarizes the content of a paper but does so in more detail. A sample executive summary is given on page 76. Whereas abstracts are read by people who are doing research, executive summaries are more likely to be read by people who need some or all of the information in the paper in order to make a decision. Many people, however, will read the executive summary to fix clearly in their minds the organization and results of a paper before reading the paper itself.

Executive Summary

Municipal parks in Springfield are deteriorating because of inadequate maintenance, and one park in particular, Oak Ridge Community Park, needs immediate attention. The problem is that parking, picnic, and rest room facilities at Oak Ridge Community Park have deteriorated as a result of normal wear, adverse weather, and vandalism, and are inadequate to meet public demand. The park was established as a public recreation "Class B" facility in 1943. Only one major renovation has occurred: in the summer of 1967 general building repair was done, and new swing sets were installed. The Park Department estimates that 10,000 square feet of new parking space, fourteen items of playground equipment, seventeen new picnic tables, and repairs on current facilities would cost about $43,700.

Three possible solutions have been given extensive consideration in this paper. One option is to do nothing. Area residents will use the area less as deterioration continues, but no immediate outlay of public funds will be necessary. The first alternative solution is to make all repairs immediately. Area residents will enjoy immediate and increased use of facilities. Taxpayers have turned down the last three tax increase requests. Revenue bonds may be acceptable to a total of $20,000, according to the City Manager, but no more than $5,000 per year is available from general city revenues.

A second alternative is to make repairs, according to a priority list, over a five-year period, using a combination of general city revenues and a $20,000 first-year bond issue that will require City Council and voter approval. Residents will enjoy the most needed improvements immediately.

The recommendation of this report is that the second alternative be adopted by the City Council. The City Council should, during its May 15 meeting, (1) adopt a resolution of intent to commit $5,000 per year for five years from the general revenue fund, dedicated to this purpose; and (2) approve for submission to public vote in the November 1998 election a $20,000 bond issue.

3.5 Outline Page

An outline page is a specific type of executive summary. Most often found in position papers and policy analysis papers, an outline page provides more information about the organization of the paper than does an executive summary. The outline shows clearly the sections in the paper and the information in each. An outline page is an asset because it allows busy decision makers to understand the entire content of a paper without reading it or to refer quickly to a specific part for more information. Position papers and policy analysis papers are written for people in positions of authority who normally need to make a variety of decisions in a short period. Outline pages reduce the amount of time they need to understand a policy problem, the alternative solutions, and the author's preferred solution. Outline pages sequentially list the complete topic sentences of the major paragraphs of a paper, in outline form. In a position paper, for example, you will be stating a problem, defining possible solutions, and then recommending the best solution. These three steps will be the major headings in your outline. (See Chapter 1 for instructions on writing an outline.) Wait until you have completed the paper before writing the outline page. Take the topic sentences from the leading (most important) paragraph in each section of your paper and place them in the appropriate places in your outline. A sample outline page is given on page 78.

3.6 Table of Contents

A table of contents does not provide as much information as an outline, but it does include the titles of the major divisions and subdivisions of a paper. Tables of contents are not normally required in student papers or papers presented at professional meetings but may be included. They are normally required, however, in books, theses, and dissertations. The table of contents should consist of the chapter or main section titles, the headings used in the text, with one additional level of titles, along with their page numbers, as the sample on page 79 demonstrates.

3.7 Tables and Figures

Lists of Tables and Figures

A list of tables or figures contains the titles of the tables or figures in the paper, in the order in which they appear, along with their page numbers. You may list tables, illustrations, and figures together under the title "Figures" (and call them all Figures in the text), or if you have more than a half page of entries, you may have separate lists for tables, illustrations, and figures (and title them accordingly in the text). An example of the format for such lists is on page 79.

Outline of Contents

I. The problem is that parking, picnic, and rest room facilities
    at Oak Ridge Community Park have deteriorated as a result of
    normal wear, adverse weather, and vandalism, and are inade-
    quate to meet public demand.
    A. Only one major renovation has occurred since 1963, when
       the park was opened.
    B. The Park Department estimates that 10,000 square feet of
       new parking space, fourteen items of playground equipment,
       seventeen new picnic tables, and repairs on current facil-
       ities would cost about $43,700.
II. Three possible solutions have been given extensive considera-
    tion:
    A. One option is to do nothing. Area residents will use the
       area less as deterioration continues, but no immediate
       outlay of public funds will be necessary.
    B. The first alternative solution is to make all repairs imme-
       diately. Area residents will enjoy immediate and increased
       use of facilities. $43,700 in funds will be needed.
       Sources include: (1) Community Development Block Grant
       funds; (2) increased property taxes; (3) revenue bonds;
       and (4) general city revenues.
    C. A second alternative is to make repairs according to a pri-
       ority list over a 5-year period, using a combination of
       general city revenues and a $20,000 first-year bond issue.
       Residents will enjoy the most needed improvements immedi-
       ately. The bond issue will require City Council and voter
       approval.
III.The recommendation of this report is that alternative C be
    adopted by the City Council. The benefit/cost analysis demon-
    strates that residents will be satisfied if basic improvements
    are made immediately. The City Council should, during its May
    15 meeting, (1) adopt a resolution of intent to commit $5,000
    per year for five years from the general revenue fund, dedi-
    cated to this purpose; and (2) approve for submission to pub-
    lic vote in the November 2000 election a $20,000 bond issue.

Contents

Figures

Tables

Tables are used in the text to show relationships among data, to help the reader come to a conclusion or understand a certain point. Tables that show simple results or "raw" data should be placed in an appendix. Tables should not reiterate the content of the text. They should say something new, and they should stand on their own. In other words, the reader should be able to understand the table without reading the text. Clearly label the columns and rows in the table. Each word in the title (except articles, prepositions, and conjunctions) should be capitalized. The source of the information should be shown immediately below the table, not in a footnote or endnote. A sample table is shown on pages 80–81.

Table 1. Projections of the Total Population of States, 1995 to 2025

(all population figures in thousands)

State	1995	2000	2005	2015	2025
Alabama	4,253	4,451	4,631	4,956	5,224
Alaska	604	653	700	791	885
Arizona	4,218	4,798	5,230	5,808	6,412
Arkansas	2,484	2,631	2,750	2,922	3,055
California	31,589	32,521	34,441	41,373	49,285
Colorado	3,747	4,168	4,468	4,833	5,188
Connecticut	3,275	3,284	3,317	3,506	3,739
Delaware	717	768	800	832	861
District of Columbia	554	523	529	594	655
Florida	14,166	15,233	16,279	18,497	20,710
Georgia	7,201	7,875	8,413	9,200	9,869
Hawaii	1,187	1,257	1,342	1,553	1,812
Idaho	1,163	1,347	1,480	1,622	1,739
Illinois	11,830	12,051	12,266	12,808	13,440
Indiana	5,803	6,045	6,215	6,404	6,546
Iowa	2,842	2,900	2,941	2,994	3,040
Kansas	2,565	2,668	2,761	2,939	3,108
Kentucky	3,860	3,995	4,098	4,231	4,314
Louisiana	4,342	4,425	4,535	4,840	5,133
Maine	1,241	1,259	1,285	1,362	1,423
Maryland	5,042	5,275	5,467	5,862	6,274

continued on page 81

Table 1 (continued)

State	1995	2000	2005	2015	2025
Massachusetts	6,074	6,199	6,310	6,574	6,902
Michigan	9,549	9,679	9,763	9,917	10,078
Minnesota	4,610	4,830	5,005	5,283	5,510
Mississippi	2,697	2,816	2,908	3,035	3,142
Missouri	5,324	5,540	5,718	6,005	6,250
Montana	870	950	1,006	1,069	1,121
Nebraska	1,637	1,705	1,761	1,850	1,930
Nevada	1,530	1,871	2,070	2,179	2,312
New Hampshire	1,148	1,224	1,281	1,372	1,439
New Jersey	7,945	8,178	8,392	8,924	9,558
New Mexico	1,685	1,860	2,016	2,300	2,612
New York	18,136	18,146	18,250	18,916	19,830
North Carolina	7,195	7,777	8,227	8,840	9,349
North Dakota	641	662	677	704	729
Ohio	11,151	11,319	11,428	11,588	11,744
Oklahoma	3,278	3,373	3,491	3,789	4,057
Oregon	3,141	3,397	3,613	3,992	4,349
Pennsylvania	12,072	12,202	12,281	12,449	12,683
Rhode Island	990	998	1,012	1,070	1,141
South Carolina	3,673	3,858	4,033	4,369	4,645
South Dakota	729	777	810	840	866
Tennessee	5,256	5,657	5,966	6,365	6,665
Texas	18,724	20,119	21,487	24,280	27,183
Utah	1,951	2,207	2,411	2,670	2,883
Vermont	585	617	638	662	678
Virginia	6,618	6,997	7,324	7,921	8,466
Washington	5,431	5,858	6,258	7,058	7,808
West Virginia	1,828	1,841	1,849	1,851	1,845
Wisconsin	5,123	5,326	5,479	5,693	5,867
Wyoming	480	525	568	641	694

Source: U.S. Census Bureau.

Illustrations and Figures

Illustrations are not normally inserted in the text of a political science paper, even in an appendix, unless they are necessary to explain the content. If illustrations are necessary, do not paste or tape photocopies of photographs or similar materials to the text or the appendix. Instead, photocopy each one on a separate sheet of paper and center it, along with its typed title, within the normal margins of the paper. The format of illustration titles should be the same as that for tables and figures.

Figures in the form of charts and graphs may be very helpful in presenting certain types of information, as the accompanying example shows.

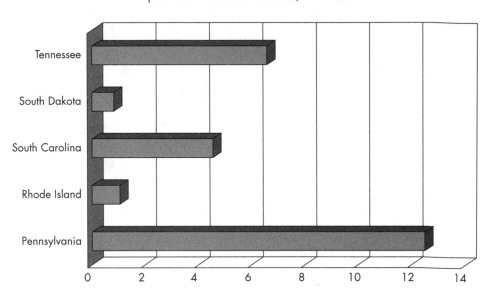

Populations of Five States in 2025, in Millions

3.8 Text

Ask your instructor for the number of pages required for the paper you are writing. The text should follow the directions explained in Chapters 1 and 2 of this manual and should conform to the format of the facsimile page shown on page 83.

Chapter Headings

Your papers should include no more than three levels of headings:

1. *Primary,* which should be centered, with each word except articles, prepositions, and conjunctions capitalized.

Facsimile Page of Text

The problem is that parking, picnic, and rest room facilities at Oak Ridge Community Park have deteriorated as a result of normal wear, adverse weather, and vandalism, and are of inadequate quantity to meet public demand. The paved parking lot has crumbled and eroded. As many as two hundred cars park on the lawn during major holidays. Only one of the five swing sets is in safe operating condition. Each set accommodates four children, but during weekends and holidays many children wait turns for the available sets. Spray paint vandalism has marred the rest room facilities, which are inadequate to meet major holiday demands.

The Department of Parks and Recreation established the park as a public recreation Class B facility in 1963. In the summer of 1987 the department conducted general building repair and installed new steel swing sets. Only minimal annual maintenance has occurred since that time.

The department estimates that 10,000 square feet of new parking lot space, fourteen items of playground equipment, seventeen new picnic tables, and repairs on current facilities would cost about $43,700 (Department of Parks and Recreation 1999). Parking lot improvements include a new surface of coarse gravel on the old paved lot and expansion of the new paved lot by 10,000 square feet. The State Engineering Office estimates the cost of parking lot improvements to be $16,200.

2. *Secondary,* which begin at the left margin, also with each word except articles, prepositions, and conjunctions capitalized.
3. *Tertiary,* which should be written in sentence style (with only the first word and proper nouns capitalized), with a period at the end, underlined.

The following illustration shows the proper use of headings:

```
                    The House of Representatives   (Primary Heading)
Impeachment Procedures of the House            (Secondary Heading)
Rules for debate in impeachment proceedings.    (Tertiary Heading)
```

3.9 Reference Page

The format for references is discussed in detail in Chapter 4. Sample reference pages for three formats—the author-date system, the documentary-note system, and the student citation system—appear on pages 103, 120–121, and 129.

3.10 Appendixes

Appendixes are reference materials provided for the convenience of the reader at the back of the paper, after the text. Providing information that supplements the important facts in the text, they may include maps, charts, tables, and selected documents. Do not place materials that are merely interesting or decorative in your appendix. Use only items that will answer questions raised by the text or are necessary to explain the text. Follow the guidelines for formats for illustrations, tables, and figures when adding material in an appendix. At the top center of the page, label your first appendix "Appendix A," your second appendix "Appendix B," and so on. Do not append an entire government report, journal article, or other publication, but only the portions of such documents that are necessary to support your paper. The source of the information should always be evident on the appended pages.

4

Citing Sources

4.1 Preliminary Decisions

One of your most important jobs as a research writer is to document your use of source material carefully and clearly. Failure to do so will cause your reader confusion, damage the effectiveness of your paper, and perhaps make you vulnerable to a charge of plagiarism. Proper documentation is more than just good form. It is a powerful indicator of your own commitment to scholarship and the sense of authority that you bring to your writing. Good documentation demonstrates your expertise as a researcher and increases your reader's trust in you and your work.

Unfortunately, as anybody who has ever written a research paper knows, getting the documentation right can be a frustrating, confusing job, especially for the writer who is not familiar with the citation system. Positioning each element of a single reference citation accurately can require what seems an inordinate amount of time looking through the style manual. Even before you begin to work on the specific citations, there are important questions of style and format to answer.

What to Document

Direct quotes must always be credited, as well as certain kinds of paraphrased material. Information that is basic—important dates, universally acknowledged facts or opinions—need not be cited. Information that is not widely known, whether fact or opinion, should receive documentation.

What if you are unsure as to whether a certain fact is widely known? You are, after all, very probably a newcomer to the field in which you are conducting your research. If in doubt, supply the documentation. It is better to overdocument than to fail to do justice to a source.

The Choice of Style

While the question of which documentation style to use may be decided for you by your instructor, others may allow you a choice. There are several styles available, each designed to meet the needs of researchers in particular fields. The reference systems approved by the Modern Language Association (MLA) and the American Psychological Association (APA) are often used in the humanities and the social sciences and could serve the needs of the political science writer, but this manual offers three styles that are most likely to be appropriate for political science papers:

- The APSA Author-Date System
- The Documentary-Note System
- The Student Citation System

The APSA Author-Date System

The American Political Science Association (APSA) has adopted a modification of the style elaborated in *The Chicago Manual of Style* (*CMS*), perhaps the most universally approved of all documentation authorities. One of the advantages of using the APSA style, which is outlined in an APSA pamphlet entitled *Style Manual for Political Science,* is that it is designed to guide the professional political scientist in preparing a manuscript for submission to a journal. The APSA style is required for all papers submitted to the *American Political Science Review,* the journal of the American Political Science Association and the most influential political science journal in publication. Learning the APSA documentation style, then, offers you as a student another crucial connection to the world of the political scientist. For this reason, there are models in section 4.2 of all formats described in the APSA *Style Manual* in addition to other models found only in the *CMS.*

NOTE. The APSA *Style Manual for Political Science* (revised edition, 1993) covers only certain basic reference and bibliographical models. For other models and for more detailed suggestions about referencing format, the APSA *Manual* refers readers to the thirteenth edition of the *CMS* (1982), which the APSA models closely follow. The formats below are based on APSA guidelines whenever such guidelines are available. Otherwise, the formats follow models taken from the fourteenth and most recent edition of the *CMS* (1993). Models based on the *CMS* are identified as such and, where helpful, section numbers for relevant passages in the fourteenth edition of the *CMS* are given in parentheses. For example, *CMS* (15.367) refers to the 367th section of Chapter 15 in the 14th edition of *The Chicago Manual of Style,* a section which shows how to cite source material taken from the United States Constitution.

The Documentary-Note System

The *documentary-note system,* or the *humanities system,* uses superscript (raised) numbers in the text, which refer to footnotes that occur at the bottom of the page or to endnotes that are found at the end of the paper. Although it is not advocated by the APSA *Manual,* the documentary-note format has a long history of use, especially in the social sciences and humanities, and your instructor may want you to follow it instead of the author-date system. It is important to remember that both formats require a *bibliography* at the end of the paper.

The Student Citation System

As an alternative to the APSA author-date and the documentary-note systems, you may want to use the Student Citation System (SCS). Be sure to get your instructor's approval before using the SCS system. Why, you may ask, would anyone want another citation system, especially since so many disciplines already have their own (MLA, APA, and others)? It is precisely because college students are currently required to use several different citation systems that the SCS was created. The SCS is the first system specifically designed for use in all undergraduate college courses. Students who use it will be able to use the same system in their English, psychology, sociology, math, science, history, political science, and other courses. How is the SCS different from other citation systems? In addition to the fact that it is designed to be used in courses in all disciplines, the SCS has several other distinctive features: The SCS is made for students, not academicians. It is simpler, has fewer rules to learn, and is easier to type than other systems. The SCS uses the punctuation and syntax of a new grammar that students are quickly learning around the world: the universal language of the Internet. The Internet is rapidly becoming the foremost means of a wide range of research and communication activities. SCS symbols are familiar to anyone who has used the Internet: / @ + . They allow citations to be constructed with a minimum of space, effort, and confusion.

The Importance of Consistency

Whichever style and format you use, the most important rule is to *be consistent.* Sloppy referencing undermines your reader's trust and does a disservice to the writers whose work you are incorporating into your own argument. And from a purely practical standpoint, inconsistent referencing can severely damage your grade.

Using the Style Manual

Read through the following pages before trying to use them to structure your notes. Unpracticed student researchers tend to ignore this section of the style manual until the moment the first note has to be worked out, and then they skim through the examples looking for the one example that perfectly corresponds to the immediate case in hand. But most style manuals do not include every possible documentation model, so the writer must piece together a coherent reference out of elements from several models. Reading through all the models before using them gives you a feel for where to find different aspects of models as well as for how the referencing system works in general.

4.2 The APSA Author-Date System

In the author-date system of citation, a note is placed in parentheses within the text, near where the source material appears. In order not to distract the reader from the argument, the reference is as brief as possible, containing just enough information to refer the reader to the full citation in the bibliography following the text. Usually the minimum information necessary is the author's name—meaning the name by which the source is alphabetized in the bibliography—and the date of the publication of the source. As indicated by the models in the following subsection, this information can be given in a number of ways.

Models of bibliographical entries that correspond to these parenthetical text references are given in the subsection that begins on page 95. A sample bibliography appears on page 103.

The Author-Dated System: Citations

Author, date, and page in parentheses

Several critics found the senator's remarks to be, in the words of one, "hopelessly off the mark and dangerously incendiary" (Northrup 1999, 28).

Note that, when it appears at the end of a sentence, the parenthetical reference is placed inside the period.

Page and chapter in notes

A text citation may refer to an entire article, in which case you need not include page numbers, since they are given in the bibliography. However, you will sometimes need to cite specific page and chapter numbers, which follow the date, and are preceded by a comma and, in the case of a chapter, the abbreviation *chap.* Note that you do not use the abbreviation *p.* or *pp.* when referring to page numbers.

Page numbers

Rudd (2000, 84–86) provides a brief but coherent description of the bill's evolution.

Chapter numbers

> Collins (1999, chaps. 9, 10) discusses at length the structure of the Roman senate.

Author and date in text

The following example focuses the reader's attention on Northrup's article:

> For a highly critical review of the senator's performance, see Northrup 1999 (28).

Author in the text, date and page in parentheses

Here the emphasis is on the author, for only Northrup's name is within the grammar of the sentence:

> Northrup (1999, 28) called the senator's remarks "hopelessly off the mark and dangerously incendiary."

Source with two authors

> The administration's efforts at reforming the education system are drawing more praise than condemnation (Younger and Petty 1998).

Notice that the names are not necessarily arranged alphabetically. Use the order that the authors themselves sanctioned on the title page of the book.

Source with three authors

> Most of the farmers in the region support the cooperative's new pricing plan (Moore, Macrory, and Traylor 2000, 132).

Source with four or more authors

Place the Latin phrase *et al.,* meaning "and others," after the name of the first author. Note that the phrase appears in roman type, not italics, and is followed by a period:

> According to Herring et al. (1996, 42), five builders backed out of the project due to doubts about the local economy.

More than one source

Note that the references are arranged alphabetically:

> Several commentators have supported the council's decision to expand the ruling (Barrere 1997; Grady 1997; Payne 1996).

Two authors with the same last name

Use a first initial to differentiate two authors with the same last name.

Few taxpayers will appreciate the new budget cuts (L. Grady 2000). The president may be right in thinking his new policy will stimulate economic growth (B. Grady 1999).

Two works by the same author

If two references by the same author appear in the same note, place a comma between the publication dates:

George (1998, 2000) argues for sweeping tax reform on the national level.

If the two works were published in the same year, differentiate them by adding lowercase letters to the publication dates. Be sure to add the letters to the references in the bibliography too.

The commission's last five annual reports pointed out the same weaknesses in the structure of the city government (Estrada 2000a, 2000b).

Reprints

It is sometimes significant to note the date when an important text was first published, even if you are using a reprint of that work. In this case, the date of the first printing appears in brackets before the date of the reprint:

During that period, there were three advertising campaign strategies that were deemed potentially useful to political campaigners (Adams [1964] 1988, 12).

Classic texts

You may use the author-date system to structure notes for classic texts, such as the Bible, standard translations of ancient Greek works, or numbers of the *Federalist Papers,* by citing the date and page numbers of the edition you are using. Or you may refer to these texts by using the systems by which they are subdivided. Since all editions of a classic text employ the same standard subdivisions, this reference method has the advantage of allowing your reader to find the citation in any published version of the text. For example, you may cite a biblical passage by referring to the particular book, chapter, and verse, all in roman type, with the translation given after the verse number. Titles of books of the Bible should be abbreviated.

"But the path of the just is as the shining light, that shineth more and more unto the perfect day" (Prov. 4:18 King James Version).

The Federalist Papers may be cited by their standard numbers:

Madison addresses the problem of factions in a republic (Federalist 10).

Newspaper articles

According to the *CMS* (16.117), references to daily newspapers should be handled within the syntax of your sentence:

In a 10 August 1999 editorial, the *New York Times* painted the new regime in glowing colors.

An article entitled "Hoag on Trial," written by Austin Fine and published in the *Tribune* on 24 November 1998, took exception to Senator Hoag's remarks.

Usually, according to the *CMS,* references to newspaper items are not included in the bibliography. If you wish to include such references, however, there is a model of a bibliography entry in the next section of this chapter.

Public documents

You may cite public documents using the standard author-date technique. The *CMS* (15.322–411, 16.148–198) gives detailed information on how to cite public documents published by national, state, county, or city governments, as well as those published by foreign governments. Corresponding bibliography entries appear in the next subsection.

Congressional journals

Parenthetical text references to either the *Senate Journal* or the *House Journal* start with the journal title in place of the author, the session year, and, if applicable, the page:

Senator Jones endorsed the proposal as reworded by Senator Edward's committee (*Senate Journal* 1999, 24).

Congressional debates

Congressional debates are printed in the daily issues of the *Congressional Record,* which are bound biweekly and then collected and bound at the end of the session. Whenever possible, you should consult the bound yearly collection instead of the biweekly compilations. Your parenthetical reference should begin with the title *Congressional Record* (or *Cong. Rec.*) in place of the author's name and include the year of the congressional session, the volume and part of the *Congressional Record,* and finally the page:

Rep. Valentine and Rep. Beechnut addressed the question of funding for secondary education (*Cong. Rec.* 1930, 72, pt. 8: 9012).

Congressional reports and documents

References to these reports and documents, which are numbered sequentially in one- or two-year periods, include the name of the body generating the material, the year, and the page:

Rep. Slavin promised from the floor to answer the charges against him within the next week (U.S. House 1999, 12).

NOTE. Any reference that begins with *U.S. Senate* or *U.S. House* may omit the *U.S.*, if it is clear from the context that you are referring to the United States. Whichever form you use, be sure to use it *consistently,* in both the notes and the bibliography.

Bills and resolutions

According to the *CMS* (15.347–48), bills and resolutions, which are published in pamphlets called "slip bills," on microfiche, and in the *Congressional Record,* are not always given a parenthetical text reference and a corresponding bibliography entry. Instead, the pertinent reference information appears in the syntax of the sentence. If, however, you wish to cite such information in a text reference, the form depends on the source from which you took your information:

Citing to a slip bill

The proposed legislation prohibits consular officials from rejecting visa requests out of hand (U.S. Senate 1998).

The proposed legislation prohibits consular officials from rejecting visa requests out of hand (*Visa Formalization Act of 1998*).

You may cite either the body that authored the bill or the title of the work itself. Whichever method you choose, remember to begin your bibliography entry with the same material.

Citing to the Congressional Record

The recent ruling prohibits consular officials from rejecting visa requests out of hand (U.S. Senate 1998, S7658).

The number following the date and preceded by an *S* (for Senate; *H* for House) is the page in the *Congressional Record.*

Laws

As with bills and resolutions, laws (also called statutes) are not necessarily given a parenthetical text reference and a bibliography entry. Instead, the identifying material is included in the text. If you wish to make a formal reference for a statute, you must structure it according to the place where you found the law published. Initially published separately in pamphlets, as slip laws, statutes are eventually collected and incorporated, first into a set of volumes called *U.S. Statutes at Large* and later into the *United States Code,* a multivolume set that is revised every six years. You should use the latest publication.

Citing to a slip law

You should either use *U.S. Public Law,* in roman type, and the number of the piece of legislation, or the title of the law:

Congress stipulates that any book deposited for copyright in the Library of Congress that suffers serious damage or deterioration due to age be rebound in library cloth (U.S. Public Law 678, 16–17).

Congress stipulates that any book deposited for copyright in the Library of Congress that suffers serious damage or deterioration due to age be rebound in library cloth (*Library of Congress Book Preservation Act of 1999,* 16–17).

Citing to the Statutes at Large

Include the page number after the year:

Congress stipulates that any book deposited for copyright in the Library of Congress that suffers serious damage or deterioration due to age be rebound in library cloth (*Statutes at Large* 1999, 466).

Citing to the United States Code

Congress stipulates that any book deposited for copyright in the Library of Congress that suffers serious damage or deterioration due to age be rebound in library cloth (*Library of Congress Book Preservation Act of 1999*).

United States Constitution

According to the *CMS* (15.367), references to the United States Constitution include the number of the article or amendment, the section number, and the clause, if necessary:

The president has the power, in extraordinary circumstances, either to convene or to dismiss Congress (U.S. Constitution, art. 3, sec. 3).

It is not necessary to include the Constitution in the bibliography.

Executive department documents

A reference to a report, bulletin, circular, or any other type of material issued by the executive department starts with the name of the agency issuing the document, although you may use the name of the author, if known:

Recent demographic projections suggest that city growth will continue to be lateral for several more years, as businesses flee downtown areas for the suburbs (Department of Labor 1984, 334).

Legal references

Supreme Court

As with laws, court decisions are rarely given their own parenthetical text reference and bibliography entry, but are instead identified in the text. If you wish to use a formal reference, however, you may place within the parentheses the title of the case, in italics, followed by the source (for cases after 1875 this is the *United States Supreme Court Reports,* abbreviated *U.S.*), which is preceded by the volume number and followed by the page number. You should end the first reference to the case that appears in your paper with the date of the case, in brackets. You need not include the date in subsequent references:

The judge ruled that Ms. Warren did have an obligation to offer assistance to the survivors of the wreck, an obligation which she failed to meet (*State of Nevada v. Goldie Warren* 324 U.S. 123 [1969]).

Before 1875, Supreme Court decisions were published under the names of official court reporters. The reference below is to William Cranch, *Reports of Cases Argued and Adjudged in the Supreme Court of the United States, 1801–1815,* 9 vols. (Washington, D.C., 1804–17). The number preceding the clerk's name is the volume number; the last number is the page:

The first case in which the Supreme Court ruled a law of Congress to be void was *Marbury v. Madison,* in 1803 (1 Cranch 137).

For most of these parenthetical references, it is possible to move some or all of the material outside the parentheses simply by incorporating it in the text:

In 1969, in State of *Nevada v. Goldie Warren* (324 U.S. 123), the judge ruled that an observer of a traffic accident has an obligation to offer assistance to survivors.

Lower courts

Decisions of lower federal courts are published in the *Federal Reporter.* The note should give the volume of the *Federal Reporter* (*F.*), the series, if it is other than the first (*2d,* in the following model), the page, and, in brackets, an abbreviated reference to the specific court (the example below is to the Second Circuit Court) and the year:

One ruling takes into account the bias that often exists against the defendant in certain types of personal injury lawsuits (*United States v. Sizemore,* 183 F. 2d 201 [2d Cir. 1950]).

Publications of government commissions

According to the *CMS* (16.169), short text references for bulletins, circulars, reports, and study papers that are issued by various government commissions should include the name of the commission, the date of the document, and the page:

This year saw a sharp reaction among large firms to the new tax law (Securities and Exchange Commission 1985, 57).

Corporate authors

Because government documents are often credited to a corporate author with a lengthy name, you may devise an acronym or a shortened form of the name and indicate in your first reference to the source that this name will be used in later citations:

Government statistics over the last year showed a continuing leveling of the inflation rate (*Bureau of Labor Statistics* 1999, 1954; *hereafter BLS*).

The practice of using a shortened name in subsequent references to any corporate author, whether a public or private organization, is sanctioned in most journals, including the *American Political Science Review,* and approved in the *CMS* (16.8). Thus, if you refer often to the *U.N. Monthly Bulletin of Statistics,* you may, after giving the publication's full name in the first reference, use a shortened form of the title—perhaps an acronym such as *UNMBS*—in all later cites.

Publications of state and local governments

According to the *CMS* (15.377), references to state and local government documents are similar to those for the corresponding national government sources:

> In arguing for the legality of cockfighting, Senator Lynd actually suggested that the "sport" served as a deterrent to crime among the state's young people (Oklahoma Legislature 1997, 24).

The *CMS* (16.178) restricts bibliographical information concerning state laws or municipal ordinances to the running text.

Interviews

According to the *CMS* (16.127, 130), citations to interviews should be handled within the syntax of a sentence rather than in parentheses. The *CMS* states that interviews need not be listed in the bibliography but may be included if you or your instructor wishes. Model bibliography formats for such material appear in the bibliography subsection.

Published interview

> In a March 1999 interview with Selena Fox, Simon criticized the use of private funds to build such city projects as the coliseum.

No parenthetical reference is necessary in this citation because sufficient information is given for the reader to find the complete citation, which will be alphabetized under Simon's name in the bibliography.

Unpublished interview conducted by the writer of the paper

> In an interview with the author on 23 April 1999, Dr. Kennedy expressed her disappointment with the new court ruling.

If you are citing material from an interview that you conducted, you should identify yourself as the author and give the date of the interview.

The Author-Date System: Bibliography

In a paper using the author-date system of referencing, the parenthetical text references point the reader to the full citations in the bibliography. This bibliography, which always follows the text, is arranged alphabetically according to the first element in each citation. Usually this element is the last name of the author or editor, but in the absence of such information, the citation is alphabetized according to the title of the work, which is then the first element in the citation (*CMS* 16.41).

The bibliography is double-spaced throughout, even between entries. As with most alphabetically arranged bibliographies, there is a kind of reverse indentation system: after the first line of a citation, all subsequent lines are indented five spaces.

Capitalization

The APSA *Manual* uses standard, or "headline style," capitalization rules for titles in the bibliographical citations. In this style, all first and last words in a title, and all other words *except* articles (*a, an, the*), coordinating words (*and, but, or, for, nor*), and all prepositions, are capitalized. The *CMS* (15.73.3), however, uses a "down" style (or sentence style) of capitalization, in which "only the first word of the main title and the subtitle and all proper nouns and proper adjectives" are capitalized. You should check with your instructor to see which capitalization style you should use. In keeping with its general policy, this manual gives examples using the APSA format.

Books

One author

> Northrup, K. Alan. 1999. *Living High off the Hog: Recent Pork Barrel Legislation in the Senate.* Cleveland: Johnstown.

First comes the author's name, inverted, then the date of publication, followed by the title of the book, the place of publication, and the name of the publishing house. For place of publication, do not identify the state unless the city is not well known. In that case, use postal abbreviations to denote the state (*OK, AR*).

Periods are used to divide most of the elements in the citation, although a colon is used between the place of publication and publisher. Custom dictates that the main title and subtitle are separated by a colon, even though a colon may not appear in the title as printed on the title page of the book.

Two authors

Only the name of the first author is reversed, since it is the one by which the citation is alphabetized:

> Spence, Michelle, and Kelly Rudd. 1998. *Education and the Law.* Boston: Tildale.

Three authors

> Moore, J. B., Jeannine Macrory, and Natasha Traylor. 2000. *Down on the Farm: Renovating the Farm Loan.* Norman: Univ. of Oklahoma Press.

According to the *CMS* (15.161), you may abbreviate the word *University* if it appears in the name of the press:

Four or more authors

> Herring, Ralph, et al. 1996. *Funding City Projects.* Atlanta: Jessup Institute for Policy Development.

Editor, compiler, or translator as author

When no author is listed on the title page, the *CMS* (16.46) calls for you to begin the citation with the name of the editor, compiler, or translator:

>Trakas, Dylan, comp. 2000. *Making the Roadways Safe: Essays on Highway Preservation and Funding.* El Paso: Del Norte Press.

Editor, compiler, or translator with author

Place the editor, compiler, or translator's name after the title, prefaced, according to the *CMS* (16.47), by the appropriate phrase: *Ed., Comp.,* or *Trans.*:

>Pound, Ezra. 1953. *Literary Essays.* Ed. T. S. Eliot. New York: New Directions.

>Stomper, Jean. 1973. *Grapes and Rain.* Trans. John Picard. New York: Baldock.

Untranslated book

If your source is in a foreign language, it is not necessary, according to the *CMS* (15.118), to translate the title into English. Use the capitalization format of the original language (see in *CMS* 9).

>Picon-Salas, Mariano. 1950. *De la Conquista a la Independencia.* Mexico D.F.: Fondo de Cultura Económica.

If you wish to provide a translation of the title, do so in brackets or parentheses following the title. Set the translation in roman type, and capitalize only the first word of the title and subtitle, proper nouns, and proper adjectives:

>Wharton, Edith. 1916. *Voyages au front* (Visits to the front). Paris: Plon.

Two or more works by the same author

According to the *CMS* (15.66, 16.28), the author's name in all citations after the first may be replaced, if you wish, by a three-em dash (six strokes of the hyphen):

>Russell, Henry. 1978. *Famous Last Words: Notable Supreme Court Cases of the Last Five Years.* New Orleans: Liberty Publications.

>———. 1988. *Great Court Battles.* Denver: Axel & Myers.

Chapter in a multiauthor collection

>Gray, Alexa North. 2000. "Foreign policy and the foreign press." In *Current Media Issues,* ed. Barbara Bonnard. New York: Boulanger.

The parenthetical text reference may include the page reference:

(Gray 2000, 191, 195–97)

You *must* repeat the name if the author and the editor are the same person:

>Farmer, Susan A. 1997. "Tax Shelters in the New Dispensation: How to Save Your Income." In *Making Ends Meet: Strategies for the Nineties,* ed. Susan A. Farmer. Nashville: Burkette and Hyde.

Author of a foreword or introduction

There is no need, according to the *CMS* (16.51), to cite the author of a foreword or introduction in your bibliography, unless you have used material from that author's contribution to the volume. In that case, the bibliography entry is listed under the name of the author of the foreword or introduction. Place the name of the author of the work itself after the title of the work:

Farris, Carla. 2000. Foreword to *Marital Stress among the Professoriat: A Case Study,* by Basil Givan. New York: Galapagos.

The parenthetical text reference cites the name of the author of the foreword or introduction, not the author of the book:

(Farris 2000)

Subsequent editions

If you are using an edition of a book other than the first, you must cite the number of the edition or the status, such as *Rev. ed.* for Revised edition, if there is no edition number:

Hales, Sarah. 1996. *The Coming Water Wars.* 2nd ed. Pittsburgh: Blue Skies.

Multivolume work

If you are citing a multivolume work in its entirety, use the following format:

Graybosch, Charles. 1988–89. *The Rise of the Unions.* 3 vols. New York: Starkfield.

If you are citing only one of the volumes in a multivolume work, use the following format:

Ronsard, Madeleine. 1998. *Monopolies.* Vol. 2 of *A History of Capitalism.* Ed. Joseph M. Sayles. Boston: Renfrow.

Reprints

Adams, Sterling R. [1964] 1988. *How to Win an Election: Promotional Campaign Strategies.* New York: Starkfield.

Modern editions of classics

It is not necessary to give the date of original publication of a classic work:

Burke, Edmond. 1987. *Reflections on the Revolution in France.* Ed. J. G. A. Pocock. Indianapolis: Hackett.

Remember, if the classic text is divided into short, numbered sections (such as the chapter and verse divisions of the Bible), you do not need to include the work in your bibliography unless you wish to specify a particular edition.

Periodicals

Journal articles

Journals are periodicals, usually published either monthly or quarterly, that specialize in serious scholarly articles in a particular field.

Journal with continuous pagination

Most journals are paginated so that each issue of a volume continues the numbering of the previous issue. The reason for such pagination is that most journals are bound in libraries as complete volumes of several issues; continuous pagination makes it easier to consult these large compilations:

> Hunzecker, Joan. 1987. "Teaching the Toadies: Cronyism in Municipal Politics." *Review of Local Politics* 4:250–62.

Note that the name of the journal, which is italicized, is followed without punctuation by the volume number, which is itself followed by a colon and the page numbers. There should be no space between the colon and the page numbers, which are *inclusive*. Do not use *p.* or *pp.* to introduce the page numbers.

Journal in which each issue is paginated separately

> Skylock, Browning. 1991. "'Fifty-Four Forty or Fight!': Sloganeering in Early America." *American History Digest* 28(3): 25–34.

The issue number appears in parentheses immediately following the volume number. Place one space between the colon and the page numbers.

Magazine articles

Magazines, which are usually published weekly, bimonthly, or monthly, appeal to the popular audience and generally have a wider circulation than journals. *Newsweek* and *Scientific American* are examples of magazines.

Monthly magazine

The name of the magazine is separated from the month of publication by a comma. According to the APSA *Manual*, inclusive page numbers are not necessary in a magazine reference:

> Stapleton, Bonnie. 1981. "How It Was: On the Campaign Trail with Ike." *Lifetime Magazine*, April.

Weekly or bimonthly magazine

The day of the issue's publication appears before the month:

> Bruck, Connie. 1999. "The World of Business: A Mogul's Farewell." *The New Yorker*, 18 October, 12–15.

Newspaper articles

The *CMS* (16.117) says that bibliographies usually do not include entries for articles from daily newspapers. If you wish to include such material, however, here are two possible formats:

New York Times. 1999. Editorial, 10 August.

Fine, Austin. 1998. "Hoag on Trial." *Carrollton (Texas) Tribune,* 24 November.

Note that *The* is omitted from the newspaper's title, as it is for all English language newspapers (*CMS* 15.242). If the name of the city in which an American newspaper is published does not appear in the paper's title, it should be appended, in italics. If the city is not well known, the name of the state is added, in italics, in parentheses, as in the second model above. The *CMS* (15.234–42) offers additional suggestions for citations of newspaper material.

Public documents

Congressional journals

References to either the *Senate Journal* or the *House Journal* begin with the journal's title and include the years of the session, the number of the Congress and session, and the month and day of the entry:

U.S. Senate Journal. 1999. 105th Cong., 1st sess., 10 December.

The ordinal numbers *second* and *third* may be represented as *d* (52d, 103d) or as *nd* and *rd,* respectively.

Congressional debates

Congressional Record. 1930. 71st Cong., 2d sess. Vol. 72, pt. 8.

Congressional reports and documents

U.S. House. 1999. *Report on Government Efficiency as Perceived by the Public.* 105th Cong., 2d sess. H. Doc. 225.

Bills and resolutions

Citing to a slip bill

U.S. Senate. 1998. *Visa Formalization Act of 1998.* 105th Cong. 1st sess. S.R. 1437.

or

Visa Formalization Act of 1998. See U.S. Senate. 1998.

The abbreviation *S.R.* in the first model above stands for *Senate Resolutions,* and the number following is the bill or resolution number. For references to House bills, the abbreviation is *H.R.* Notice that the second model refers the reader to the more complete entry above. The choice of formats depends upon the one you used in the parenthetical text reference.

Citing to the Congressional Record

Senate. 1999. *Visa Formalization Act of 1999.* 105th Cong., 1st sess., S.R. 1437. *Congressional Record* 135, no. 137, daily ed. (10 December): S7341.

Laws

Citing to a slip law

U.S. Public Law 678. 105th Cong., 1st sess., 4 December 1999. *Library of Congress Book Preservation Act of 1999.*

or

Library of Congress Book Preservation Act of 1999. U.S. Public Law 678. 105th Cong., 1st sess., 4 December 1999.

Citing to the Statutes at Large

Statutes at Large. 2000. Vol. 82, p. 466. *Library of Congress Book Preservation Act of 1999.*

or

Library of Congress Book Preservation Act of 1999. Statutes at Large 82:466.

Citing to the United States Code

Library of Congress Book Preservation Act. 1999. *U.S. Code.* Vol. 38, sec. 1562.

United States Constitution

According to the *CMS* (16.172), the Constitution is not listed in the bibliography.

Executive department documents

Department of Labor. 2000. *Report on Urban Growth Potential Projections.* Washington, D.C.: GPO.

The abbreviation for the publisher in the preceding model, *GPO,* stands for the *Government Printing Office,* which prints and distributes most government publications.

According to the *CMS* (15.327), you may use any of the following formats to refer to the GPO:

Washington, D.C.: U.S. Government Printing Office, 1984.
Washington, D.C.: Government Printing Office, 1984.
Washington, D.C.: GPO, 1984.
Washington, D.C., 1984.
Washington, 1984.

Remember to *be consistent* in using the form you choose.

Legal references

Supreme Court

According to the *CMS* (16.174), Supreme Court decisions are only rarely listed in bibliographies. If you do wish to include such an entry, here is a suitable format:

State of Nevada v. Goldie Warren. 1969. 324 U.S. 123.

For a case prior to 1875, use the following format:

Marbury v. Madison. 1803. 1 Cranch 137.

Lower courts

United States v. Sizemore. 1950. 183 F. 2d 201 (2d Cir.).

Publications of government commissions

U.S. Securities and Exchange Commission. 1984. *Annual Report of the Securities and Exchange Commission for the Fiscal Year.* Washington, D.C.: GPO.

Publications of state and local governments

Remember that references for state and local government publications are modeled on those for corresponding national government documents:

Oklahoma Legislature. 1997. Joint Committee on Public Recreation. *Final Report to the Legislature, 1997, Regular Session, on Youth Activities.* Oklahoma City.

Interviews

According to the *CMS* (16.127), interviews need not be included in the bibliography, but if you or your instructor wants to list such entries, here are possible formats:

Published interview

Untitled interview in a book

Jorgenson, Mary. 2000. Interview by Alan McAskill. In *Hospice Pioneers.* Ed. Alan McAskill, 62–86. Richmond: Dynasty Press.

Titled interview in a periodical

Simon, John. 1999. "Picking the Patrons Apart: An Interview with John Simon." By Selena Fox. *Media Week,* 14 March, 40–54.

Interview on television

Snopes, Edward. 2000. Interview by Kent Gordon. *Oklahoma Politicians.* WKY Television, 4 June.

Unpublished interview

Kennedy, Melissa. 1999. Interview by author. Tape recording. Portland, ME, 23 April.

Unpublished sources

Theses and dissertations

Hochenauer, Klint. 1980. "Populism and the Free Soil Movement." Ph.D. diss. University of Virginia.

Sharpe, Ellspeth Stanley. 1998. "Black Women in Politics: A Troubled History." Master's thesis. Oregon State University.

Material from the Internet and World Wide Web

Instructions for citing online sources are printed on pages 336 and 337 of this manual.

Sample Bibliography: Author-Date System

Bibliography

Ariès, Philippe. 1962. <u>Centuries of Childhood: A Social History of Family Life</u>. Trans. Robert Baldock. New York: Knopf.

Cesbron, Henry. 1909. <u>Histoire critique de l'hystérie</u>. Paris: Asselin et Houzeau.

Farmer, Susan A. 1997. "Tax Shelters in the New Dispensation: How to Save Your Income." In <u>Making Ends Meet: Strategies for the Nineties,</u> Ed. Susan A. Farmer. Nashville: Burkette and Hyde.

Herring, Ralph, et al. 1996. <u>Funding City Projects</u>. Atlanta: Jessup Institute for Policy Development.

Hunzecker, Joan. 1987. "Teaching the Toadies: Cronyism in Municipal Politics." <u>Review of Local Politics</u> 4:250-62.

Moore, J. B., Jeannine Macrory, and Natasha Traylor. 2000. <u>Down on the Farm: Renovating the Farm Loan</u>. Norman: Univ. of Oklahoma Press.

Northrup, Alan K. 1999. <u>Living High off the Hog: Recent Pork Barrel Legislation in the Senate</u>. Cleveland: Johnstown.

Skylock, Browning. 1991. "'Fifty-Four Forty or Fight!': Sloganeering in Early America." <u>American History Digest</u> 28(3): 25-34.

Stapleton, Bonnie. 1981. "How It Was: On the Campaign Trail with Ike." <u>Lifetime Magazine,</u> April.

U.S. Securities and Exchange Commission. 1984. <u>Annual Report of the Securities and Exchange Commission for the Fiscal Year</u>. Washington, D.C.: Government Printing office.

Manuscript in the author's possession

> Borges, Rita V. "Mexican-American Border Conflicts, 1915–1970." University of Texas at El Paso. Photocopy.

The entry includes the institution with which the author is affiliated and ends with a description of the format of the work (typescript, photocopy, etc.).

4.3 The Documentary-Note System: Numbered References

In the documentary-note system, instead of putting text references in parentheses, you place a superscript (raised) number after the passage that includes source material. The number refers to a full bibliographical citation given either at the foot of the page (a footnote) or in a list at the end of the paper (an endnote). Because the APSA *Manual* does not advocate the use of the documentary-note reference system, all the information in this section comes from the *CMS* (Chapter 15).

Numbering System

Number the notes consecutively throughout the paper, starting with [1]. In other words, do not begin again with [1] at the beginning of each chapter or section, as seen in some published works.

Placement of Superscript Numeral

Whenever possible, the superscript numeral should go at the end of the sentence:

> Architectural styles for municipal libraries are undergoing radical change.[1]

If it is necessary to place the reference within a sentence instead of at the end, position the numeral at the end of the pertinent clause:

> In his last editorial Bagley denounces the current city administration[13]— and thousands of others feel the same way.

Notice in the example that the superscript numeral occurs *before* the dash. With all other pieces of punctuation—comma, semicolon, period, exclamation mark, question mark—the superscript numeral *follows* the punctuation.

The numeral also follows the terminal quotation mark of a direct quote:

> "This election," claimed Senator Lindley, "is the most crucial one in the state."[20]

Multiple Notes

When a passage refers to more than one source, do not place more than one superscript numeral after the passage. Instead use only one numeral, and combine all the references into a single footnote or endnote:

> Separate studies by Lovett, Morrison, Collins, and the Anderson Group all corroborate the state's findings.[4]

Models for Documentary Notes and Bibliography Citations

In each pair of models in this section, the first example is for a documentary note, and the second is for the corresponding bibliographical entry. A note may appear either as a *footnote,* placed at the bottom of the page of text on which the reference occurs, or as an *endnote,* placed, in numerical order, in a list following the text of the paper. The bibliography is usually the final element in the paper. Because its entries are arranged alphabetically, the order of entries in the bibliography will differ from the order of the endnotes, which are arranged according to the appearance of the references within the text.

Pay attention to the basic differences between the note format and the bibliography format. Notes are numbered; bibliographical entries are not. The first line of a note is indented; all lines in a bibliography are indented *except* the first. While the author's name is printed in normal order in a note, the order is reversed in the bibliography to facilitate alphabetizing. There are also other variations within the individual references. A sample bibliography appears on page 120–21.

If the note refers to a book or an article in its entirety, you need not cite page numbers in your references. If, however, you wish to cite material on a specific page or pages, give those in the note.

Books

One author

> *Note*

> 1. Amanda Collingwood, *Architecture and the Public* (Detroit: Zane Press, 1999), 235–38.

> *Bibliography*

> Collingwood, Amanda. *Architecture and the Public.* Detroit: Zane Press, 1999.

Two authors

> *Note*

> 6. Delbert P. Grady and Jane Ryan Torrance, *Embassies and Their Secrets* (New York: Holograph Press, 1989).

Bibliography

Grady, Delbert P., and Jane Ryan Torrance. *Embassies and Their Secrets.* New York: Holograph Press, 1989.

Three authors

Note

2. Samuel Howard, William J. Abbott, and Jane Hope, *Powerbase: How to Increase Your Hold on Your Constituency* (Los Angeles: Gollum and Smythe, 1986).

Bibliography

Howard, Samuel, William J. Abbott, and Jane Hope. *Powerbase: How to Increase Your Hold on Your Constituency.* Los Angeles: Gollum and Smythe, 1986.

Four or more authors

The Latin phrase *et al.,* meaning "and others," appears in roman type after the name of the first author:

Note

21. Angela Genessario et al., *Alimony and the Child: A National Survey* (Baltimore: Colgate, 1997), 16–18, 78–82.

Bibliography

Genessario, Angela, et al. *Alimony and the Child: A National Survey.* Baltimore: Colgate, 1997.

Editor, compiler, or translator as author

Note

6. Dylan Trakas, comp., *Making the Roadways Safe: Essays on Highway Preservation and Funding* (El Paso: Del Norte Press, 2000).

Bibliography

Trakas, Dylan, comp. *Making the Roadways Safe: Essays on Highway Preservation and Funding.* El Paso: Del Norte Press, 2000.

Editor, compiler, or translator with author

Note

15. Ezra Pound, *Literary Essays,* ed. T. S. Eliot (New York: New Directions, 1953), 48.

47. Jean Stomper, *Grapes and Rain,* trans. John Picard (New York: Baldock, 1973).

Bibliography

Pound, Ezra. *Literary Essays.* Ed. T. S. Eliot. New York: New Directions, 1953.

Stomper, Jean. *Grapes and Rain.* Trans. John Picard. New York: Baldock, 1973.

Untranslated book

Note

       8. Mariano Picon-Salas, *De la Conquista a la Independencia* (Mexico, D.F.: Fondo de la Cultura Económica, 1950).

Bibliography

Picon-Salas, Mariano. *De la Conquista a la Independencia,* Mexico, D.F.: Fondo de la Cultura Económica, 1950.

Translated book

Note

       53. Edith Wharton. *Voyages au front* (Visits to the front) (Paris: Plon, 1916).

Bibliography

Wharton, Edith. *Voyages au front* (Visits to the front). Paris: Plon, 1916.

Two or more works by the same author

In the notes, subsequent works by an author are handled exactly as the first work. In the bibliography, the works are listed alphabetically, with the author's name replaced, in all entries after the first, by a three-em dash (six strokes of the hyphen):

Bibliography

Russell, Henry. *Famous Last Words: Notable Supreme Court Cases of the Last Five Years.* New Orleans: Liberty Publications, 1978.

————. *Great Court Battles.* Denver: Axel & Myers, 1988.

Chapter in a multiauthor collection

Note

       23. Alexa North Gray, "Foreign Policy and the Foreign Press," in *Current Media Issues,* ed. Barbara Bonnard (New York: Boulanger, 2000), 189–231.

Bibliography

Gray, Alexa North. "Foreign Policy and the Foreign Press." In *Current Media Issues.* Ed. Barbara Bonnard, 189–231. New York: Boulanger, 2000.

You may, if you wish, place the inclusive page numbers either in the note, following the publication information, or in the bibliography entry, following the name of the editor. If the author of the article is also the editor of the book, you must place her or his name in both locations. If the entire book is written by the same author, do not specify the chapter in the bibliography reference.

Author of a foreword or introduction

> *Note*

> 4. Carla Farris, foreword to *Marital Stress among the Professoriat: A Case Study*, by Basil Givan (New York: Galapagos, 2000).

> *Bibliography*

> Farris, Carla. *Foreword to Marital Stress among the Professoriat: A Case Study*, by Basil Givan. New York: Galapagos, 2000.

It is not necessary to cite the author of a foreword or introduction in the bibliography unless you have used material from that author's contribution to the volume.

Subsequent editions

If you are using an edition of a book other than the first, you must cite the number of the edition or the status, such as *Rev. ed.* for *Revised edition,* if there is no edition number:

> *Note*

> 43. Sarah Hales, *The Coming Water Wars,* 2d ed. (Pittsburgh: Blue Skies, 1996).

> *Bibliography*

> Hales, Sarah. *The Coming Water Wars.* 2d ed. Pittsburgh: Blue Skies, 1996.

Multivolume work

If you are citing the multivolume work in its entirety, use the following format:

> *Note*

> 49. Charles Graybosch, *The Rise of the Unions,* 3 vols. (New York: Starkfield, 1988–89).

> *Bibliography*

> Graybosch, Charles. *The Rise of the Unions.* 3 vols. New York: Starkfield, 1988–89.

If you are citing only one of the volumes in a multivolume work, use the following format:

Note

9. Madeleine Ronsard, *Monopolies,* vol. 2 of *A History of Capitalism,* ed. Joseph M. Sayles (Boston: Renfrow, 1998).

Bibliography

Ronsard, Madeleine. *Monopolies.* Vol. 2 of *A History of Capitalism.* Ed. Joseph M. Sayles. Boston: Renfrow, 1998.

Reprints

Note

8. Sterling R. Adams, *How to Win an Election: Promotional Campaign Strategies* (1964; reprint, New York: Starkfield, 1988).

Bibliography

Adams, Sterling R. *How to Win an Election: Promotional Campaign Strategies.* 1964. Reprint, New York: Starkfield, 1988.

Modern editions of classics

It is not necessary to give the date of original publication of a classic work:

Note

24. Edmond Burke, *Reflections on the Revolution in France,* ed. J. G. A. Pocock (Indianapolis: Hackett, 1987).

Bibliography

Burke, Edmond. *Reflections on the Revolution in France.* Ed. J. G. A. Pocock. Indianapolis: Hackett, 1987.

Periodicals

Journal articles

Journals are periodicals, usually published either monthly or quarterly, that specialize in serious scholarly articles in a particular field. One significant distinction between the note format and the bibliography format for a journal article is that in the note you cite only those pages from which you took material, while in the bibliography you report the inclusive pages of the article.

Journal with continuous pagination

Most journals are paginated so that each issue of a volume continues the numbering of the previous issue. The reason for such pagination is that most journals are bound in libraries as complete volumes of several issues; continuous pagination makes it easier to consult these large compilations:

Note

17. Joan Hunzecker, "Teaching the Toadies: Cronyism in Municipal Politics," *Review of Local Politics* 4 (1987): 253, 260–62.

Bibliography

Hunzecker, Joan. "Teaching the Toadies: Cronyism in Municipal Politics." *Review of Local Politics* 4 (1987): 250–62.

Note that the name of the journal, which is italicized, is followed without punctuation by the volume number, which is itself followed by the year, in parentheses, then a colon and the page numbers. Do not use *p.* or *pp.* to introduce the page numbers.

Journal in which each issue is paginated separately

Note

8. Browning Skylock, "'Fifty-Four Forty or Fight!': Sloganeering in Early America," *American History Digest* 28, no. 3 (1997): 27, 29.

Bibliography

Skylock, Browning. "'Fifty-Four Forty or Fight!': Sloganeering in Early America." *American History Digest* 28, no. 3 (1997): 25–34.

The issue number follows the volume number, introduced by *no.* It is also permissible to enclose the issue number in parentheses, without the *no.*, moving the year to the end of the entry and placing it in a second parentheses:

. . . *American History Digest* 28 (3): 25–34 (1997).

Whichever format you use, *be consistent.*

Magazine articles

Magazines, which are usually published weekly, bimonthly, or monthly, appeal to the popular audience and generally have a wider circulation than journals. *Newsweek* and *Scientific American* are examples of magazines.

Monthly magazine

Note

10. Bonnie Stapleton, "How It Was: On the Campaign Trail with Ike," *Lifetime Magazine,* April 1981, 22–25.

Bibliography

Stapleton, Bonnie. 1981. "How It Was: On the Campaign Trail with Ike." *Lifetime Magazine,* April 1981, 19–30.

Weekly or bimonthly periodical

The day of the issue's publication appears before the month:

Note

    37. Connie Bruck, "The World of Business: A Mogul's Farewell," *The New Yorker,* 18 October 1999, 13.

Bibliography

Bruck, Connie. "The World of Business: A Mogul's Farewell." *The New Yorker,* 18 October 1999, 12–15.

    If an article begins in the front of the magazine and finishes at the back, the *CMS* (15.232) states that there is no point in recording inclusive page numbers in the bibliography entry. The specific pages used in your paper, however, must still be cited in the note.

Newspaper articles

    The *CMS* (16.117) says that bibliographies usually do not include entries for articles from daily newspapers. If you wish to include such material, however, here is a possible format:

Note

    5. Editorial, *New York Times,* 10 August 1999.

    14. Austin Fine, "Hoag on Trial," *Carrollton (Texas) Tribune,* 24 November 1998.

    Note that *The* is omitted from the newspaper's title, as it is for all English language newspapers (*CMS* 15.242). If the name of the city in which an American newspaper is published does not appear in the paper's title, it should be appended, in italics. If the city is not well known, the name of the state is added, in italics, in parentheses, as in the second model above.

Bibliography

    Although the *CMS* (15.235) maintains that news stories from daily papers are rarely included in a bibliography, it does suggest that you may, if you wish, give the name of the paper and the relevant dates in the bibliography:

Carrollton (Texas) Tribune, 22–25 November 1998.

    The *CMS* (15.234–42) offers additional suggestions for citations of newspaper material.

Public documents

Congressional journals

    References to either the *Senate Journal* or the *House Journal* begin with the journal's title and include the years of the session, the number of the Congress and session, and the month and day of the entry:

Note

19. *Senate Journal.* 105th Cong., 1st sess., 10 December 1999, 46–47.

Bibliography

Senate Journal. 105th Cong., 1st sess., 10 December 1999.

or

U.S. Congress. *Senate Journal.* 105th Cong., 1st sess., 10 December 1999.

You may dispense with the *U.S.* at the beginning of an entry if it is clear from the context that you are talking about the United States Congress, Senate, or House. Again, *be consistent* in your use of format.

The endings of the ordinal numbers *second* and *third* may be represented as *d* (52d, 103d) or as *nd* and *rd*, respectively.

Congressional debates

The debates are printed in the daily issues of the *Congressional Record,* which are bound biweekly and then collected and bound at the end of the session. Whenever possible, you should consult the bound yearly collection of the journal instead of the biweekly compilations.

Note

The number following the year is the volume, followed by the part and page numbers:

6. *Congressional Record,* 71st Cong., 2d sess., 1930, 72, pt. 8:9012.

Bibliography

Congressional Record. 71st Cong., 2d sess., 1930. Vol. 72, pt. 8.

Congressional reports and documents

Note

31. House, *Report on Government Efficiency as Perceived by the Public,* 105th Cong., 2d sess., 1999, H. Doc. 225, 12.

Bibliography

House. *Report on Government Efficiency as Perceived by the Public.* 105th Cong., 2d sess., 1999. H. Doc. 225, 12.

The abbreviation *H. Doc.* refers to *House Document.* Likewise, *S. Doc.* refers to *Senate Document.*

Bills and resolutions

Bills and resolutions are published in pamphlets called slip bills, on microfiche, and in the *Congressional Record.*

Citing to a slip bill

Note

      53. Senate, *Visa Formalization Act of 1998,* 105th Cong., 1st sess., S.R. 1437.

or

      53. *Visa Formalization Act of 1998,* 105th Cong., 1st sess., S.R. 1437.

Bibliography

Senate. *Visa Formalization Act of 1998.* 105th Cong., 1st sess., S.R. 1437.

or

*Visa Formalization Act of 1998.*105th Cong., 1st sess., S.R. 1437.

The abbreviation *S.R.* in these models stands for *Senate Resolution,* and the number following is the bill or resolution number. For references to House bills, the abbreviation is *H.R.*

Citing to the Congressional Record

Note

      53. Senate, *Visa Formalization Act of 1999,* 105th Cong., 1st sess., S.R. 1437, *Congressional Record* 135, no. 137, daily ed. (10 December): S7341.

Bibliography

Senate. *Visa Formalization Act of 1999.* 105th Cong., 1st sess., S.R. 1437. *Congressional Record* 135, no. 137, daily ed. (10 December 1999): S7341.

Laws

If you wish to make a formal reference for a statute, you must structure it according to the place where you found the law published. Initially published separately in pamphlets, as slip laws, statutes are eventually collected and incorporated, first into a set of volumes called *U.S. Statutes at Large* and later into the *United States Code,* a multivolume set that is revised every six years. You should use the latest publication.

Citing to a slip law

Note

      16. Public Law 678, 105th Cong., 1st sess. (4 December 1999), 16–17.

or

      16. Public Law 678, 103th Cong., 1st sess. (4 December 1999), *Library of Congress Book Preservation Act of 1999,* 16–17.

or

16. *Library of Congress Book Preservation Act of 1999,* Public Law 678, 103th Cong., 1st sess. (4 December 1999), 16–17.

Bibliography

U.S. Public Law 678. 105th Cong., 1st sess., 4 December 1999.

or

U.S. Public Law 678. 105th Cong., 1st sess., 4 December 1999. *Library of Congress Book Preservation Act of 1999.*

or

Library of Congress Book Preservation Act of 1999. Public Law 678. 105th Cong., 1st sess., 4 December 1999.

Citing to the Statutes at Large

Note

10. *Statutes at Large* 82 (1999): 466.

or

10. *Library of Congress Book Preservation Act of 1999, Statutes at Large* 82 (1999): 466.

Bibliography

Statutes at Large 82 (1999): 466.

or

Library of Congress Book Preservation Act of 1999. Statutes at Large 82 (1999): 466.

Citing to the United States Code

Note

42. *Library of Congress Book Preservation Act, U.S. Code,* vol. 38, sec. 1562 (1999).

Bibliography

Library of Congress Book Preservation Act. U.S. Code. Vol. 38, sec. 1562 (1999).

United States Constitution

In the documentary-note format, according the *CMS* (15.367), the Constitution is cited by article or amendment, section, and, if relevant, clause. The Constitution is not listed in the bibliography.

Note

23. U.S. Constitution, art. 3, sec. 3.

Executive department documents

A reference to a report, bulletin, circular, or any other type of material issued by the executive department starts with the name of the agency issuing the document, although you may use the name of the author, if known:

Note

39. Department of Labor, *Report on Urban Growth Potential Projections* (Washington, D.C.: GPO, 2000), 334.

Bibliography

U.S. Department of Labor. *Report on Urban Growth Potential Projections.* Washington, D.C.: GPO, 2000.

The abbreviation for the publisher in the model, *GPO,* stands for the Government Printing Office, which prints and distributes most government publications. According to the *CMS* (15.327), you may use any of the following formats to refer to the GPO:

Washington, D.C.: U.S. Government Printing Office, 1984.
Washington, D.C.: Government Printing Office, 1984.
Washington, D.C.: GPO, 1984.
Washington, D.C., 1984.
Washington, 1984.

Remember to *be consistent* in using the form you choose.

Legal references

Supreme Court

Note

73. *State of Nevada* v. *Goldie Warren,* 324 U.S. 123 (1969).

The *U.S.* in the entry refers to *United States Supreme Court Reports,* which is where decisions of the Supreme Court have been published since 1875. Preceding the *U.S.* is the volume number; following is the page number and the year in parentheses.

Before 1875, Supreme Court decisions were published under the names of official court reporters. The following reference is to William Cranch, *Reports of Cases Argued and Adjudged in the Supreme Court of the United States,* 1801–15, 9 vols. (Washington, D.C., 1804–17). The number preceding the clerk's name is the volume number; following the clerk's name is the page number and year, in parentheses:

8. *Marbury* v. *Madison,* 1 Cranch 137 (1803).

Bibliography

According to the *CMS* (15.369), Supreme Court decisions are only rarely listed in bibliographies.

Lower courts

Decisions of lower federal courts are published in the *Federal Reporter*. The note should give the volume of the *Federal Reporter* (*F.*), the series, if it is other than the first series (2d, in the following model), the page, and, in parentheses, an abbreviated reference to the specific court and the year:

Note

> 58. *United States v. Sizemore,* 181 F. 2d 200 (2d Cir. 1950).

The reference is to the Second Circuit Court.

Bibliography

According to the *CMS* (15.369), court decisions are only rarely listed in bibliographies.

Publications of government commissions

Note

> 63. Securities and Exchange Commission, *Annual Report of the Securities and Exchange Commission for the Fiscal Year* (Washington, D.C.: GPO, 1985), 57.

Bibliography

Securities and Exchange Commission. *Annual Report of the Securities and Exchange Commission for the Fiscal Year.* Washington, D.C.: GPO, 1985.

Publications of state and local governments

Remember that references for state and local government publications are modeled on those for corresponding national government documents:

Note

> 2. Oklahoma Legislature, Joint Committee on Public Recreation, *Final Report to the Legislature, 1997, Regular Session, on Youth Activities* (Oklahoma City, 1997), 24.

Bibliography

Oklahoma Legislature. Joint Committee on Public Recreation. *Final Report to the Legislature, 1997, Regular Session, on Youth Activities.* Oklahoma City, 1997.

Interviews

According to the *CMS* (15.263), citations to interviews in the documentary-note system should be handled by references within the text. If, however, you wish to include references to interviews in the notes or bibliography, you may use the following formats:

Published interview

Untitled interview in a book

Note

30. Mary Jorgenson, interview by Alan McAskill, in *Hospice Pioneers,* ed. Alan McAskill (Richmond: Dynasty Press, 2000), 68.

Bibliography

Jorgenson, Mary. Interview by Alan McAskill. In *Hospice Pioneers.* Ed. Alan McAskill, 62–86. Richmond: Dynasty Press, 2000.

Titled interview in a periodical

Note

7. John Simon, "Picking the Patrons Apart: An Interview with John Simon," interview by Selena Fox, *Media Week,* 14 March 1999, 43–44.

Bibliography

Simon, John. "Picking the Patrons Apart: An Interview with John Simon." By Selena Fox. *Media Week,* 14 March 1999, 40–54.

Interview on television

Note

4. Edward Snopes, interview by Kent Gordon, *Oklahoma Politicians,* WKY Television, 4 June 2000.

Bibliography

Snopes, Edward. Interview by Kent Gordon. *Oklahoma Politicians.* WKY Television, 4 June 2000.

Unpublished interview

Note

17. Melissa Kennedy, interview by author, tape recording, Portland, ME, 23 April 1999.

Bibliography

Kennedy, Melissa. Interview by author. Tape recording. Portland, ME, 23 April 1999.

Unpublished sources

Theses and dissertations

Dissertation

Note

16. Klint Hochenauer, "Populism and the Free Soil Movement" (Ph.D. diss., University of Virginia, 1980), 88–91.

Bibliography

Hochenauer, Klint. "Populism and the Free Soil Movement." Ph.D. diss., University of Virginia, 1980.

Thesis

Note

5. Ellspeth Stanley Sharpe, "Black Women in Politics: A Troubled History" (master's thesis, Oregon State University, 1998), 34, 36, 112–14.

Bibliography

Sharpe, Ellspeth Stanley. "Black Women in Politics: A Troubled History." Master's thesis, Oregon State University, 1998.

Paper presented at a meeting

Note

82. Kim Zelazny and Ed Gilmore, "Art for Art's Sake: Funding the NEA in the Twenty-First Century" (presented at the annual meeting of the Conference of Metropolitan Arts Councils, San Francisco, April 1999).

Bibliography

Zelazny, Kim, and Ed Gilmore. "Art for Art's Sake: Funding the NEA in the Twenty-First Century." Presented at the annual meeting of the Conference of Metropolitan Arts Councils, San Francisco, April 1999.

Material from the Internet and Worldwide Web

Instructions for citing online sources are printed on pages 336 and 337 of this manual.

Subsequent or shortened references in notes

After you have given a complete citation for a source in a note, it is possible, if the citation is lengthy, to shorten later references to that source. One convenient method of shortening subsequent references, described in the *CMS* (15.249), is to give only the last name of the author, followed by a comma and the page number of the reference:

One work by an author in notes

First reference

21. Angela Genessario et al., *Alimony and the Child: A National Survey* (Baltimore: Colgate, 1997), 16–18, 78–82.

Later reference

35. Genessario, *Alimony and the Child,* 46.

More than one work by an author in notes

If there are citations to more than one work by the author, you will have to include a shortened form of the title in all later references:

First references

23. John George, *Fringe Groups I Have Known: The Radical Left and Right in American Society* (New York: Lear Press, 1997), 45.

26. John George, "Onward Christian Soldiers: Evangelism on the Plains," *Radical Wind Magazine,* March 2000, 35, 37.

Later references

32. George, *Fringe Groups,* 56.

48. George, "Christian Soldiers," 34.

Government documents

Methods for shortening references to government documents vary, depending on the type of source. One rule is to make sure there is sufficient information in the shortened reference to point the reader clearly to the full citation in the bibliography.

Statute cited to slip law

First reference

16. Public Law 678, 105th Cong., 1st sess. (4 December 1999), *Library of Congress Book Preservation Act of 1999,* 16–17.

Later reference

19. Public Law 678, 17.

or

19. PL 678, 17.

Publications of state and local governments

First reference

2. Oklahoma Legislature, Joint Committee on Public Recreation, *Final Report to the Legislature, 1997, Regular Session, on Youth Activities* (Oklahoma City, 1997), 24.

Later reference

14. Oklahoma, Joint Committee, *Final Report*, 22.

Court decisions

First reference

58. *United States v. Sizemore*, 183 F. 2d 201 (2d Cir. 1950).

Later reference

67. *United States v. Sizemore*, 203.

Consult the *CMS*, chapter 15, for details on shortening other types of references.

Use of Ibid.

Ibid., an abbreviation of the Latin term *ibidem*, meaning "in the same place," can be used to shorten a note that refers to the source in the immediately preceding note:

First reference

14. Samuel Howard, William J. Abbott, and Jane Hope, *Powerbase: How to Increase Your Hold on Your Constituency* (Los Angeles: Gollum and Smythe, 1986), 35–36.

Following reference

15. Ibid., 38.

Sample Bibliography: Documentary–Note System

Bibliography

<u>Congressional Record</u>. 71st Cong., 2d sess., 1930. Vol. 72, pt. 8.

Farris, Carla. Foreword to <u>Marital Stress among the Professoriat: A Case Study,</u> by Basil Givan. New York: Galapagos, 2000.

Gray, Alexa North. "Foreign Policy and the Foreign Press." In <u>Cur-</u>
<u>rent Media Issues</u>. Ed. Barbara Bonnard, 189-231. New York:
Boulanger, 2000.

Hunzecker, Joan. "Teaching the Toadies: Cronyism in Municipal Politics." <u>Review of Local Politics</u> 4 (1987): 250-62.

<u>Library of Congress Book Preservation Act. U.S. Code</u>. Vol. 38, sec.
1562 (1993).

Ronsard, Madeleine. <u>Monopolies</u>. Vol. 2 of <u>A History of Capitalism</u>.
Ed. Joseph M. Sayles. Boston: Renfrow, 1998.

Russell, Henry. <u>Famous Last Words: Notable Supreme Court Cases of</u>
<u>the Last Five Years</u>. New Orleans: Liberty Publications, 1978.

Senate. <u>Visa Formalization Act of 1998</u>. 105th Cong., 1st sess.,
S.R. 1437.

Skylock, Browning. "'Fifty-Four Forty or Fight!': Sloganeering in
Early America." <u>American History Digest</u> 28, no. 3 (1997):
25-34.

Stapleton, Bonnie. 1981. "How It Was: On the Campaign Trail with
Ike." <u>Lifetime Magazine,</u> April 1981, 19-30.

<u>Statutes at Large</u> 82 (1993): 466.

Trakas, Dylan, comp. <u>Making the Roadways Safe: Essays on Highway</u>
<u>Preservation and Funding</u>. El Paso: Del Norte Press, 1994.

U.S. Public Law 678. 105th Cong., 1st sess., 4 December 1999.

4.4 The Student Citation System (SCS)

General Rules and Rules for Notes

Like other citation systems, the Student Citation System, or SCS, requires
that each source citation include (1) a note in the text in which the reference to
the source cited occurs, and (2) an entry in a reference page. Notes in the text
are always placed at the end of the sentence in which the reference is made.
Examine the models that accompany the following list of rules for notes.

RULE	EXAMPLE
1. Notes in the text always contain, in this order: a forward slash (/); a source reference numeral (1, 2, 3 etc.); and a dot (.) that ends the sentence.	Reagan waved to the convention /1. (Notice that there is a space before the /, but no spaces between the / and the 1, or between the 1 and the dot.)
2. Direct quotes and references to materials on a specific page both require a page number.	Reagan waved to the convention /1.23. (Note that no spaces occur between the dots and the page number.)
3. You may indicate a range of pages or a page and a range of pages.	Reagan waved to the convention /1.23–25. Reagan waved to the convention /1.19.23–25.
4. Indicate chapters, sections, parts, and volumes in the note with appropriate abbreviations. Note that there is no dot between the abbreviation and the number of the chapter, section, part, or volume.	Reagan waved to the convention /1.c3. Reagan waved to the convention /1.s3. Reagan waved to the convention /1.pt3. Reagan waved to the convention /1.v3.
5. You may cite more than one source in a single note. Separate sources by the / without spaces between any of the characters.	Reagan waved to the convention 1.v3.23/4/13c6. (This note refers to source 1, volume 3, page 23; source 4; and source 13, chapter 6.)
6. Once used, reference numbers always refer to the same source. They may be used again to refer to a different quote or idea from that same source.	Reagan waved to the convention /1.19. Nancy, who had had a severe headache the evening before, came to join him /5/7. One source reported that they had argued about the color suit he was to wear /1.33. (The second note in this passage refers the reader to two different sources, numbers 5 and 7. The third note is another reference to the first source used in the paper.)
7. Refer to a constitution with article and section number.	Bill Clinton fulfilled his obligation to address the state of the nation /18.2.3.
8. Refer to passages in the Bible, the Koran, and other ancient texts that are divided into standard verses with the verse citation in the note.	Jake forgot that "the seventh day shall be your Holy day" /6.Exodus 35.2. (This example refers to the book of Exodus, chapter 35, verse 2. The 6 indicates that this is the sixth source cited in the paper. There is a dot between the source number and the verse citation.)

Rules for Reference Pages

General Format Rules

The reference list is usually the final element in the paper. It is entitled "References." Its entries are arranged in the order that citations appear in the paper. The references page has standard page margins (one inch from all sides of the paper). All lines are double-spaced. A sample bibliography appears on page 129.

Rules of Punctuation and Abbreviation

1. Punctuation imitates the format used on the Internet.
2. No spaces occur between entry elements (author, date, and so on) or punctuation marks (/ . + @ ").
3. Dots (.) always follow entry elements with exceptions for punctuation rules 5 and 6.
4. The number of the source is always followed immediately by a dot.
5. Dots are also used to separate volume and edition numbers in journals.
6. Additional authors are denoted by a plus (+) sign.
7. Subtitles of books and articles are separated from main titles by a colon and a single space: "Crushing Doubt: Pascal's Bleak Epiphany."
8. Book chapters and periodical articles are enclosed in quotation marks (" ").
9. Use the following abbreviations:

c	chapter
comp	compiler
ed	editor
NY	New York (Use postal abbreviations for all states. Note that NY is unique in that when it is used alone it always means New York City. Cite other New York State locations in this form: "Oswego NY". Cite cities in other states like this: "Chicago IL" "Los Angeles CA" "Boston MA.")
pt	part
s	section
sess	session
tr	translator
v	volume
S	September (Months: Ja F Mr Ap My Je Jl Au S Oc N D)
C	College
I	Institute
U	University

10. Use full names instead of initials of authors whenever they are used in the original source. When listing publishers you may use the commonly used names instead of full titles. For example, use "Yale" for "Yale University Press"; use "Holt" for Holt, Rinehart and Winston." Use Internet abbrevia-

tions when known, such as "Prenhall" for "Prentice Hall, Inc." When abbreviating universities in dissertation and thesis citations, place no dot between the names of the state or city and the university. For example, use "MaIT" for the Massachusetts Institute of Technology and "UMa" for the University of Massachusetts. Always use the second letter of the state abbreviation, in lowercase, to avoid the following type of confusion: "OSU" could be a university in Ohio, Oklahoma, or Oregon.

Rules of Order

Elements are always entered in the order shown in the following list of examples. Not all elements are available for every citation (authors are sometimes not provided), and the list provides directions for these cases. Further, not all entries are appropriate for every citation. For example, cities of publication are not required for magazines. Carefully examine the order of elements in the examples.

SOURCE	CITATION ELEMENTS AND EXAMPLES
Books	
One author	3.Edna Applegate.1997.My Life on Earth.4th ed.Howard Press.St. Louis MO.
	[Note the order of elements:
	—Reference number of note (1, 2, 3, etc.), followed by a dot
	—Author's name
	—Year of publication
	—Title of book
	—Number of edition, if other than the first
	—Name of publisher
	—City of publication
	—State of publication (not necessary for New York City)
Two to three authors	10.William Grimes+Joan Smith+Alice Bailey.1998.Philosophy and Fire.Harvard.Cambridge MA.
More than three authors	42.Lois Mills+others.1989.Revolution in Thought.Agnew.NY.
Editor, compiler, or translator in place of author	1.Michael Schendler ed.1992.Kant's Cosmology.Bloom.NY.
	(Remember that the citation for New York City does not require a state abbreviation.)

SOURCE	CITATION ELEMENTS AND EXAMPLES
Editor, compiler, or translator with author	9.Elena White.1999.Nietzsche Was Right.Alexander Nebbs tr.Spartan.Biloxi MS.
No author, editor, compiler, or translator	5.The Book of Universal Wisdom. 1995.4th ed.Northfield Publications.Indianapolis IN. (Reverse the placement of the date and title of the book, beginning the entry with the title.)
Separately authored foreword, afterword, or preface as source	17.Beulah Garvin.1992.Preface.Down in the Hole by James Myerson.Philosopher's Stone Press.Boston MA.
Separately authored chapter, essay, or poem as source	5.Jack Wittey.1996."Chickens and People."Animal Rights Anthology.3rd ed.Gene Cayton comp.Palo Duro Press.Canyon TX.73–90.
One volume in a multivolume work	9.Astrid Schultz+others.1991.The Myth of the West.v3 of The Development of European Thought.8 vols.Muriel Hodgson ed.University of Rutland Press.Rutland ME.

Encyclopedias

Citation from an encyclopedia that is regularly updated	24.Ronald Millgate.1985."Mill, John Stuart."Encyclopedia Americana. (The date refers to the edition of the encyclopedia. Cite the name of the article exactly as it appears in the encyclopedia.)
When no name is given for the article's author	2. "Mill, John Stuart."1946.Hargreave's Encyclopedia.

Ancient texts

Bible, Koran, etc.	24.Holy Bible.New International Version. (Because the book, chapter, and verse numbers are given in the textual reference, it is not necessary to repeat them here. Remember to cite the traditional divisions of the work instead of the page number and publication information of the specific edition you used.)

SOURCE	CITATION ELEMENTS AND EXAMPLES

Periodicals

Journal articles

Article with author or authors named	30.Ellis Michaels+Andrea Long.1998. "How We Know: An Exercise in Cartesian Logic."Philosopher's Stone.12.4.213–227.
	(This citation refers to an article published in a journal entitled *Philosopher's Stone,* volume 12, number 4, pages 213–227.)
Article with no author named	7."Odds and Ends."1997.Philosopher's Stone.12.4.198–199.

Magazine articles

Article in a weekly or biweekly magazine	11.Lorraine Bond.1996."The Last Epicurean."Mental Health.6Jn.34–41.
	(This citation refers to an article published in the June 6, 1996, issue of *Mental Health.*)
Article in a monthly magazine	3.Allan Hull.1998."My Secret Struggle."Pathology Digest.Mr.17–30.
	(The difference between a citation for a monthly magazine and one for a weekly or biweekly magazine is that the former does not include a reference to the specific day of publication.)

Newpapers

Article with named author	10.Anne Bleaker.1997."Breakthrough in Artificial Intelligence."New York Times.10My.14.
	(The word *The* is omitted from the newspaper's title.)
Article with unnamed author	22."Peirce Anniversary Celebration Set."1998.Kansas City Times-Democrat.1Ap.14.

SOURCE	CITATION ELEMENTS AND EXAMPLES
When city is not named in newspaper title	13.Boyd Finnell.1998."Stoic Elected Mayor."(Eugenia, TX) Daily Equivocator.30D.1.
	(Place the name of the city, and the abbreviation for the state if the city is not well known, in parentheses before the name of the paper.)

Government documents

Agency publications	28.U.S. Department of Commerce.1998.Economic Projections: 1997–2004.GPO.
	(Note that when no author's name is given, the government department is considered the author. Because the Government Printing Office [GPO], the government's primary publisher, is located in Washington,D.C., you need not list the city of publication.)
Legislative journals	31.Senate Journal.1995.103Cong. sess1.D10.
	(This citation refers to the record, published in the *Senate Journal,* of the first session of the 103rd Congress, held on December 10, 1995.)
	8.Congressional Record.71 Cong. sess2.72.8.
	(This citation refers to the account, published in the *Congressional Record,* of the second session of the 71st Congress, volume 72, page 8.)
Bills in Congress	13.U.S. Senate.1999.Visa Formalization Act of 1999.105Cong.sess1. SR.1437.
	(This citation refers to Senate Resolution 1437, originated in the first session of the 105th Congress. Bills originating in the House of Representatives are designated by the abbreviation HR.)

SOURCE	CITATION ELEMENTS AND EXAMPLES
Laws	17.U.S. Public Law 678.1995.Library of Congress Book Preservation Act of 1995.U.S.Code.38.1562.
	(The law referred to in this citation is recorded in section 1562 of volume 38 of the *U.S. Code.*)
Constitutions	31.U.S.Constitution.
	8.MO.Constitution.
	(This citation refers to the Missouri State Constitution.)
Internet documents	4.Akiko Kasahara and K-lab, Inc.1997. ArtScape of the Far East: Seminar on the Philosophy of Art.Shinshu. University Nagano.Japan.http:// Pckiso3.cs.Shinshu-u.ac.jp/artscape/ index.html.
	(The last item in an Internet citation is always the web site at which the document was found.)
Unpublished materials	
Interview	12.Lily Frailey.1996.Interview with Clarence Parker.Santa Fe NM.10Ag.
Thesis or dissertation	21.Gregory Scott.1973.Mysticism and Politics in the Thought of Bertrand Russell.MA thesis.UVa.
Paper presented at a meeting	5.Celia Hicks.1997."What Whitehead Would Say."Conference on the Western Imagination.14Ja.Boston MA.
	(The citation includes the name of the conference and the date on which the paper was presented, and ends with the city where the conference took place.)
Monograph housed in a collection	32.Jose Sanchez.1953?–1982. Journal.Southwest Collection.Arial Library.Chisum Academy.Canyon TX.

SOURCE   CITATION ELEMENTS AND EXAMPLES

(Unpublished manuscripts are sometimes left unnamed and undated by
their authors. Use any relevant information supplied by the repository catalog to complete the citation. When a
date is hypothesized, as in this example, place a question mark after it.)

Manuscript in the author's possession.   14.Jane Fried.1998.Life in Califor-
                                          nia.UTx.Photocopy.

(The citation includes the institution
with which the author is affiliated and
ends with a description of the format
of the work: typescript, photocopy,
and so on.)

Sample Bibliography: Student Citation System

```
                        Bibliography
1.Amanda Collingwood.1995.Architecture and Philosophy.Carlington
     Press.Detroit MI.
2.Tom Barker+Betty Clay, eds.1987.Swamps of Louisiana.Holt.NY.
3.Joan Garth+Allen Sanford.1963."The Hills of Wyoming."Critical
     Perspectives on Landscape.Prentice Hall.Upper Saddle River
     NJ.49-75.
4.Hayley Trakas, ed.1996.Russell on Space.3rd ed.Harmony Press.El
     Paso.TX.
5.Philippe Ariès.1962.Centuries of Childhood: A Social History of
     Family Life.Robert Baldock tr.Knopf.NY.
6.Jesus Gonzolez.1997."The Making of the Federales."Mexican Stories
     Revisited.Jules Frank ed.Comanche Press.San Antonio TX.54-79.
7.Carla Farris.2000.Foreword.Marital Stress among the Professo-
     riat: A Case Study by Basil Givan.Galapagos.NY.
8.Jasper Craig.1995."The Flight from the Center of the
     Cities."Time.10S.67-69.
```

9.Matthew Moen.1998."Evolving Politics of the Christian
     Right."PS:Political Science and Politics.29.3.461-464.

10.Patrick Swick.1998."Jumping the Gun on the Federal Reserve."New
     York Times.10My.78.

11.Frances Muggeridge.1995."The Truth Is Nowhere."Conundrum
     Digest.Mr.40-54.

12.Alan McAskill.1996."Interview with Mary Jordan."Hospice Pio-
     neers of New Mexico.Dynasty Press.Enid.OK.62-86.

13.Jane Smith.1999.Interview with Jerry Brown.San Francisco
     CA.15Oc.

14.Jacob Lynd.1973.Perfidy in Academe: Patterns of Rationalization
     in College Administrations.Ph.D. diss.UVA.

15.Holy Bible.New King James Version.

16.Paula Thomas.1970-1976.Diary.Museum of the Plains.Fabens TX.

17.U.S. Department of Labor.1931.Urban Growth and Population Pro-
     jections:1930-1939.GPO.

18.Senate Journal.1995.103Cong.sess1.D10.

19.U.S.Senate.1998.Visa Formalization Act of 1998.105Cong.
     sess1.SR.1437.

20.Peter Bolen.1997."Creating Designs in Social Systems."The
     Internet Journal of Sociological Welfare.14.6.
     http://www.carmelpeak.com.

NOTE. Most of the sources used as models in this chapter are not references to actual publications.

5
Principles of Argument

5.1 An Introduction
to Effective Argument

We have all heard sloppy thinking as people express it in speech or in writing. Sloppy thinking is a signal that no critical thinking has taken place. It makes inappropriate comparisons and draws unjustified conclusions. When we hear someone say, "Congress always messes things up," we know that someone has made an overly broad generalization, a sure sign of sloppy thinking. In politics, sloppy thinking can be dangerous. It can lead to stereotypes and to blaming people for causing problems over which they had no influence. Racism, in which all people of a certain skin color are blamed either for the actions of a few or for imagined actions that did not occur at all, is a prime example of dangerous sloppy thinking.

Critical thinking is the opposite of sloppy thinking. Critical thinking draws appropriate conclusions from phenomena we observe in the world around us. If we say, "The weight of evidence tends to indicate that President Clinton had an affair with Monica Lewinsky," we are probably demonstrating critical thinking because we have drawn a conclusion that is directly related to explicit observations about the president's behavior. Critical thinking does not provide us with the answers to all questions, however. It merely gives us a better chance of coming to the right conclusions. If we accept as valid the conclusion that Monica Lewinsky had an affair with President Clinton, for example, critical thinking may still lead to different conclusions concerning what should be done about the president's actions: censure, removal from office, or no action at all. Different conclusions come from similar patterns of critical thinking because different values are brought to bear in the judgment process. In any case, however, critical thinking sharpens our ability to see clearly the values we hold and the consequences of the choices we make.

How do we develop our critical thinking abilities? Philosophers have been working on this problem for centuries, and they have many answers. Probably the best way to begin is to understand the principles for making effective arguments. Effective arguments are expressions of logic, properly applied. In this chapter and the next, Anthony Graybosch, professor of philosophy at the University of California at Chico, explains how to use logic properly to make effective arguments and avoid fallacies that lead to sloppy thinking. As you read these chapters and apply the concepts they contain to your own writing about politics, you will increasingly demonstrate your command of critical thinking and thereby become more effective in your work as a student and in your career.

Arguments are discussions in which we strive to attain an objective. There are all sorts of objectives: selling our favorite political candidate, gaining a couple of points on an exam, selecting the movie we want to see, returning an item to a department store, or discovering the truth on an important matter. Verbal and non-verbal exchanges of reasons, threats, emotions, or even bricks, in the interest of reaching an objective, are normally called arguments.

The language in which we talk about argument suggests that we conceive argument metaphorically as a war to be won. Words such as *demolish, overwhelm, destroy,* and *thrust* make frequent appearances in our accounts of arguments. And we know that all is fair in love and war. So the very idea that there are rules governing argument may seem questionable from the start, unless the rules are going to show us how to attain our objectives more effectively.

Let us consider arguments to be verbal wrestling matches. Protagoras (490–421 B.C.E.), a Sophist, boasted that he could make equally strong cases for any side of an argument. Sophists were in great demand in ancient Athens, just as lawyers are in great demand today. People then, like today, needed to know how to argue to defend their lives and property. Sophists knew how to argue well and made a good deal of money by teaching others and by bringing the rich to court. Arguments, especially legal arguments, are more than mere sport. Unlike the Sophists, who argued for money, the Athenian philosopher Socrates argued for truth. He believed that knowing the truth about matters such as the nature of social justice, piety, the nature of god, and the justification of punishment was essential to living a good and happy life. Socrates was skilled in two strategies essential to good philosophical argument. First, he was adept at keeping the point of an argument from being lost. The Sophists often engaged in long flowery speeches on topics such as the nature of love or justice. Socrates was quick to bring his partners in argument back to the point at issue. This can be a maddening practice for those more interested in style than substance.

Second, during an argument Socrates was skillful at devising examples that undermined definitions offered by his opponents. Socratic dialectic is a method of argument in which a definition of an important concept, such as *justice* or *truth,* is subjected to a series of questions aimed at testing it. In the Socratic dialogues that Plato wrote, Socrates tests definitions offered by other participants in the discussion. For instance, early in Socrates' dialogue with Euthyphro, Euthyphro defines piety as "that which is pleasing to the gods." Socrates tests this definition by pointing out that the traditional stories of the gods are full of conflicts, and this fact suggests that what pleases one god may well displease another. While one god may be pleased by a person's action, another may be offended by that same action. If this is the case, what happens to Euthyphro's definition of piety? Is it possible for one action to be both pious and impious? Of course not, and so the definition must be given up because it leads to an inconsistency.

5.2 Argument Validity and Soundness

Before you can argue effectively, you must know how to identify and analyze arguments presented to you. The first requirement is to determine whether a series of statements is an argument. If it is an argument, you must then discern whether the argument is valid.

An argument is a series of statements that include at least one premise, a conclusion, and material that links the premises to a conclusion. A premise is a statement, offered as evidence for a conclusion, that is assumed or taken for granted. For example, the statements "Cats eat mice" and "Jake is a cat" are premises. Some expressions that indicate premises are *if, since, because, on the basis of, on the basis of the following observations,* and *the following observation supports my claim.* There are also other words that indicate premises.

Philosophers use the expression *connective* to designate the basic linking expressions of logic. The basic connectives are *it's not the case that, and, or,* and *if . . . then.* The first connective, which is represented by the negation sign, does not really connect statements. Instead, it negates a statement or a group of statements connected by the other connectives. *And* joins two or more statements. *Or* also joins two or more statements and is understood in logic in its inclusive sense. A better rendering of this connective would be "at least one." *If . . . then* does double duty in arguments. It connects two statements. The statement before *then* is the antecedent, the statement after *then* is the consequent. Compound sentences formed by *if . . . then* are called conditionals. Conditionals often are found as premises in arguments either expressly stated or implied. But *if . . . then* also functions as the basic connective in any argument connecting the premises to the conclusion. An argument can always be translated into a long conditional sentence in which the premises are the antecedent and the conclusion is the consequent. It is important to know the meanings of *antecedent* and *consequent* because they appear in the names of several valid and invalid argument forms.

A conclusion is a reasoned judgment resulting from understanding the implications of the premises. For example, if we accept the premises that (1) cats eat mice and (2) Jake is a cat, we may reasonably conclude that Jake eats mice. The following are all linking expressions that indicate conclusions: *it follows that, therefore, if . . . then, hence, my conclusion is, consequently, it is (probably) the case that,* and *so.* Here is one of many ways in which we can frame our little discussion about Jake's dining habits in the form of an argument complete with premises, conclusion, and linking material. Here's another phrasing for the argument: "Because cats eat mice and Jake is a cat, it follows that Jake eats mice." How many other ways can you devise for stating the argument, using the connectives that we have just given? Both premises and conclusions make a claim on us for acceptance. Arguments call for us to take the truth or probable truth of the premises for granted for a moment so that we may determine whether the purported truth of the premises is sufficient to guarantee the truth or probability of the conclusion. In addition to premises and conclusions, arguments may contain extraneous material such as jokes, biographical data, or even personal attacks. Narratives, which are simply chronological stories of actions or events, are not arguments.

Arguments are either deductive or nondeductive. An argument is deductive if it claims that the conclusion must be true if the premises are true. The conclusion is, therefore, guaranteed by the truth of the premises. A deductive argument spends no time, in other words, inquiring into the accuracy of the premises: If they are true, then the conclusion must also be true. The argument about Jake the cat is phrased as a deductive argument. The following argument is deductive because its conclusion, given its premises, is presented as being an unarguable matter of fact:

> Two million and thirty-seven lottery tickets were sold for Wednesday's drawing. I bought two tickets. So my chance of winning Wednesday is 2 in 2,000,037.

An argument is nondeductive (inductive) if it claims only a high degree of probability for the conclusion. An inductive argument, then, allows for some doubt of the truth of the conclusion, and it bases its claim of accuracy on the very good chance that its premises are correct. Here is a way to phrase our argument about Jake the cat inductively:

> All cats that I have ever seen will eat mice. Jake is a cat. Therefore, Jake will probably eat mice.

Whether we knew it or not at the time, most of us have had the following inductive argument with ourselves:

> Because most commercial aircraft do not crash on routine flights, the flight that I have booked myself on for Christmas break will probably not crash.

It is important to know the difference between deductive and inductive arguments because we must know what an argument demands of us. Does the argument ask us to accept something as true, or only as probably true? The actions we take based upon certainty are different from the actions we take that are based upon mere probability, and we may hold deductive arguments liable for much stronger bases of proof.

There are two slightly different definitions of validity, which correspond to the two different types of argument, deductive and nondeductive. An argument is deductively valid if it is deductive and if the truth of the premises would make it necessary that the conclusion is true also. In other words, an argument is deductively valid if it is deductive and if it cannot be the case that the premises are true and the conclusion is false. The following argument is deductively valid:

PREMISE 1	If Santa Claus lives at the South Pole, then Tesla invented the light bulb.
PREMISE 2	Santa Claus lives at the South Pole.
CONCLUSION	Tesla invented the light bulb.

Even though the two premises are false, the argument is still deductively valid; that is, the deduction from the assumed true premises is valid. The argument is deductive because it claims certainty for the conclusion, and it is valid because its conclusion would have to be true if the premises were true. When you evaluate an argument for deductive validity, you do not yet check for the truth of the premises. The factual truth of the premises is irrelevant to the validity of an argument. Consequently, a deductively valid argument may have false premises and a true conclusion, or it may have false premises and a false conclusion.

In a deductively valid argument, the relation between premises and conclusions is not a causal relationship. Premises do not cause a conclusion to be true; they merely explain why, if they are true, the conclusion is also true.

Nondeductive arguments make claims in their conclusions that go beyond the evidence of the premises. If I claim, for example, that "since my chances of winning the lottery are 2 million to 1, then I will probably lose the lottery," then I am making a nondeductive argument because I am claiming only the probability, not the certainty, of my conclusion. An argument is nondeductively valid if it is nondeductive and if the truth or high probability of its premises makes the conclusion highly probable also. My argument about the probability of my losing the lottery is nondeductively valid because the high odds against winning do indeed produce a high likelihood that I will lose.

Checking for validity is important because it is the first step in examining an argument in order to see if it is worthwhile to check the actual truth of the premises. If an argument is not valid, there is no point in finding out whether or not the premises are true. If an argument is valid, however, the premises become important.

Imagine you are a member of the National Science Foundation and someone presents a grant for funding. The grant's hypothesis is that, since mosquitoes carry malaria, then the people of Kentucky are vulnerable to malaria. As you read the grant, you realize that the argument guiding the proposed research is not arranged in a valid way. Not all mosquitoes carry malaria, and the mosquitoes that carry malaria have not been found in Kentucky. You would not have to consider funding it, because the project would probably produce invalid information. It needs to be reformulated if it is to be worth funding.

Consider the following deductive arguments. Are they valid?

If President Clinton did what Paula Jones charged in her deposition that he did, then he is guilty of sexual harassment in the workplace. Paula Jones did indeed speak the truth. Therefore, Clinton is a harasser.

Republican candidate Bob Dole said he would not raise taxes. But Dole voted many times to raise taxes while he was a senator even while Republicans were in control of the presidency. So Dole was lying.

When I am in Memphis, I always go to the services at Al Green's church. If I go to Al Green's church, then I will visit Graceland afterward, since it is nearby. So if I go to Memphis, then I will visit Graceland.

If you found yourself asking whether Al Green has a church, how Dole voted, whether Paula Jones spoke the truth, or if Graceland is indeed close to Al Green's church (it is), then you missed the point. It does not matter to the question of validity whether the statements you questioned are in fact true or false. It matters only whether, if they and the other premises in their respective arguments were true, the truth of the premise would make it necessary that the conclusion be true also. The anti-Clinton bias of the first argument and the anti-Dole bias of the second argument may irritate you, but these biases have nothing to do with the validity of the arguments. Try to filter out your worries about my bias and attend to the arguments.

Are the following nondeductive arguments nondeductively valid?

The United States has never elected a third-party candidate as president. So Perot will probably not be elected in 2000.

When people are transferred to Calvary Hospital they usually die within a week or two. Helene's physician has recommended that she be transferred to Calvary. So the physician has decided she is beyond recovery.

Cogency

To this point, we have discussed three questions that need to be raised when evaluating a passage to test its qualities as an argument:

1. Does it have the components (at least one premise and a conclusion) of an argument?
2. Is the argument deductive (purporting certainty) or nondeductive (purporting probability)?
3. Is the argument valid (the premises lead to the conclusions) or invalid (the premises do not lead to the conclusions)?

A fourth question remains to be asked: "Is the argument cogent?" An argument is cogent if it is valid and if its premises are true. We may then say that an argument is deductively cogent (or sound) if it is deductive, if it is deductively valid, and if the premises are in fact true. An argument is nondeductively cogent (often called *strong* or *correct*) if it is nondeductive, if it is nondeductively valid, and if its premises are true or highly probable.

The following argument is deductively cogent:

The electric company charges for electricity. I used electricity from the electric company last month. I will be charged for the use of electricity.

The following argument is nondeductively cogent:

Thousands of tickets are sold for each drawing of the California lottery. I bought one ticket for the next drawing on Wednesday. I will probably lose.

Now that we know how to ask four questions that will help us test the quality of an argument, we can add to our argument-testing capabilities by understanding sound and unsound patterns of reasoning. When we discussed validity, we relied upon simple examples to elicit your agreement on when the premises would guarantee the truth or high probability of a conclusion. Some intuitively appealing forms of argument, however, are invalid. There are mathematically objective ways of demonstrating when an argument form is valid or invalid, but we will not provide mathematical proofs here, for the attempt to do so would take us too far beyond the compass of this book. If you are interested in mathematical proofs, take a course in symbolic logic or look at a good logic textbook.

The practical benefit of learning the valid and invalid argument forms lies in the ways in which the forms facilitate argumentative discussion. Once you have isolated the author's major thesis and premises for the thesis, you can summarize the argument in argument form. You may discover that the author has structured the argument in a valid form such as modus ponens or a reductio. And so you would not criticize the author's form of argument, but turn immediately to investigate the premises. But if the author has relied upon eliminative induction, then it may be the case that a possibility has been overlooked and a false dilemma presented. Or, if the author relies upon an invalid form such as affirming the consequent, you can identify her error and perhaps find a way to repair the argument. And, of course, if you can cast summaries of your own arguments in valid forms, your writing will be more effective. It is a daunting task to cast most extended arguments in argumentative form, although you might enjoy looking at the attempt to do so found in Spinoza's *Ethics*. It is considerably easier to work with argument summaries. So how do we exhibit the forms of arguments?

In *sentential logic,* ordinary language statements are given letters as their names. Each statement gets only one name, one letter. Take the sentence: "If this is Tuesday, this must be Brussels." This is a compound sentence containing two statements: "This is Tuesday" and "This is Brussels." Some systems of sentential logic use capital letters and begin with the letter A. Others use small letters and begin with p. Whether "This is Tuesday" is named A or p is a convention. The important thing is that in an argument form it keeps the same name and no other statement is given the same name. So "This is Brussels" is going to be B or q, but certainly not A or p. Could we have called it A before we baptized the other statement A? Sure, provided we baptized the other one something else.

When an argument in ordinary language is translated replacing its statements with sentence letters and the connectives with their appropriate symbols, then we have exhibited its form. The connectives in sentential logic connect sentences. The connectives are *and, or, it is not the case that,* and *if . . . then.* They are represented by an upside-down V, a right-side-up V, the − or —, and an arrow, respectively. Punctuation is also provided in the form of parentheses and brackets.

Two arguments in ordinary language that have the same representation when translated have the same logical or argument form. This fact is handy because once you know a form is valid and are practiced in recognizing it, you can immediately recognize valid arguments about matters you never heard of. Take my argument about Clinton, Paula Jones, and sexual harassment and make it about Rush Limbaugh, Oprah Winfrey, and unfair competition. If one argument is valid, the other one is too.

Common Valid Logical Forms

Tautologies

A *tautology* is a sentence that must be true in all possible worlds. A contradiction is a sentence that must be false in all possible worlds. You can recognize tautologies and contradictions by their forms. "*P* and not *P*" is a contradiction. "It is snowing in hell, and it is not snowing in hell" is a contradiction. Tautologies are redundant and boring, but they are valid. "*P* or not *P*" is a tautology: "It is raining right now in Chico, or it is not raining right now in Chico." Notice that a tautology requires no premises. It is true on the basis of form alone. So perhaps tautologies are exceptions to the rules we have looked at governing argument: Tautologies are valid argument forms that require no premises. However, philosophers disagree on the question of whether tautologies assert any conclusions at all when sentence names are replaced with ordinary language statements. After all, how much information about the weather is included in the tautology about Chico?

Modus Ponens

A common valid form of argument, *modus ponens* is, as its Latin name implies, a "method of putting." A modus ponens argument takes the following symbolic form:

If p, then q
p
Therefore q

If July 15 is Graybosch's birthday, then he is a Cancer just like O. J. Simpson, Bill Clinton, and Phyllis Diller.

July 15 is Graybosch's birthday.

Therefore he is a Cancer just like O. J. and the others.

More complicated modus ponens follow patterns such as the following:

If p and q and r, then s or t
P and q and r
Therefore s or t

Hypothetical Syllogisms

Hypothetical syllogisms are arguments that have the following symbolic form:

If p, then q
If q, then r
Therefore if p, then r

Here is an example of a valid simple hypothetical syllogism:

If the Yankees win the pennant, then Darryl Strawberry will get a raise.

If Darryl Strawberry gets a raise, then his ex-wife will take him to court.

So if the Yankees win the pennant, then Strawberry's ex-wife will take him to court.

Syllogisms come in many forms. One is known as the *disjunctive syllogism,* which has the following symbolic form:

P or *q*
Not *p*
Therefore *q*

EXAMPLE

Jill is a lawyer or Jill is a psychologist.

Jill is not a lawyer.

Therefore Jill is a psychologist.

A knowledge of traditional syllogisms will be helpful to you if you are taking a standardized test for graduate or professional school. Here are several valid syllogisms. Notice that traditional syllogisms are not in sentential form.

All *A*'s are *B*'s.
All *B*'s are *C*'s
Therefore all A's are *C*'s.

EXAMPLE

All talk show hosts are well paid.

All well-paid people are happy.

Therefore all talk show hosts are happy.

Another valid syllogism follows:

All *A*'s are *B*'s.
This is an *A*.
This is therefore also a *B*.

EXAMPLE

All Rolling Stones albums have one song on which Keith sings lead.

This is a Rolling Stones album.

Therefore this album has one song on which Keith sings lead.

Here is a third valid syllogism:

All *A*'s are *B*'s.
No *B*'s are *C*'s.
Therefore no *A*'s are *C*'s.

EXAMPLE

All lovers of Champion Jack Dupree are lovers of Jerry Lee Lewis.

No lovers of Jerry Lee Lewis are lovers of Johnny Mathis.

Therefore no lovers of Champion Jack are lovers of Johnny Mathis.

A fourth valid syllogism is this:

No A's are B's.
Some C's are A's.
Therefore some C's are not B's.

EXAMPLE

No supporters of President Clinton are Bosnian Serbs.

Some Croatians are supporters of Clinton.

Therefore some Croatians are not Bosnian Serbs.

Some syllogisms sound valid but are not. What is wrong with the following syllogism?

God is love.

Love is blind.

Ray Charles is blind.

Ray Charles is God.

Modus Tollens

Modus tollens, latin for "method of removing," is an argument that takes the following symbolic form. Can you see the reason for its name?

If p, then q
Not q
Therefore not p

EXAMPLE

If Graybosch finds the Holy Grail, then he will be famous.

Graybosch will not be famous.

Then Graybosch will not find the Holy Grail.

Dilemmas

A *dilemma* is an argument in which there is a choice between two alternatives, neither of which is particularly desirable. A dilemma takes the following symbolic form:

P or q
If p, then r

If *q*, then *s*

Therefore, *r* or *s*

EXAMPLE

Peter either forgot that it was Christmas or did not care enough for his kids to buy them gifts.

If Peter forgot it was Christmas, then he needs to see a doctor.

If Peter did not care enough for his kids to buy them a gift, then he needs counseling.

Therefore, Peter either needs to see a doctor or get counseling.

This is a handy form of argument for use when you know that someone is guilty of one of several offenses but you cannot say which one. You do not have to determine which offense is the real one to convict the person.

Indirect Proof, or Reductio ad Absurdum

An *indirect proof,* also known as *reductio ad absurdum,* or "reduction to the absurd," complies with the following form:

Suppose: *p*

If *p*, then *q*

If *q*, then *r*

Not *r*

Therefore not *p*

EXAMPLE

Suppose Pat Paulsen becomes president.

If he becomes president, then he will sell the White House to his cousin Maxine.

If he sells the White House to his cousin Maxine, then Maxine will live forever.

Maxine will not live forever.

Therefore, Pat Paulsen will not become president.

The reductio looks like an extended version of modus tollens. The difference is that the reductio is purposely used to throw doubt on a particular premise. This is a very effective form of argument because it forces an opponent to speak to a matter she might just as soon pass over in silence.

Contradictions

A *contradiction* is a sentence form that must be false no matter what statements are substituted for the statement names. It has the symbolic form "*p* and not *p*." For example, the statement "It is raining right now in Chico, and it is not raining right now in Chico" is a contradiction. The negation of a contradiction

must be true. So if you find a contradiction, you should conclude that its negation is true: "It is not the case that it is raining and not raining in Chico right
now." In a charge of atheism against Socrates, we would agree with Socrates that
it is not the case that he is both an atheist and a believer in gods.

Analogies

In an *analogy* we draw a comparison between the known qualities of a sample population and the partially known qualities of a target population. If, for
example, we have several friends who like heavy metal music, alternative rock,
mosh pits, and tattoos, and if we make a new friend who likes three of those
things, then it would be reasonable to infer by analogy that the new friend will
like the fourth thing.

Our analogy works on the basis of similarities. If our friends are similar in
three respects, they are probably similar in the fourth. The cogency of this
reasoning depends in part on the similar qualities being related to each other.
Our first three friends might also like Chopin or falafel, but I would be less
inclined to infer that the fourth person shares those likes because an appreciation of falafel does not seem related to an appreciation of mosh pits. Analogies
often lead to unsound conclusions because they are not properly grounded.

Induction by Elimination

Induction by elimination is a popular nondeductive form of reasoning in
philosophy. It requires three steps. The first is to canvas the alternative perspectives on a question. The second step is to find reasons why all alternatives but one
cannot be true. Finally, having eliminated all the unacceptable alternatives, you
take step three, which is to accept the remaining alternative as the most probable
one. The crucial step in this form of reasoning is the first step. If you have not
included all the alternatives, you will commit an informal fallacy called a *false
dilemma*. We will talk a little more about false dilemmas in Chapter 6.

Induction by Enumeration

In *induction by enumeration* we infer that a quality probably belongs to a
whole population on the basis of a finite number of instances.

EXAMPLE

Farmer Jones's turkey believes that Farmer Jones will come to feed him
every morning on the basis of a finite number of previous feedings.

This is a fairly reliable inference for the turkey; it is correct every morning except
the last.

Statistical Induction

A *statistical induction* is similar to induction by enumeration. It involves attributing the statistical frequency of a quality in a sample population to the
population as a whole.

EXAMPLE

Since 75 percent of the camels we have seen have two humps, we infer that 75 percent of all camels have two humps.

Both induction by enumeration and statistical induction uncover connections that may be more than coincidences. They may be connections that are based on an underlying causal relationship. Is it a mere coincidence that students begin to fidget in their seats when the end of class approaches? Could it be that the clock makes them fidget? Higher-level inductions consider a wider variety of objects in their samples than those considered in the inductions, enumerative or statistical, that generate the initial connections that become candidates for causes and effects.

Inference to the Best Explanation

Some philosophers accept *inference to the best explanation* as a valid form of nondeductive inference. Suppose there is a series of events whose occurrence can be most reasonably explained if you posit another event as their cause.

EXAMPLE

You notice that every time you play cards with me you lose. But when you play cards with other people you do reasonably well. Your losing streak with me might be best explained if you posit that I am a cheat. Perhaps I have marked the cards.

Certainly the explanation will have a stronger initial probability if you have seen me cheat in the past or if you remember that when we play cards we always use my deck. Your inability to imagine another explanation for your losses does not prove that I am cheating. But it does not follow from the fact that another explanation does not occur to us that the one that does occur is the only possible explanation. An explanation, therefore, is only as good as our knowledge of the conditions and circumstances of the phenomenon that we are trying to explain. Good background knowledge might justify our claim that the explanation that occurs to us is the only possible one, but because our knowledge is so often more limited than we think, we should normally give low probability to conclusions from this form of reasoning.

The hypothetical-deductive method is usually attributed to Karl Popper but dates at least from the work of the nineteenth-century American philosopher Chauncey Wright. Popper popularized the method with philosophers of science as his original criterion for differentiating science from nonscience. Popper points out that one can never conclusively verify a universal statement by empirical means, but one can falsify it.

For instance, induction by enumeration cannot establish once and for all that all swans are white. One nonwhite swan can falsify the universal claim about white swans. It may sound odd, but falsifiability is actually more helpful to science than verification by means of induction. After all, if you can falsify a claim, then you need not pursue it any longer and can move on to another claim.

Popper urges that scientific investigators select the hypothesis with the lowest initial probability, given our background beliefs, for further investigation. It is the hypothesis that has the highest likelihood to turn out to be wrong when empirically tested. If it survives frequent tests, it is considered corroborated.

Argumentation is the means by which most philosophy gets done. As you read philosophical essays, try to determine which particular modes of argumentation the writers are using. The premises may be more complicated than the ones I have used in my examples in this chapter, but the basic forms will be there. Remember, arguing is like wrestling. Learning the throws now will enhance your ability not only to understand philosophical positions but also to find ways to question and, perhaps, improve upon them in your own writing.

6
Avoiding Fallacies

6.1 Types of Fallacies

Fallacies are errors in reasoning that lead us to accept conclusions that are not soundly based upon valid premises. Formal fallacies are reasoning errors that occur because the form or structure of an argument is incorrect. There are an infinite number of formal fallacies, yet a few may be identified that are commonly encountered when analyzing arguments. The ability to recognize them may make your job as a critical writer easier.

Denying the Antecedent

Remember the way we formulated arguments in Chapter 5. Consider an argument in this form:

If p, then q
Not p
Therefore, not q

EXAMPLE

If Graybosch wins the lottery, then he can take a vacation.

Graybosch cannot win the lottery.

Therefore, Graybosch cannot take a vacation.

It would be a lot easier to take a vacation if I won the lottery, but maybe I will take one anyway. The error in the argument is in assuming that the antecedent (winning the lottery) is necessary to my conclusion (taking a vacation). In actuality, my taking a vacation does not depend upon winning the lottery. Now, it may be true that if I win the lottery, I will take a vacation, but this statement does not mean the opposite, that if I do not win the lottery, I will not take a vacation. Winning the lottery is one sufficient, but not necessary, condition of taking a vacation.

Affirming the Consequent

Here is another invalid form of reasoning:

If p, then q
Therefore, p

Just because p always leads to q does not mean that q always leads to p. Other sufficient conditions may also result in q. The consequent q is a necessary condition of p in the sense that if p does occur, q must also occur.

The Exclusive Fallacy

The *exclusive fallacy* takes the following form:

p or q
p
Therefore, not q

The fallacy lies in confusing the inclusive and exclusive sense of *or*. Example: You are at a party and ask who brought the wine. The host says Fred or Jack brought the wine. If *or* is meant exclusively, then once you know that Fred brought wine you could conclude that Jack did not. But if *or* is used inclusively then it means at least Fred and possibly Jack brought wine. Since logic uses the inclusive sense of *or*, you ought not to infer from the fact that Fred brought wine that Jack did not.

Here is an example of the exclusive fallacy:

Either Newt Gingrich is guilty of ethics violations, or Bill Clinton is guilty of ethics violations.
Newt Gingrich is guilty of ethics violations.
Therefore, Bill Clinton is not guilty of ethics violations.

Alas, dear Democrats, the guilt of Newt does not establish Bill's innocence. The inclusive sense of *or* allows both disjuncts to be true. They both could be guilty; both disjuncts could be true.

Of course, we are familiar with detective stories in which each suspect is eliminated until there is only one left who must be guilty. There are eliminative arguments in which the truth or falsity of a disjunct is relevant to the truth or falsity of others. But they must be carefully phrased to show the relevance of the disjuncts to each other. And you will note that the Gingrich-Clinton example did not include a premise that said they both could not be guilty. If it did, it would have been a valid argument. But it would also have had a different argument form.

Informal Fallacies

Informal fallacies are errors in reasoning based in the content of an argument and not in the argument's form. It is possible to construct arguments with valid forms but still fail to have reasoned properly in one of three general ways. First, the premises of the argument could be false or lack the proper degree of probability. Second, our reasoning could leave out evidence that is in our possession or evidence that is not in our possession that we are still responsible for gathering. Ignorance of contrary evidence is not an acceptable excuse. Third, our argument could mistakenly assert that the premises give more support to the conclusion than the truth or probability of the premises would warrant. These three general types of fallacies are found in a number of more specific forms, which we shall now describe.

Our human desires make us susceptible to fallacies. A common gambling fallacy is to bet on a number that is due because it has not occurred recently. If the dice or the roulette wheel is fair, each outcome has the same probability on each roll or spin regardless of how long it has been since it last occurred. If I throw six snake eyes (two ones) in a row, on the seventh throw it is just as likely that I will throw snake eyes again as it was on the first throw. Snake eyes are not less likely because they have occurred six times in a row, if the dice are fair.

Psychologists have cataloged a number of impediments to reasoning. I am pretty good at math, but I make an increasing number of errors of subtraction in my checkbook toward the end of the month. Wishful thinking infects my math. Two other interesting impediments to reasoning are our tendencies to have a confirmation bias and to expect one cause for any given event. The confirmation bias allows us to accept horoscopes and psychic hot lines because we remember only the instances when the "predictions" come true and forget the times when they do not. The expectation that every event has just one cause blinds us to other contributing causes and makes us especially prone to give up good causal connections when we run into one exception. For example, "Smoking does not cause cancer because my dad smoked until he was 97." Perhaps your dad was lucky and had a genetic endowment that helped him resist cancer.

There is also an interesting error made consistently with statistical reasoning that could be called a formal error. Suppose you read of a study that says that 35 percent of people convicted of heroin possession said they had smoked marijuana before becoming involved with heroin. This correlation might lead you to infer that marijuana use causes heroin use; or you might infer that whatever causes marijuana use also causes heroin use. And people commonly make such inferences. The 35 percent is impressive until you notice that 65 percent did not say that they smoked marijuana before becoming involved with heroin. When you are presented with a statistical correlation between two factors such as marijuana use and heroin use, you really want to know four correlations before drawing a conclusion about the relevance of one to the other:

What percent of marijuana users also use heroin?
What percent of marijuana users do not use heroin?
What percent of the population use heroin only?
What percent of the population use neither marijuana nor heroin?

But if you studied further, you might find that 50 percent of people convicted of heroin possession are women, 90 percent are coffee drinkers, and 98 percent have at least ten teeth. These figures might lead you to want to test for heroin all the women you can find who drink coffee and have at least ten teeth.

Our human tendency to accept fallacies is, fortunately, counteracted by our ability to identify them. The following subsections on informal fallacies have been constructed to assist you in identifying fallacies in arguments.

Invalid Appeal to Authority

An *invalid appeal to authority* occurs when we rely on defective expertise. Defective expertise is a source of knowledge that presents itself as authoritative but is not. Michael Jordan is an expert basketball player, but he does not necessarily know the best brand of ice cream. Experts may be subject to bias that can cause them consciously or unconsciously to render unfair judgment. A Toyota salesman will probably not provide an unbiased evaluation of a Nissan. And sometimes the experts disagree, leaving us forced to reason for ourselves. The two founders of the philosophical tradition known as pragmatism, Charles Peirce and William James, could not agree on a common definition. So Peirce renamed his view pragmaticism.

The fact that people have positions of authority does not automatically make their beliefs, or our premises, false or unjustified. When the president or the pope speaks, he does not commit a fallacy of invalid appeal to authority just by saying something. Perhaps their offices do not give them expertise in all matters, but each has a sphere of expertise—politics or religion—where it is appropriate to speak and be cited as an authority. And, when they venture into other areas such as the philosophy of love, the arguments they offer ought to be considered. It would be simply unfair to convict them of the fallacy of invalid appeal to authority unless they claim that their position gives them some special expertise. In other words, authorities should have the chance to offer arguments and be given a fair hearing.

Straw Person

A *straw person* is a misrepresentation of the position of an opponent. A straw person is a position or concept that you have formulated because it is more easily attacked than your opponent's real position. The phrase "What so-and-so really means to say" often introduces a straw person argument. Consider this example: "What Pat Robertson really means to say is that if we don't join his church, we will all burn in hell."

Inconsistency

You commit the error of *inconsistency* when you use inconsistent premises to support a conclusion. If you accept as a premise the idea that smoking does not lead to death but admit that diseases caused by smoking lead to death, your two premises conflict. You can also commit this fallacy by being inconsistent in your words and actions. Or you could argue for inconsistent conclusions. Sometimes people change a belief over time without offering an explanation why. And, finally, organizations such as corporations or political parties sometimes take inconsistent positions with different audiences or have spokespersons who take differing stands. You and a friend might take opposing viewpoints on an important issue, send letters to a politician, and compare the replies you receive. In many cases, it will look like the politician agrees with both of you.

False Dilemma

A *false dilemma* occurs when all the available alternatives are not considered. Consider this example of a false dilemma often used by parents: "Do you want to go to bed now or after your bath?" Faced with what seem to be only two possible courses of action, the five-year-old child will take the bath and go to bed, without realizing that there may be other, less undesirable alternatives. When she reaches the age of eight or nine, different courses of action, such as continuing to watch television, may occur to her.

In politics, even in the most sophisticated commentaries, false dilemmas appear in such questions as "Should the United States use military force or economic sanctions against Iraq?"

Complex Question

In the fallacy of the *complex question,* you ask a question in a way that begs the answer to another, usually negatively perceived, question. The idea is to make your opponents grant a premise that will be useful in constructing an argument against a conclusion they wish to resist. "When are you going to become responsible?" If you answer that question, you admit that you have not been responsible in the past and grant a premise that may then be used against you.

Begging the Question

When you *beg the question,* you argue for a conclusion by assuming at least part of it in your premises. "Why do you doubt that God is good? Does not the Koran say so?" The question assumes that God exists and that the Koran provides an authoritative description of the deity's characteristics.

Suppressed Evidence

Because we cannot spend all our lives in doubt, we must eventually draw conclusions on the basis of the evidence available to us. But whenever we *suppress evidence,* whether we have it available or not, we engage in fallacious reasoning. It is easier to know when you have suppressed relevant evidence in your possession than it is to know when you have done enough investigation to conclude that there is no conflicting evidence that you have not uncovered. Do you need to have read everything William James ever wrote to know that he believed in free will? Or is reading "The Dilemma of Determinism" enough? The correct answer depends upon your social role and responsibilities, on whether you are a beginning student or an advanced scholar. We often suppress evidence for good motives. When we tell children that bad things will happen to them when they lie, we suppress evidence that not all lies lead to negative consequences.

Lack of Proportion

When we over- or underestimate actions, interests, or outcomes, we are guilty of applying a *lack of proportion* in our arguments. Consider the following exhortation, addressed to a typical teenager: "Go ahead and buy the Smashing Pumpkins concert ticket for $300.00. You only live once!"

Appeal to Unknowable Statistics

It is tempting to insert into our arguments *appeals to unknowable statistics.* For example: "Let's have one more drink. Nobody has ever died from a six-pack!" Another example: "Battlefield deployment of tactical nuclear weapons has prevented 17 major wars in Europe since 1950."

Ad Hominem

Ad hominem is Latin for "to the person." It is a fallacy that involves attacking people's character, looks, tastes, or some other irrelevant aspect of their lives to avoid dealing with their arguments. Examples: "Clinton's health plan is no good. We know he is a liar." "Dole's tax plan will never work. He's too old."

Guilt by Association.

Guilt by association is a form of ad hominen argument in which a person's associates are attacked in attempt to reflect negatively upon that person or her argument. The target person may be beyond reproach, but her associates may be easy targets. Vice presidential candidate Richard Nixon used this strategy in his famous 1952 "Checkers" speech to attack Adlai Stevenson, a politician beyond reproach, by associating Stevenson with President Harry Truman, who was very controversial. Although Truman had endorsed Stevenson's candidacy for president, Truman and Stevenson were not constant companions. Politicians commonly employ the opposite of this phenomenon, something I call innocence by association. When wealthy politicians have themselves photographed with the poor, they take advantage of innocence by association.

Two Wrongs Make a Right

A common fallacy involves defending a wrong action by claiming that someone else has done the same thing or has done something just as bad: "Tommy hit me first!" When we base our argument on the wrong behavior of more than two people, this fallacy is called *common practice:* "It's not so bad to cheat on the test; all my friends do it." When a way of doing wrong has become so accepted that it has attained the status of a proverb, it is called *traditional wisdom:* "The real speed limit is ten miles per hour above the posted speed limit."

Equivocation

Equivocation is the practice of using different meanings of a term that has more than one meaning to derive a conclusion: "Jesus loved prostitutes, and so do I. That's why I pay them well for their services."

Appeal to Ignorance

We *appeal to ignorance* when we try to get someone to believe that his conclusion is false because he has failed to prove it is true. We may even try to get him to believe that because he has failed to prove his conclusion to be true, then the opposite of his conclusion is true. The failure to prove the existence of extraterrestrial humanoids does not demonstrate that there are none, and the failure to prove that there are no extraterrestrial humanoids does not demonstrate that there are some.

Composition

Composition is a fallacy that occurs when we reason that if the members of a group have a property or characteristic, then the whole group has that characteristic. We might believe, for example, that if all the players on the Oklahoma Sooners football team are individually good players, then the team must be good also. They may not, however, play well together.

Division

Division is the fallacy that occurs when we expect a member of a group to have all the characteristics of a group as a whole: "Native Americans care about the environment." Even if most Native Americans do care about the environment, this fact does not mean that any individual Native American will.

Hasty Conclusion

When you accept a sweeping conclusion on the basis of a single or small number of incidents, you reach a *hasty conclusion.* For instance, someone may conclude that all New York City taxi drivers are dishonest if she has been overcharged for a ride from the airport to downtown. A hasty conclusion is the result of making a judgment on the basis of too small a sample of experiences. Another example: "From what I've seen, atheists are easier to live with than Christians." Sometimes hasty conclusions are referred to as *small samples.* A sample can be too small to reveal a representative trend. You would probably be less likely to accept the conclusion of a survey about pornography and sexual assault if you found out that only twenty-five offenders were surveyed. A sample can also be faulted for being unrepresentative. A survey of New York City cab drivers ought not to be taken as a fair indication of the behaviors of all cab drivers no matter how many cabbies are surveyed.

Humans are inclined to make inductions from single experiences, but rationally we ought not to do so. Calculating a sufficiently large sample size depends on both the size of the population we study and its diversity. I heard a psychologist on the radio this morning say that she had spoken to over fifty women before drawing her conclusion about how best to end a relationship. A sample of fifty is not enough to draw a conclusion about such a large group of persons. Also, people are more complex entities than Ping-Pong balls. One may expect a greater diversity of opinions within the population of women or men, and this expectation should affect sample size. Statisticians would want you to check with at least 1,200 people in a rigorous, scientifically designed study before drawing a conclusion about a country like the United States.

The sample should also be representative of the population. So, if you want to talk about women in general, then you should make sure your sample is not just about a particular ethnic or economic group.

Questionable Cause

The *questionable cause* fallacy is committed when we take an event as the cause of another on the basis of token evidence, such as a correlation that has not been subjected to further investigation. Political candidates are fond of attributing economic improvements to their economic policies. But they rarely consider that there might have been even greater improvements in the economy if their policies had not been followed: that the economy improved despite their policies and not because of them.

Questionable Analogy

A *questionable analogy* is the result of drawing a conclusion on the basis of similarities while ignoring or overlooking relevant differences. For example, electric discharges occur both in a computer that is processing "information" and in the human brain when it is thinking. This similarity might lead us to draw analogies between what goes on in the brain and the computer as support for the conclusion that computers and humans both process information in the same sense. But there are many dissimilarities between human brains and computers; in fact, there may be too many relevant dissimilarities to compare "artificial intelligence" to human intelligence.

Appeal to Pity

Sometimes we are tempted to accept a conclusion or a premise because we have sympathetic feelings either for the person who advances it or for the person's current situation. Perhaps we may accept a job applicant's argument that he deserves a teaching position because, if he does not receive it, he and his family will suffer.

Appeal to the Stick

Appeals to the stick are actions that mistake threats for arguments. When we appeal to the stick we urge someone to accept a conclusion or else suffer stated or implied negative consequences. "Why should I attend class?" asks the student. "Because if you do not, I will lower your grade one level for each absence in excess of two," replies the authoritarian philosophy instructor. The instructor has not persuaded the student of the reasonableness of attending class but instead has tried to supply a motivation.

Appeal to Loyalty

Sometimes we accept a conclusion because it comes from a revered public figure, or it is crucial to our national interest, or its contradiction reflects unfavorably on our nation or another cherished institution such as a church, school, or family. Some Americans have refused, for example, to believe that their country's armed forces have committed atrocities.

Provincialism

Like the appeal to loyalty, *provincialism* blinds us to the value of beliefs and practices of other cultures. We are provincial when we reject the ideas of others not for verified reasons but simply because we are familiar with our own practices but not theirs. We may attend a Christian communion service without questioning its value but reject a harvest dance as having no religious value.

Popularity

We rely upon *popularity* or *appeal to the crowd (argumentum ad baculum)* when we argue for a conclusion on the grounds of its widespread acceptance or acceptance by an important group that is not composed of appropriate experts. If we go to church because all our neighbors do, we are basing our actions upon popularity.

Double Standard

A *double standard* occurs when we treat similar cases in a dissimilar manner. If we expect men but not women to experience premarital sex, we subscribe to a double standard.

Invincible Ignorance

Some people actually take pride in refusing to listen to argument. This severe form of evading the issue is usually fed by faith, frustration, and self-righteousness. Extremists on both sides of the abortion issue, for example, sometimes exhibit *invincible ignorance* by demonstrating pride in not listening to arguments of the other side.

6.2 An Exercise in Identifying Fallacies

Here is an exercise to sharpen your argument skills. Although the example presented here may not at first appear to be an argument, if you examine it closely you will find an argument within it that contains a fallacy. Your task, to identify the fallacy, will be easier if you take the following steps, in this order:

1. Identify the conclusion that you are being asked to accept.
2. Identify the reasons (premises) that are offered for accepting the conclusion.
3. Determine the appropriateness of the premises, that is, the extent to which the premises lead to the conclusion.
4. Determine the adequacy of the premises, that is, the extent to which the premises provide sufficient reason to accept the conclusion.
5. If the premises are inappropriate or inadequate, select the fallacy from the preceding subsections that most adequately explains the error in the argument.

EXERCISE   *Identifying Fallacies*

The following is an excerpt from a letter to the editor of a newspaper addressing reparations to Japanese Americans interned in camps in California during World War II:

> There is no question that these people of Japanese ancestry were wronged, and for this I am truly sorry. But the idea that this specific historical act should be selected for me to help pay for, when I had absolutely nothing to do with it nor even know of anyone who did is outrageous. . . . As for American historical wrongs that should be righted, coming from ancestors of the old cotton South, I personally would rather give the money to American blacks. . . . But finally, I don't believe that the sins of the father should be exacted from his children. One man's sin is another man's virtue.

7

Organizing the Research Process

7.1 Gaining Control
of the Research Process

The research paper is where all your skills as an interpreter of details, an organizer of facts and theories, and a writer of clear prose come together. Building logical arguments on the twin bases of fact and hypothesis is the way things are done in political science, and the most successful political scientists are those who master the art of research.

Students new to the writing of research papers sometimes find themselves intimidated by the job ahead of them. After all, the research paper adds what seems to be an extra set of complexities to the writing process. As any other expository or persuasive paper does, a research paper must present an original thesis using a carefully organized and logical argument. But a research paper also investigates a topic that is outside the writer's own experience. As a result, writers must locate and evaluate information that is new, in effect educating themselves as they explore their topics. A beginning researcher sometimes feels overwhelmed by the basic requirements of the assignment or by the authority of the source material being investigated.

As you begin a research project, it may be difficult to establish a sense of control over the different tasks you are undertaking. You may have little notion of where to search for a thesis or even for the most helpful information. If you do not carefully monitor your own work habits, you may find yourself, unwittingly, abdicating responsibility for the research paper's argument by borrowing it wholesale from one or more of your sources.

Who is in control of your paper? The answer must be *you*—not the instructor who assigned you the paper, and certainly not the published writers and interviewees whose opinions you solicit. If all your paper does is paste together the opinions of others, it has little use. It is up to you to synthesize an original idea from a judicious evaluation of your source material. At the beginning of your research project, you will of course be unsure about many elements of your paper—for example, you will probably not yet have a definitive thesis sentence or even much understanding of the shape of your argument. But you *can* establish a measure of control over the process you will go through to complete the paper. And, if you work regularly and systematically, keeping yourself open to new ideas as they present themselves, your sense of control will grow. Here are some suggestions to help you establish and maintain control of your paper:

1. *Understand your assignment.* It is possible for a research assignment to go badly simply because the writer did not read the assignment carefully. Considering how much time and effort you are about to put into your project, it is a very good idea to make sure you have a clear understanding of what your instructor wants you to do. *Be sure to ask your instructor about any aspect of the assignment that is unclear to you—but only after you have read it carefully.* Recopying the assignment in your own handwriting is a good way to start, even though your instructor may have already given it to you in writing. Make sure, before you dive into the project, that you have considered the questions listed in the following paragraphs.

2. *What is your topic?* The assignment may give you a great deal of specific information about your topic, or you may be allowed considerable freedom in establishing one for yourself. In a government class in which you are studying issues affecting American foreign policy, your professor might give you a very specific assignment—a paper, for example, examining the difficulties of establishing a viable foreign policy in the wake of the collapse of international communism—or she may allow you to choose for yourself the issue that your paper will address. You need to understand the terms, set up in the assignment, by which you will design your project.

3. *What is your purpose?* Whatever the degree of latitude you are given in the matter of your topic, pay close attention to the way your instructor has phrased the assignment. Is your primary job to *describe* a current political situation or to *take a stand* on it? Are you to *compare* political systems, and if so, to what end? Are you to *classify, persuade, survey, analyze?* To determine the purpose of the project, look for such descriptive terms in the assignment.

4. *Who is your audience?* Your own orientation to the paper is profoundly affected by your conception of the audience for which you are writing. Granted, your main reader is your instructor, but who else would be interested in your paper? Are you writing for the voters of a community? a governor? a city council? A paper that describes the proposed renovation of city buildings may justifiably contain much more technical jargon for an audience of contractors than for a council of local business and civic leaders.

5. *What kind of research are you doing?* You will be doing one if not both of the following kinds of research:

- *Primary research,* which requires you to discover information firsthand, often by conducting interviews, surveys, or polls. In primary research, you are collecting and sifting through raw data—data that have not already been interpreted by researchers—which you will then study, select, arrange, and speculate on. These raw data may be the opinions of experts or of people on the street, historical documents, the published letters of a famous politician, or material collected from other researchers. It is important to set up carefully the methods by which you collect your data. Your aim is to gather the most accurate information possible, from which sound observations may be made later, either by you or by other writers using the material you have uncovered.

- *Secondary research,* which uses published accounts of primary materials. While the primary researcher might poll a community for its opinion on the outcome of a recent bond election, the secondary researcher will use the material from the poll to support a particular thesis. Secondary research, in other words, focuses on interpretations of raw data. Most of your college papers will be based on your use of secondary sources.

PRIMARY SOURCE	SECONDARY SOURCE
A published collection of Thurgood Marshall's letters	A journal article arguing that the volume of letters illustrates Marshall's attitude toward the media
An interview with the mayor	A character study of the mayor based on the interview
Material from a questionnaire	A paper basing its thesis on the results of the questionnaire

6. *Keep your perspective.* Whichever type of research you perform, you must keep your results in perspective. There is no way that you, as a primary researcher, can be completely objective in your findings. It is not possible to design a questionnaire that will net you absolute truth, nor can you be sure that the opinions you gather in interviews reflect the accurate and unchanging opinions of the people you question. Likewise, if you are conducting secondary research, you must remember that the articles and journals you are reading are shaped by the aims of their writers, who are interpreting primary materials for their own ends. The farther you are removed from a primary source, the greater the possibility for distortion. Your job as a researcher is to be as accurate as possible, which means keeping in view the limitations of your methods and their ends.

7.2 Effective Research Methods

In any research project there will be moments of confusion, but you can prevent this confusion from overwhelming you by establishing an effective research procedure. You need to design a schedule that is as systematic as possible, yet flexible enough so that you do not feel trapped by it. By always showing you what to do next, a schedule will help keep you from running into dead ends. At the same time, the schedule helps you retain the focus necessary to spot new ideas and new strategies as you work.

Give Yourself Plenty of Time

You may feel like delaying your research for many reasons: unfamiliarity with the library, the press of other tasks, a deadline that seems comfortably far away. But do not allow such factors to deter you. Research takes time. Working in a library seems to speed up the clock, so that the hour you expected it would take you to find a certain source becomes two. You must allow yourself the time needed not only to find material but also to read it, assimilate it, and set it in the context of your own thoughts. If you delay starting, you may well find yourself distracted by the deadline, having to keep an eye on the clock while trying to make sense of a writer's complicated argument.

The following schedule lists the steps of a research project in the order in which they are generally accomplished. Remember that each step is dependent on the others and that it is quite possible to revise earlier decisions in the light of later discoveries. After some background reading, for example, your notion of the paper's purpose may change, a fact that may in turn alter other steps. One of the strengths of a good schedule is its flexibility. Note that this schedule lists tasks for both primary and secondary research; you should use only those steps that are relevant to your project.

Research Schedule

```
TASK    DATE OF COMPLETION

Determine topic, purpose, and audience             _____

Do background reading in reference books           _____

Narrow your topic; establish a tentative hypothesis  _____

Develop a working bibliography                     _____

Write for needed information                       _____

Read and evaluate written sources, taking notes    _____

Determine whether to conduct interviews or surveys  _____

Draft a thesis and outline                         _____

Write a first draft                                _____

Obtain feedback (show draft to instructor,
if possible)                                       _____

Do more research, if necessary                     _____

Revise draft                                       _____

Correct bibliographical format of paper            _____

Prpeare final draft                                _____

Proofread                                          _____

Proofread again, looking for characteristic errors  _____

Deadline for final draft                           _____
```

Do Background Reading

Whether you are doing primary or secondary research, you need to know what kinds of work have already been done in your field. A good way to start is by consulting general reference works, though you do not want to overdo it (see warning). Chapter 8 lists specialized reference works on topics of interest to political scientists. You might find help in such volumes even for specific local problems, such as how to restructure a city council or finance an antidrug campaign in area schools.

WARNING. Be very careful not to rely too exclusively on material in general encyclopedias, such as the *Encyclopaedia Britannica* or *Collier's Encyclopedia.* You may wish to consult one for an overview of a topic with which you are unfamiliar, but students new to research are often tempted to import large sections, if not entire articles, from such volumes, and this practice is not good scholarship. One major reason your instructor has assigned a research paper is to let you experience the kinds of books and journals in which the discourse of political science is conducted. Encyclopedias are good places for instant introductions to subjects; some even include bibliographies of reference works at the ends of their articles. But to write a useful paper you will need much more detailed information about your subject. Once you have learned what you can from a general encyclopedia, move on to other sources.

A primary rule of source hunting is to *use your imagination.* Determine what topics relevant to your study might be covered in general reference works. If, for example, you are looking for introductory readings to help you with a research paper on antidrug campaign financing, you might look into such specialized reference tools as the *Encyclopedia of Social Work.* Remember to check articles in such works for lists of references to specialized books and essays.

Narrow Your Topic and Establish a Working Thesis

Before exploring outside sources, you should find out what you already know or think about your topic, a job that can be accomplished well only in writing. You might wish to investigate your own attitude toward your topic by using one or more of the prewriting strategies described in Chapter 1. You might also be surprised by what you know—or don't know—about the subject. This kind of self-questioning can help you discover a profitable direction for your research.

For a research paper in a course in American government, Charlotte Goble was given the topic category of grassroots attempts to legislate morality in American society. She chose the specific topic of textbook censorship. Here is the path she took as she looked for ways to limit the topic effectively and find a thesis:

GENERAL TOPIC   Textbook censorship
POTENTIAL TOPICS   How a local censorship campaign gets started
                     Funding censorship campaigns

	Reasons behind textbook censorship
	Results of censorship campaigns
WORKING THESIS	It is disconcertingly easy in our part of the state to launch a textbook censorship campaign.

Specific methods for discovering a thesis are discussed in Chapter 1. It is unlikely that you will come up with a satisfactory thesis at the beginning of your project. You need a way to guide yourself through the early stages of research as you work toward discovering a main idea that is both useful and manageable. Having in mind a *working thesis*—a preliminary statement of your purpose—can help you select the material that is of greatest interest to you as you examine potential sources. The working thesis will probably evolve as your research progresses, and you should be ready to accept such change. You must not fix on a thesis too early in the process, or you may miss opportunities to refine it.

Develop a Working Bibliography

As you begin your research, you will look for published sources—essays, books, interviews with experts—that may help you. This list of potentially useful sources is your *working bibliography*. There are many ways to develop this bibliography. The cataloging system in your library will give you sources, as will published bibliographies in your field. (Some of these bibliographies are listed in Chapter 8.) The general references in which you did your background reading may also list such works, and each specialized book or essay you find will itself have a bibliography that its writer used, which may be helpful to you.

It is from your working bibliography that you will select the items for the bibliography that will appear in the final draft of your paper. Early in your research you will not know which of the sources will help you and which will not, but it is important to keep an accurate description of each entry in your working bibliography so that you will be able to tell clearly which items you have investigated and which you will need to consult again. Establishing the working bibliography also allows you to practice using the bibliographical format you are required to follow in your final draft. As you make your list of potential sources, be sure to include all the information about each one, in the proper format, using the proper punctuation. (Chapter 4 describes in detail the bibliographical formats most often required for political science papers.)

Write for Needed Information

In the course of your research you may need to consult a source that is not immediately available to you. Working on the antidrug campaign paper, for example, you might find that a packet of potentially useful information may be obtained from a government agency or public interest group in Washington. Or you may discover that a needed book is not owned by your university library or by any other local library, or that a successful antidrug program has been implemented in the school system of a city of comparable size in another state. In such situations, it may be tempting to disregard potential sources because of the difficulty of consulting them. If you ignore this material, however, you are not doing your job.

It is vital that you take steps to acquire the needed data. In the first case in the preceding paragraph, you can simply write to the Washington agency or interest group; in the second, you may use your library's interlibrary loan procedure to obtain the book; in the third, you can track down the council that manages the antidrug campaign, by mail, phone, or Internet, and ask for information. Remember that many businesses and government agencies want to share their information with interested citizens; some have employees or entire departments whose job is to facilitate communication with the public. Be as specific as possible when asking for information by mail. It is a good idea to outline your own project briefly—in no more than a few sentences—to help the respondent determine the types of information that will be useful to you.

Never let the immediate unavailability of a source stop you from trying to consult it. And be sure to begin the job of locating and acquiring such long-distance material as soon as possible, to allow for the various delays that often occur.

Evaluate Written Sources

Fewer research experiences are more frustrating than trying to recall information found in a source that you can no longer identify. You must establish an efficient method of examining and evaluating the sources in your working bibliography. Suggestions for compiling an accurate record of your written sources are described in the following paragraphs.

Determine Quickly the Potential Usefulness of a Source

For books, you can read the front material (the introduction, foreword, and preface) looking for the author's thesis; you can also examine chapter headings, dust jackets, and indexes. A journal article should announce its intention in its introduction, which in most cases will be a page or less in length. This sort of preliminary examination should tell you whether a more intensive examination is worthwhile. *Whatever you decide about the source, photocopy its title page,* making sure that all important publication information (including title, date, author, volume number, and page numbers) is included. Write on the photocopied page any necessary information that is not printed there. Without such a record, later in your research you might forget that you have consulted a text, in which case you might find yourself repeating your work.

When you have determined that a potential source is worth closer inspection, explore it carefully. If it is a book, determine whether you should invest the time needed to read it in its entirety. Whatever the source, make sure you understand not only its overall thesis, but also each part of the argument that the writer sets up to illustrate or prove the thesis. You need to get a feel for the writer's argument—how the subtopics form (or do *not* form) a logical defense of the main point. What do you think of the writer's logic and the examples used? More than one reading may be needed to arrive at an accurate appraisal.

As you read, try to get a feel for the larger argument in which the source takes its place. Its references to the works of other writers will show you where to look for additional material and indicate the general shape of scholarly opinion concerning your subject. If you can see the source you are reading as only one element of an ongoing dialogue, instead of the last word on the subject, then you can place its argument in perspective.

Use Photocopies

Periodicals and most reference works cannot be checked out of the library. Before the widespread availability of photocopy machines, students could use these materials only in the library, jotting down information on note cards. Although there are advantages to using the note card method (see the next subsection), photocopying saves you time in the library and allows you to take the original information home, where you can decide how to use it at your convenience.

If you do decide to copy source material, you should do the following:

- Be sure to follow all copyright laws.
- Have the exact change for the photocopy machines. Do not trust the change machines at the library. They are usually battle-scarred and cantankerous.
- Record all necessary bibliographical information on the photocopy. If you forget to do so, you might find yourself making an extra trip to the library just to get a date of publication or page numbers.

Remember that photocopying a source is not the same as examining it. You will still have to spend time going over the material, assimilating it to use it accurately. It is not enough merely to have the information close at hand or even to have read it once or twice. You must understand it thoroughly. Be sure to give yourself time for this kind of evaluation.

The Note Card—A Thing of the Past?   In many ways, note cards are an old-fashioned method of recording source material, and for unpracticed researchers, they may seem unwieldy and unnecessary, because the information jotted on them—one fact per card—will eventually have to be transmitted again, in the research paper. However, before you decide to abolish the note card system once and for all, consider its advantages:

1. Using note cards is a way of forcing yourself to think productively as you read. In translating the language of the source into the language of your notes, you are assimilating the material more completely than you would by merely reading it.
2. Note cards give you a handy way to arrange and rearrange your facts, looking for the best possible organization for your paper. Not even a computer gives you the flexibility of a pack of cards as you try to order your paper.

Determine Whether Interviews or Surveys Are Needed

If your project calls for primary research, you may need to use a questionnaire to interview experts on your topic or to conduct a survey of opinions among a select group. Be sure to prepare yourself as thoroughly as possible for any primary research. Here are some tips:

Conducting an Interview

Establish a purpose for each interview, bearing in mind the requirements of your working thesis. In what ways might your interview benefit your paper? Write down your description of the interview's purpose. Estimate its length, and inform your subject. Arrive for your interview on time and dressed appropriately. Be courteous.

Learn as much as possible about your topic by researching published sources. Use this research to design your questions. If possible, learn something about the backgrounds of the people you interview. This knowledge may help you establish rapport with your subjects and will also help you tailor your questions. Take with you to the interview a list of prepared questions. However, be ready during the interview to depart from your list in order to follow any potentially useful direction that the questioning may take.

Take notes. Make sure you have extra pens. Do not use a tape recorder, because it will inhibit most interviewees. If you must use tape, *ask for permission from your subject* before beginning the interview. Follow up your interview with a thank-you letter and, if feasible, a copy of the paper in which the interview is used.

Designing and Conducting a Survey

If your research requires a survey, see Chapter 17 for instructions on designing and conducting surveys, polls, and questionnaires.

Draft a Thesis and Outline

No matter how thoroughly you may hunt for data or how fast you read, you will not be able to find and assimilate every source pertaining to your subject, especially if it is popular or controversial, and you should not unduly prolong your research. You must bring this phase of the project to an end—with the option of resuming it if the need arises—and begin to shape both the material you have gathered and your thoughts about it into a paper. During the research phase of your project, you have been thinking about your working thesis, testing it against the material you have discovered, and considering ways to improve it. Eventually, you must formulate a thesis that sets out an interesting and useful task, one that can be satisfactorily managed within the limits of your assignment and that effectively employs much, if not all, of the material you have gathered.

Once you have formulated your thesis, it is a good idea to make an outline of the paper. In helping you to determine a structure for your writing, the outline is also testing the thesis, prompting you to discover the kinds of work your paper will have to do to complete the task set out by the main idea. Chapter 1 discusses the structural requirements of the formal and the informal outline. (If you have used note cards, you may want to start outlining by organizing your cards according to the headings you have given them and looking for logical connections among the different groups of cards. Experimenting with structure in this way may lead you to discoveries that will further improve your thesis.)

No thesis or outline is written in stone. There is still time to improve the structure or purpose of your paper even after you have begun to write your first draft or, for that matter, your final draft. Some writers actually prefer to write a first draft before outlining, and then study the draft's structure to determine what revisions need to be made. *Stay flexible,* always looking for a better connection, a sharper wording of your thesis. All the time you are writing, the testing of your ideas continues.

Write a First Draft

Despite all the preliminary work you have done on your paper, you may feel a resistance to beginning your first draft. Integrating all your material and your ideas into a smoothly flowing argument is indeed a complicated task. It may help to think of your first attempt as only a *rough draft,* which can be changed as necessary. Another strategy for reducing reluctance to start is to begin with the part of the draft about which you feel most confident, instead of with the introduction. You may write sections of the draft in any order, piecing the parts together later. But, however you decide to start writing—**START.**

Obtain Feedback

It is not enough that you understand your argument; others have to understand it, too. If your instructor is willing to look at your rough draft, you should take advantage of the opportunity and pay careful attention to any suggestions for improvement. Other readers may also be of help, although having a friend or a relative read your draft may not be as helpful as having it read by someone who is knowledgeable in your field. In any event, be sure to evaluate any suggestions carefully. Remember, the final responsibility for the paper rests with you.

7.3 Ethical Use of Source Material

You want to use your source material as effectively as possible. This will sometimes mean that you should quote from a source directly, whereas at other times you will want to express such information in your own words. At all times, you should work to integrate the source material skillfully into the flow of your written argument.

When to Quote

You should quote directly from a source when the original language is distinctive enough to enhance your argument, or when rewording the passage would lessen its impact. In the interest of fairness, you should also quote a passage to which you will take exception. Rarely, however, should you quote a source at great length (longer than two or three paragraphs). Nor should your paper, or any substantial section of it, be merely a string of quoted passages. The more language you take from the writings of others, the more the quotations will disrupt the rhetorical flow of your own words. Too much quoting creates a choppy patchwork of varying styles and borrowed purposes in which your sense of your own control over your material is lost.

Quotations in Relation to Your Writing

When you do use a quotation, make sure that you insert it skillfully. According to the *Style Manual for Political Science*, published by the American Political Science Association, quotations of four lines or fewer should be integrated into your text and set off with quotation marks:

"In the last analysis," Alice Thornton argued in 1997, "we cannot afford not to embark on a radical program of fiscal reform" (12).

Quotations longer than four lines should begin on a new line and be indented five spaces from the left margin:

Blake's outlook for the solution to the city's problem of abandoned buildings is anything but optimistic:

If the trend in demolitions due to abandonments continues, the cost of doing nothing may be too high. The three-year period from 1994 to 1997 shows an annual increase in demolitions of roughly twenty percent. Such an upward trend for a sustained period of time would eventually place a disastrous hardship on the city's resources. And yet the city council seems bent on following the tactic of inaction. (1998, 8)

Acknowledge Quotations Carefully

Failing to signal the presence of a quotation skillfully can lead to confusion or choppiness:

The U.S. Secretary of Labor believes that worker retraining programs have failed because of a lack of trust within the American business culture. "The American business community does not visualize the need to invest in its workers" (Winn 1997, 11).

The first sentence in the preceding passage seems to suggest that the quote that follows comes from the Secretary of Labor. Note how this revision clarifies the attribution:

According to reporter Fred Winn, the U.S. Secretary of Labor believes that worker retraining programs have failed because of a lack of trust within the American business culture. Summarizing the secretary's view, Winn writes, "The American business community does not visualize the need to invest in its workers" (1997, 11).

The origin of each quote must be indicated within your text at the point where the quote occurs as well as in the list of works cited, which follows the text. Chapter 4 describes the appropriate documentation formats.

Quote Accurately

If your transcription of a quotation introduces careless variants of any kind, you are misrepresenting your source. Proofread your quotations very carefully, paying close attention to such surface features as spelling, capitalization, italics, and the use of numerals.

Occasionally, in order either to make a quotation fit smoothly into a passage, to clarify a reference, or to delete unnecessary material, you may need to change the original wording slightly. You must, however, signal any such change to your reader. Some alterations may be noted by brackets:

"Several times in the course of his speech, the attorney general said that his stand [on gun control] remains unchanged" (McAffrey 1998, 2).

Ellipses indicate that words have been left out of a quote:

"The last time voters refused to endorse one of the senator's policies . . . was back in 1982" (Laws 1996, 143).

When you integrate quoted material with your own prose, it is unnecessary to begin the quote with ellipses:

Benton raised eyebrows with his claim that "nobody in the mayor's office knows how to tie a shoe, let alone balance a budget" (Williams 1999, 12).

Paraphrasing

Your writing has its own rhetorical attributes, its own rhythms and structural coherence. Inserting several quotations into one section of your paper can disrupt the patterns of your prose and diminish its effectiveness. Paraphrasing, or recasting source material in your own words, is one way to avoid the choppiness that can result from a series of quotations.

Remember that a paraphrase is to be written in your language; it is not a near-copy of the source writer's language. Merely changing a few words of the original does justice to no one's prose and frequently produces stilted passages. This sort of borrowing is actually a form of plagiarism. To integrate another's material into your own writing fully, *use your own language.*

Paraphrasing may actually increase your comprehension of source material, because in recasting a passage you will have to think very carefully about its meaning—more carefully, perhaps, than if you had merely copied it word for word.

Avoiding Plagiarism

Paraphrases require the same sort of documentation as direct quotes. The words of a paraphrase may be yours, but the idea belongs to someone else. Failure to give that person credit, in the form of references within the text and in the bibliography, may make you vulnerable to a charge of plagiarism.

Plagiarism is the use of someone else's words or ideas without proper credit. Although some plagiarism is deliberate, produced by writers who understand that they are guilty of a kind of academic thievery, much of it is unconscious, committed by writers who are not aware of the varieties of plagiarism or who are careless in recording their borrowings from sources. Plagiarism includes the following:

- Quoting directly without acknowledging the source
- Paraphrasing without acknowledging the source
- Constructing a paraphrase that closely resembles the original in language and syntax

One way to guard against plagiarism is to keep careful notes of when you have directly quoted source material and when you have paraphrased—making sure that the wording of the paraphrases is yours. Make sure that all direct quotes in your final draft are properly set off from your own prose, either with quotation marks or in indented blocks.

What kind of paraphrased material must be acknowledged? Basic material that you find in several sources need not be documented by a reference. For example, it is unnecessary to cite a source for the information that Franklin Delano Roosevelt was elected to a fourth term as president of the United States shortly before his death, because this is a commonly known fact. However, Professor Smith's opinion, published in a recent article, that Roosevelt's winning of a fourth term hastened his death is not a fact, but a theory based on Smith's research and defended by her. If you wish to use Smith's opinion in a paraphrase, you need to credit her, as you should all judgments and claims from another source. Any information that is not widely known, whether factual or open to dispute, should be documented. This includes statistics, graphs, tables, and charts taken from sources other than your own primary research.

8

Information Resources:
Library and Internet

8.1 Information in Your
College Library

You will find a vast amount of information about writing, politics, and government in your college library. There is in fact so much information that discovering where to start looking can be a substantial task in itself. This section lists some important guides to information about politics and government that may help you launch your research project.

Reference Books: American Government and Politics

Barone, Michael, and Grant Ujifusa. *The Almanac of American Politics*. Washington, D.C.: National Journal. Annual. This compendium of information on national and state governments and officeholders includes essays, organized alphabetically by state, on U.S. governors, senators, and representatives. Charts summarize yearly voting records of each official. An index is included.

Budget of the United States Government. Washington, D.C.: Government Printing Office. Annual. The yearly government printing of the budget organizes its discussion of federal spending by specific current issues, then details the budgets of the specific government agencies. There is an index.

Congressional Quarterly Almanac. Washington, D.C.: Congressional Quarterly. Annual. This overview of legislation for the year's session of Congress is organized by subject headings, for example "Economics & Finance" and "Government/Commerce." There are three indexes: a bill number index, a roll call vote index, and a general index.

Gimlin, Hoyt, ed. *Historic Documents*. Washington, D.C.: Congressional Quarterly. Annual. This series of yearly volumes publishes a selection of the current year's government documents. Chosen to reflect the editor's assessment of important events, the documents are organized chronologically, and the volumes are indexed every five years.

Graham, Judith, ed. *Current Biography Yearbook*. New York: H. W. Wilson. Annual. The essays in this series, some of them more than a page in length, sketch biographies of distinguished individuals from a variety of fields. Each entry includes a list of references. Contents are indexed by profession.

Inventory of Information Sources and Services Available to the U.S. House of Representatives. 1977. Westport, CT: Greenwood. This volume lists the tremendous number of information sources, both public and private, used by representatives. There is a general index.

Kay, Ernest. *Dictionary of International Biography.* Cambridge, MA: Melrose Press. Annual. This volume publishes brief biographical citations of individuals of interest in several fields. There is no index.

Mooney, Louis, ed. *The Annual Obituary.* Detroit: St. James Press. Annual. This series prints brief essays on notable individuals who died during the year. Each entry includes references. The volumes are indexed by profession.

Morris, Dan, and Inez Morris. 1974. *Who Was Who in American Politics.* New York: Hawthorn Books. A one-volume reference identifying approximately 4,200 national political figures currently either inactive in politics or deceased. Brief biographical descriptions list offices held. There is no index.

The National Cyclopedia of American Biography. New York: James T. White. Annual to 1978. This series of volumes, the first of which was published in 1888, offers biographical essays on living Americans of note, surveying a variety of fields. An index of names is included.

Plano, Jack C., and Milton Greenburg. 1996. *The American Political Dictionary.* 10th ed. Fort Worth: Harcourt Brace Jovanovich. This dictionary offers concise definitions of over 4,000 terms of interest in politics and political science. Important terms are given more in-depth treatment. There is an index.

Public Papers of the Presidents. Washington, D.C.: Government Printing Office. This government series publishes the papers and speeches of every U.S. president since Herbert Hoover, except for Franklin D. Roosevelt, whose papers were published privately. There is a separate set of volumes for each president.

Schwarzkopf, LeRoy, comp. *Government Reference Books: A Biennial Guide to U.S. Government Publications.* Englewood, CO: Libraries Unlimited. Biennial. This listing of government reference books is the latest in a series that began in 1968/1969. Entry for each government publication includes address, publication information, and a brief description of the contents. The entries are arranged by topic.

United States Code. Washington, D.C.: Government Printing Office. This massive, multivolume publication, updated every six to eight years, prints all of the country's laws that are currently in force. Separate volumes index the contents.

Who Was Who in America, with World Notables. 1993. 10 vols. New Providence, NJ: Marquis Who's Who. This series publishes brief biographies of national international figures who are no longer living. The first volume surveys the years 1897 to 1942; the twelfth, 1996–1998. A separate volume contains a name index.

Who's Who in America. New Providence, NJ: Marquis Who's Who. Annual. This series contains brief biographies of noteworthy living Americans in a variety of fields, listing achievements and home and office addresses.

Who's Who in American Politics. 2 vols. New Providence, NJ: Bowker. Biennial. This series offers brief biographical summaries of the lives of Americans currently active in national, state, and local government. There are sections representing U.S. holdings: Guam, Puerto Rico, and the Virgin Islands. Information included for each individual includes party affiliation, offices held, publications, memberships in various organizations, and religion. There is a name index.

Who's Who of American Women. New Providence, NJ: Marquis Who's Who. Biennial. This biographical dictionary surveys notable American women. There is no index.

Reference Books: International Politics and the World

Amnesty International. *Report on Human Rights around the World*. Alameda, CA: Hunter House. Annual. This volume offers reports on the status of human rights in various countries. The entries, organized alphabetically by name of country, include essays, maps, and illustrations dealing with such topics as the use of the death penalty, voting rights and restrictions, and the treatment of minorities. There is no index.

Banks, Arthur S., ed. *Political Handbook of the World*. Binghamton, NY: CSA Publications. The essays in this volume, which is revised every one or two years, summarize the political history and current political situation of a variety of countries, arranged alphabetically. The essays profile political parties, list current government officials by name, and discuss issues such as local media. Also included is a chronology of important political events for the year and UN conferences. There is a general index.

Bowen, Thomas F., and Kelly S. Bowen, *Countries of the World and Their Leaders Yearbook*. 2 vols. Detroit: Gale Research. Annual. This twenty-year-old series prints a variety of information, taken from U.S. State Department reports, relating to selected countries. Each entry includes tables and an essay profiling the country's history, ethnic makeup, and current political condition.

Brune, Lester H. 1981. *Chronological History of United States Foreign Relations: 1776 to January 20, 1981*. 2 vols. New York: Garland. This set of volumes is an extensive timeline of events, each briefly summarized, in the history of American foreign policy. Also discussed are international political events that affected U.S. policy. For example, an entry for September 14, 1812, notes the French occupation of Moscow. Volume 2 includes a bibliography of references and a general index.

Central Intelligence Agency. *The World Factbook*. Washington, D.C.: Central Intelligence Agency. Annual. Published primarily for the use of government officials, this CIA compendium gives various kinds of information about different countries. Broad categories, represented by charts and maps as well as by written summaries, include agricultural development, import information, inflation profiles, and population growth. Entries are arranged alphabetically by name of country.

Clements, John. *Clements' Encyclopedia of World Governments*. Dallas: Political Research. The essays in this series offer analyses of historical events, current government programs, and economic and foreign affairs, among other topics. Each volume includes a chronological listing of important political events occurring during the years surveyed by the volume. There are appendixes and a geographical index.

Demographic Yearbook. New York: United Nations. Annual. This series publishes international demographic statistics from the United Nations. A dual-language text, the volume is printed in French and English. There is a subject index.

The Europa World Year Book. 2 vols. London: Europa. Annual. This publication examines the current status of political, economic, and commercial institutions of various countries. Contents are alphabetized by country, and entries include charts and tables listing vital statistics for each country surveyed.

Flanders, Stephen A., and Carl N. Flanders. 1993. *Dictionary of American Foreign Affairs*. New York: Macmillan. The entries in this volume cover terms, events, documents, and individuals involved with U.S. foreign policy now or at any time from 1776 to the present. Appendix A is a useful timeline of American foreign affairs. There is a bibliography of references, but no index.

Hunter, Brian, ed. *The Statesman's Yearbook*. New York: St. Martin's. Annual. There are two main divisions, one discussing international organizations, the other profiling countries around the world, summarizing their history and present economic, technical, educational, and cultural status. Each entry includes a bibliography of references. There are three indexes: place and international organizations; product index; and names of individuals.

The International Who's Who. London: Europa. Annual. This series offers paragraph-long biographies of notable individuals from different nations. The volumes are not indexed.

Kurian, George Thomas. 1992. *Encyclopedia of the Third World*. 4th ed. 3 vols. New York: Facts on File. For each country surveyed, Kurian's book compiles data on various factors, including energy, labor, education, law enforcement, history, government, human rights, and foreign policy. Volume 3 includes appendixes, a bibliography of references, and a general index.

Lawson, Edward. 1991. *Encyclopedia of Human Rights*. New York: Taylor & Francis. Various topics concerning international human rights activities from 1945 to 1990 are discussed, and significant government documents are reprinted, such as the text of the Convention Relating to the Status of Refugees (1951). The appendixes include a chronological list of international human rights documents and a list of worldwide human rights institutions. There is a subject index.

Mackie, Thomas T., and Richard Rose. *The International Almanac of Electoral History*. 2nd ed. New York: Facts on File. Annual. This volume publishes information, represented in both statistical charts and written analyses, of election results in Western nations from the late nineteenth century to the present. The information is arranged alphabetically by country. There is no index.

Staar, Richard F., ed. *Yearbook on International Communist Affairs*. Stanford, CA: Hoover Institution. Annual. Communism as it develops in both communist and noncommunist countries is surveyed in this publication. Countries are divided into broad geographical regions and then dealt with alphabetically. There is a name index and a subject index.

The World Almanac and Book of Facts. Mahwah, NJ: World Almanac/Funk & Wagnalls. Annual. This almanac publishes a wide variety of information on U.S. and world affairs. Many tables and charts are included. There is an index.

World Debt Tables: External Debt of Developing Countries. Washington, D.C.: World Bank. Annual. The tables in this volume, summarizing data for the World Bank, break down and analyze debts owed by the developing nations. There is no index.

Other Reference Books

Wesserman, Paul, ed. *Consumer Sourcebook*. 2 vols. Detroit: Gale Research. Biennial. This guide to information sources for consumers is arranged according to the types of organizations profiled. Subheadings include "Government Organizations," "Information Centers," "Associations," and "Media Services." Contents are indexed by name of organization, subject, and publications put out by the various organizations.

Wiener, Philip P., ed. 1973. *Dictionary of the History of Ideas*. 5 vols. New York: Scribner's. The essays in these volumes discuss ideas that have helped to shape and continue to shape human culture. The essays are arranged alphabetically by topic, within a series of broad subheadings. One subheading covers politics and includes sixty essays on such topics as "Authority," "Democracy," "Legal Concept of Freedom," "Liberalism," and "Social Attitudes towards Women." Volume 5 consists of a subject and name index.

Woy, James, ed. 1998. *Encyclopedia of Business Information Sources*. 12th ed. Detroit: Gale Research. This guide to information on over 1,100 business topics is arranged by subject and surveys both print and electronic sources, such as online databases. Headings include "Customs House," "Government Publications," "Laws," and "United States Congress." There is no index.

Other Directories

The Index and Abstract Directory: An International Guide to Services and Serials Coverage. 1990. 2nd ed. Birmingham, AL: Ebsco. *The Index and Abstract Directory* gives information on the over 35,000 serial publications represented in Ebsco's publishing database. Entries are arranged alphabetically by subject. Included are twenty pages of listings for national and international political science periodicals. There are two indexes: one for titles and one for subjects.

Montney, Charles, ed. *Directories in Print.* Detroit: Gale Research. Annual. According to the Introduction to the two-volume 1994 edition, Volume 1 "describes 15,900 directories, rosters, guides, and other print and nonprint address lists published in the United States and worldwide" (vii). Each entry includes address, fax number, price of the directory, and a description of its contents. Arrangement is by subject. Chapter 19 covers "Law, Military, and Government" directories. Volume 2 contains subject and title/keyword indexes.

Olson, Stan. *The Foundation Directory.* New York: The Foundation Center. Annual. This publication lists and describes more than 6,300 foundations with at least $2 million in assets or $200,000 in annual giving. Listed alphabetically, by state, each entry includes financial information, names of donors, and brief descriptions of the purpose and activities of the foundation, as well as a list of officers. Indexed.

Government and Politics Periodicals

Clements' International Report. Dallas: Political Research. This monthly newsletter comprises essays on current international political and historical concerns. There is a biannual subject index.

Congressional Digest

Congressional Quarterly Weekly Report

Congressional Record

Federal Register. Washington, D.C.: Government Printing Office. Daily issues of the *Federal Register* print the regulations and legal notices issued by federal agencies.

GPO Monthly Catalog of United States Government Publications. This publication of the Government Printing Office includes citations from the annual *Periodicals Supplement* and the *United States Congressional Serial Set Supplement.* Topics covered include finance, business, and demographics.

Library of Congress. *Monthly Checklist of State Publications.* Washington, D.C.: Government Printing Office. This checklist, organized alphabetically by state, lists state documents received by the Library of Congress over the preceding month. There is a subject index.

Office of the Federal Register/National Archives and Records. *Code of Federal Regulations.* Washington, D.C.: Government Printing Office. Annual. As explained in the brief introduction to each issue, this mammoth set of volumes, updated yearly, constitutes "a codification of the general and permanent rules published in the Federal Register by the Executive departments and agency of the Federal Government." The code is divided into fifty "titles," which are, in turn, further subdivided.

PACs & Lobbies. This semimonthly newsletter reports on federal developments affecting campaign finance and lobbying activities.

The United States Law Week: A National Survey of Current Law. Washington, D.C.: Bureau of National Affairs. This weekly newsletter summarizes important court decisions and prints articles on current legal topics.

U.S. Code Congressional & Administrative News. St. Paul, MN: West. Annual. This series of volumes reprints selected laws made during the current session of Congress. A subject index is included.

World of Politics: Taylor's Encyclopedia of Government Officials, Federal and State. Dallas: Political Research. This monthly newsletter publishes articles discussing responses from the various branches of government to current issues. The periodical is indexed three times a year.

Political Science Periodicals

Administration
Administration and Society
Administrative Science Quarterly
African Affairs
Africa Quarterly
American Behavioral Scientist
American Journal of International Law
American Journal of Political Science
American Political Science Review
American Politics Quarterly
Annals of the American Academy of Political and Social Science
Armed Forces and Society
Asian Affairs
Asian Quarterly
Asian Survey
Atlantic Community Quarterly
Australian Journal of Politics and History
Australian Journal of Public Administration
Behavioral Science
Behavior Science Research
Black Politician
British Journal of International Studies
British Journal of Law and Society
British Journal of Political Science
Bureaucrat
Campaign and Elections
Canadian Journal of Behavioral Science
Canadian Journal of Political Science
Canadian Public Administration
Canadian Public Policy
China Quarterly
Communist Affairs
Comparative Political Studies
Comparative Politics
Comparative Strategy
Comparative Studies in Society and History
Conflict

Conflict Bulletin
Conflict Management and Peace Science
Conflict Studies
Congress and the Presidency
Contemporary China
Cooperation and Conflict
Daedalus
Democracy
Development and Change
Diplomatic History
Dissent
East European Quarterly
Electoral Studies
Environmental Policy and Law
European Journal of Political Research
European Journal of Political Science
European Studies Review
Experimental Study of Politics
Foreign Affairs
Foreign Policy
General Systems
German Foreign Policy
German Political Studies
Global Political Assessment
Governance: An International Journal of Policy and Administration
Government & Opposition
Government Finance
Growth and Change
Harvard Journal on Legislation
History and Theory
History of Political Thought
Human Organization
Human Relations
Human Rights Review
Indian Journal of Political Science
Indian Journal of Public Administration
Indian Political Science Review
International Affairs
International Development Review
International Interactions
International Journal of Political Education
International Journal of Public Administration
International Organization
International Political Science Review (Revue Internationale de Science Politique)
International Relations
International Review of Social History
International Security
International Studies
International Studies Quarterly
Interpretation: Journal of Political Philosophy

Jerusalem Journal of International Relations
Journal of African Studies
Journal of Applied Behavioral Science
Journal of Asian Studies
Journal of Common Market Studies
Journal of Commonwealth and Comparative Politics
Journal of Conflict Resolution
Journal of Constitutional and Parliamentary Studies
Journal of Contemporary History
Journal of Developing Areas
Journal of Development Studies
Journal of European Integration
Journal of Health Politics, Policy and Law
Journal of International Affairs
Journal of Japanese Studies
Journal of Law & Politics
Journal of Libertarian Studies
Journal of Modern African Studies
Journal of Modern History
Journal of Peace Research
Journal of Peace Science
Journal of Policy Analysis and Management
Journal of Policy Modeling
Journal of Political and Military Sociology
Journal of Political Economy
Journal of Political Science
Journal of Politics
Journal of Public Policy
Journal of Social History
Journal of Social Issues
Journal of Social, Political, and Economic Studies
Journal of Strategic Studies
Journal of the History of Ideas
Journal of Theoretical Politics
Journal of Urban Analysis
Law and Contemporary Problems
Law and Policy Quarterly
Law & Society Review
Legislative Studies Quarterly
Mathematical Social Sciences
Micropolitics
Middle Eastern Studies
Middle East Journal
Millennium
Modern China
Multivariate Behavioral Research
New Political Science
Orbis: A Journal of World Affairs
Pacific Affairs
Parliamentarian

Parliamentary Affairs
Parliaments, Estates, and Representation
Peace and Change
Peace Research
Perspectives on Political Science
Philosophy & Public Affairs
Philosophy of the Social Sciences
Planning and Administration
Policy Analysis
Policy and Politics
Policy Review
Policy Sciences
Policy Studies Journal
Policy Studies Review
Political Anthropology
Political Behavior
Political Communication and Persuasion
Political Geography Quarterly
Political Psychology
Political Quarterly
Political Science
Political Science Quarterly
Political Science Review
Political Science Reviewer
Political Studies
Political Theory
Politics
Politics & Society
Polity
Presidential Studies Quarterly
Public Administration
Public Administration (Australia)
Public Administration Review
Public Choice
Public Finance
Public Finance Quarterly
Public Interest
Public Law
Public Opinion Quarterly
Public Policy
Publius: The Journal of Federalism
Quarterly Journal of Administration
Res Publica
Review of International Studies; formerly *British Journal of International Studies*
Review of Law and Social Change
Review of Politics
Revolutionary World
Round Table
Russian Review
Scandinavian Political Studies

Science and Public Affairs
Science and Public Policy
Science and Society
Simulation and Games
Slavic Review
Slavonic and East European Review
Social Forces
Social Indicators Research
Socialism and Democracy
Social Policy
Social Praxis
Social Research
Social Science Journal
Social Science Quarterly
Social Science Research
Social Theory and Practice
Sociological Analysis and Theory
Sociological Methods and Research
Sociology and Social Research
Soviet Review
Soviet Studies
Soviet Union
Strategic Review
Studies in Comparative Communism
Studies in Comparative International Development
Survey
Talking Politics
Technological Forecasting and Social Change
Terrorism
Theory and Decision
Theory and Society
Third World
Urban Affairs Quarterly
Urban Studies
War & Society
Washington Quarterly: A Review of Strategic and International Studies
Western Political Quarterly
West European Politics
Wilson Quarterly
Women & Politics: A Quarterly Journal of Research and Policy Studies
World Development
World Policy Journal
World Politics
Youth and Society

Newspaper Indexes

The following major newspapers have indexes available either in print or on microfilm:

The Chicago Tribune
The Houston Post
The Los Angeles Times
The National Observer
The New Orleans Times-Picayune
The New York Times
The Times of London
The Wall Street Journal
The Washington Post

Periodical Indexes

America: History and Life (article abstracts and citations of reviews and dissertations on life in the United States and Canada)
The American Humanities Index
Bibliographic Index
Biography Index
Book Review Index
Book Reviews in Historical Periodicals
Combined Retrospective (the combined retrospective index to journals in political science, 1886–1974. 6 vols.)
Historical Abstracts
Humanities Index
An Index to Book Reviews in the Humanities
Index to U.S. Government Periodicals
International Political Science Abstracts
The New York Times Biographical Service (a monthly compilation of obituaries photocopied from the *New York Times,* arranged chronologically, with an index on the front cover of each issue)
PAIS International in Print (subject index to international periodical articles in the social and political sciences)
Public Affairs Information Service PAIS
Reader's Guide to Periodical Literature
Social Sciences Index
Sociological Abstracts
Ulrich's International Periodicals Directory 1999. 5 vols.
United States Political Science Documents
Urban Affairs Abstracts
Weekly Compilation of Presidential Documents (weekly publication including "remarks, news conferences, messages, statements"—all public presidential utterances for that week)

Statistics

Government Finance Statistics Yearbook. Washington, D.C.: International Monetary Fund. Annual. This reference volume publishes tables that document revenues and spending by governments around the world. There is no index.

Stanley, Harold W., and Richard G. Niemi. 1992. *Vital Statistics on American Politics.* 3rd ed. Washington, D.C.: Congressional Quarterly. The charts and tables in this reference guide for political statistics cover a wide range of topics related to American politics, including the media (newspaper endorsements of presidential candidates, from 1932 to 1988, are graphed), interest groups, and the geographical and ethnic makeup of political bodies. There is an index.

Statistical Reference Index Annual: Abstracts. Bethesda, MD: Congressional Information Service. Annual. This volume is a guide to American statistical publications from private organizations and state government sources. Contents are organized by the type of organization publishing the reports. Each publication listed is briefly described in an abstract. An accompanying volume includes four separate indexes: subject and name, category, issuing sources, and title index.

Statistical Yearbook. New York: United Nations. Annual. Published in French and English, this yearly volume summarizes data from several United Nations reports in order to provide an analysis of the world's socioeconomic development over a twelve-month period. Contents are arranged by topic. The book is not indexed.

Statistical Yearbook. Paris: UNESCO. Annual. The statistical charts in this yearly publication cover education, science, and aspects of cultural life for 200 member nations of UNESCO. Material is generated from UNESCO questionnaires answered by a wide variety of respondents. The text is printed in three languages. There is no index.

U.S. Bureau of the Census. *Statistical Abstract of the United States.* Washington, D.C.: Department of Commerce. Annual. This volume, part of a series published since 1878, summarizes statistics on the country's social, political, and economic organization. There is an index.

Vital Statistics of the United States. 2 vols. Hyattsville, MD: U.S. Department of Health and Human Services. Annual. Each of the two volumes of this yearly series publishes statistics under a different heading. Volume 1 covers natality: tables of the year's birth statistics at the national and local levels and for U.S. holdings. Volume 2 covers mortality: death statistics.

Yearbook of Labour Statistics. Geneva: International Labour Office. Annual. This publication offers statistical tables on the economic development of countries around the world. There is an index of countries.

Statistical and political abstracts are also published by public and private organizations for each state.

Government Agencies

For most papers you will write in other subjects, such as biology, history, or a foreign language, the library is the place where you will find most if not all of the information you will need. As a student of political science you will most certainly find much valuable information on the library shelves. However, topics in political science afford an unusual opportunity to get information from other sources, because many political science topics require recent information about state and local governments, the U.S. government, and governments of other nations. When topics like these are assigned or selected, government agencies, research centers, and public interest groups often have more recent and more detailed information than is available in most college and university libraries. In fact, in most cases, for whatever topic you select, someone in a public agency or private organization has probably already conducted significant research. If you can find the right person, you may be able to secure much more information in much less time than you can by looking in your local library.

Did you know, for example, that the members of the U.S. Senate and House of Representatives constantly use the services of the Congressional Research Service (CRS) and that, upon request to your representative or senator, CRS materials on the topic of your choice may be sent to you? Further, every local, state, and national government agency has employees who are hired primarily to gather information to help their managers make decisions. Much of the research done by these employees is available upon request.

National Government Agencies

Congressional Yellow Book: Who's Who in Congress, Including Committees and Key Staff. Washington, D.C.: Monitor Leadership Directories. This quarterly publication, which is bound yearly, identifies senators and representatives by state and district, respectively. It lists committee assignments for each member of Congress and gives addresses and phone numbers of congressional committees and staff. State maps identify members of Congress by district. There is an index of staff.

The Government Directory of Addresses and Telephone Numbers. 1994. 2nd ed. Detroit: Omnigraphics. Entries give names, addresses, and phone numbers for national, state, county, and municipal government officials.

Lauber, Daniel. 1994. *Government Job Finder 1994–1995.* River Forest, IL: Planning/Communications. Lauber's manual offers tips on how to find a job in national, state, or local government. A list of directories of various agencies is included. There is an index.

Office of the Federal Register/National Archives and Records Administration. *The United States Government Manual.* Washington, D.C: Government Printing Office. Annual. A special edition of the *Federal Register,* the volume gives brief descriptions of the agencies of all three branches of the government and peripheral agencies and organizations. The annotations summarize each agency's history and describe its function and activities.

Office of Management and Budget. *Catalog of Federal Domestic Assistance.* Washington, D.C.: Government Printing Office. Annual. Government programs offering social and economic assistance to citizens are listed and described briefly in this guide. There is an index.

Orvedahl, Jerry A., ed. *Washington Information Directory.* Washington, D.C.: Congressional Quarterly. This directory, published every two years, lists and describes various kinds of organizations located in Washington, D.C. Contents of the book are divided into eighteen chapters, with such titles as "National Security," "Law & Justice," "Advocacy & Public Services," and "Education & Culture." There are separate subject and name indexes, and address lists for foreign embassies and U.S. ambassadors.

Robinson, Judith Shiek. 1993. *Tapping the Government Grapevine: The User-Friendly Guide to U.S. Government Information Sources.* 2nd ed. Phoenix: Oryx. Robinson's manual offers practical help on finding information published by the government, including discussions of electronic media, such as CD-ROMs, databases, and electronic bulletin boards. There are chapters on how to access information from each branch of the government. An index is included.

International Agencies

Yearbook of the United Nations. Dordrecht: Martinus Nijhoff. Annual. This publication contains essays describing the United Nations' participation in various world events.

Information about Private Political and Research Organizations

Daniels, Peggy Kneffel, and Carol A. Schwartz, eds. *Encyclopedia of Associations.* Detroit: Gale Research. Annual. This guide lists entries for approximately 23,000 national and international organizations. Contents are organized into chapters by subject. Typical chapter titles are "Environmental and Agricultural Organizations" and "Legal, Governmental, Public Administration, and Military Organizations." Each entry includes a brief description of the organization's function and the publications available. There are several indexes.

Dresser, Peter D., and Karen Hill, eds. *Research Centers Directory.* Detroit: Gale Research. Annual. Over 11,700 university-related and other nonprofit research organizations are listed and briefly profiled in the two-volume 14th edition of this yearly publication (1990). The entries are listed in sections by topics. Volume 2 includes four subsections under the general heading "Private and Public Policy and Affairs." There is a subject index and a master index, as well as a supplemental volume.

Maxfield, Doris Morris, ed. 1993. *Charitable Organizations of the U.S.: A Descriptive and Financial Information Guide.* 2nd ed. Detroit: Gale Research. Approximately 800 major public charities are profiled in this guide. Information given includes summaries of each organization's history and purpose, its activities and programs, and financial data. There are three indexes: subject, geographic, and personnel.

National Directory of Nonprofit Organizations. 1991. 2nd ed. 2 vols. Rockville, MD: The Taft Group. This guide gives brief listings of over 167,000 nonprofit organizations in the United States, citing addresses, phone numbers, and IRS filing status. Volume 1 lists organizations with annual revenues of $100,000 or over; Volume 2 lists organizations with revenues of $25,000 to $99,000. The contents of both volumes are organized alphabetically by title. Included are an activity index and a geographic index.

Wilson, Robert, ed. 1990. *American Lobbyists Directory.* Detroit: Gale Research. Over 65,000 registered federal and state lobbyists are listed in this guide, along with the businesses they represent. Included are indexes for lobbyists, their organizations, and general subjects and specialties.

Zuckerman, Edward. *Almanac of Federal PACs.* Washington, D.C.: Amward. Annual. This directory profiles campaign contributions of every political action committee that gave $50,000 or more to candidates for election to the U.S. Senate or House of Representatives. PACs are arranged alphabetically within chapters devoted to different target groups. Each entry includes a brief description of the goals and yearly activities of the PAC. There is a name index.

8.2 Internet Resources for Writing Well

The preceding chapters of this book have given you much information about research and writing, but the Internet offers even more. A particularly good place to start your Internet search is a web site called Researchpaper.com (http://www.researchpaper.com). Created by an Internet publishing company, Researchpaper.com provides free electronic access to a book entitled *10,000 Ideas for Term Papers, Projects, Reports & Speeches.*

When you visit Researchpaper.com, you will find

- *Information about Infonautics,* the Internet publishing company that developed Researchpaper.com.
- *Idea Directory,* a list of more than 4,000 research topics in over 100 categories. You can type in a key word, and the directory will find interesting ways of approaching the subject you have chosen.
- *Researchpaper.com Chat,* a chat room where you will find the thoughts and suggestions of other people and where you can reply to the ideas of others and contribute your own.
- *Research Central,* a page providing help searching for information and suggestions about good web sites.
- *Writing Center,* a series of guides to more effective writing, containing ideas for writing techniques and answers to commonly asked questions about grammar and style.
- *Membership Page,* a place to sign up for news, announcements, and other materials related to research and writing.

Researchpaper.com also helps you find many other resources for researching and writing term papers. One of the sites that Researchpaper.com will introduce you to is the Purdue University On-line Writing Lab (OWL) (http://owl.english.purdue.edu/). Several universities now offer their own OWLs, and you may want to check your own college's home page to see if it provides one. The Purdue University OWL home page features many links such as the following:

- "Our Resources for Writing" includes handouts on topics related to writing as well as links to other relevant sites.
- A collection of search tools and indexes to "Search the 'Net"
- If you want to know what makes OWL tick, read "About Our OWL."
- On-line Resources for Writers
- Writing Labs on the Internet
- Indexes for Writers
- On-line Reference Resources
- Guides to Style and Editing
- Business and Technical Writing
- Children and Writing
- Professional Organizations
- ESL-Related Sites
- Listserv Groups
- Indexes for Writers

OWL's guide to writing resources on the Web includes such sites as the following:

- Writer's Resources on the Web
- Carnegie-Mellon On-line Reference Works for the worldwide Internet community

- The International Federation of Library Associations' Citation Guide for Electronic Documents
- William Strunk's *Elements of Style,* courtesy of the Bartleby project
- Editorial Esoterica
- Grammar Hotline Directory
- Editorial Eye Internet
- Internet Resources for Technical Communicators
- "Punctuation" and "Capitalization," two chapters of *Grammar, Punctuation, and Capitalization—A Handbook for Technical Writers and Editors,* by Mary McCaskill
- Society for Technical Communication
- The Institute of Electric and Electrical Engineers Professional Communication Society
- The Children's Writing Resource Center
- Alliance for Computers & Writing (ACW)
- Assembly on Computers in English
- The National Writing Centers Association
- The National Writers' Union

OWL also lists electronic discussion groups, including the Alliance for Computers and Writing, and the MegaByte University (MBU) Writing Center.

8.3 Politics and Government Resources on the Internet

Even large catalogs cannot now hold all the potential Internet resources for politics, government, and political science. Fortunately, many Internet sites specialize in creating lists of links to excellent resources. Our purpose in this chapter is to help you locate a few good sites that will in turn lead you to thousands of sources of information for your government and politics research projects.

Internet sources of information about government and politics may be grouped into three major groups:

1. Government agencies
2. Universities, private interest groups and research organizations
3. News agencies

The very best place to start for information about American government agencies is *Thomas* (thomas.loc.gov/). Named for President Thomas Jefferson, Thomas is the home page for Congress. It provides dozens of direct links to representatives, senators, legislation, committees, and historical documents, as well as links to the executive and judicial branches and state and local government agencies.

When we choose the Thomas link labeled "Executive," we arrive at "A Library of Congress Internet Resource Page: Executive Branch." Here we may choose from the following links to agencies in the executive branch of the federal government. The list begins with the Executive Office of the President (EOP):

- White House
- Council of Economic Advisers
- Council on Environmental Quality
- National Performance Review
- National Security Council (NSC)
- Office of Management and Budget (OMB)
- Office of the First Lady
- Office of National Drug Control Policy
- Office of Science and Technology Policy
- President's Council on Sustainable Development
- United States Trade Representative (USTR)

The executive agencies are next, beginning with the Department of Agriculture (DOA), which has the following bureaus within it (each with its own link):

- Agricultural Research Service
- Animal and Plant Health Inspection Service
- Economic Research Service
- Farm Service Agency
- Forest Service
- National Agricultural Library
- National Resources Conservation Service
- Research, Economics, and Education
- Rural Development

After the Department of Agriculture, each of the other federal agencies is listed, and each of these has a list of bureaus attached to it. For the sake of brevity, we list here only the departments, not the bureaus that are listed with them in the actual Internet page:

- Department of Commerce (DOC)
- Department of Defense (DOD)
- Department of Education
- Department of Energy
- Department of Health and Human Services (HHS)
- Department of Housing and Urban Development (HUD)
- Department of the Interior (DOI)
- Department of Justice (DOJ)
- Department of Labor (DOL)

In the Spirit of
Thomas
Jefferson,
a service of
The Library of
Congress

Frequently Asked
Questions (FAQ's)

(example:
How to search THOMAS)

Congress in the
News

106th Congress:
House Directories
Senate Directories

**Congressional Internet
Services:**
House – Senate
Library of Congress
GPO – GAO – CBO
AOC – OTA – More

**Library of Congress
Web Links:**
Legislative
Executive
Judicial
State/Local

**The Legislative
Process:**
House
Senate

Historical
Documents

Congressional
Documents and
Debates
1774 – 1870

House Floor This Week   House Floor Now

Search CURRENT CONGRESS for Text of Bills:
By Bill Number [   ]   By Word/Phrase [   ]   [Search]   [Clear]

LEGISLATION

**Bill Summary &
Status:**
106th or Previous

Bill Text:
106th or Previous

Major Legislation:
Definition
106th or Previous

**Public Laws By
Law Number:**
106th or Previous

Roll Call Votes:
House   (Help)
Senate   (Help)

CONGRESSIONAL RECORD

**Congressional Record
Text:**
Most Recent Issue
106th or Previous

**Congressional Record
Index:**
106th or Previous

**Résumés of Congressional
Activity:**
Previous

NEW
**Days In Session
Calendars:**
Previous

COMMITTEE INFORMATION

Committee Reports:
106th, 105th,
104th

**Committee Home
Pages:**
House or Senate

House Committees:
Schedules and
Oversight Plans
Hearing Transcripts

Senate Committees:
Hearings Schedule

Impeachment Documents:
Independent Counsel's Report, H.Res. 581, House Rpt. 105-795,
H. RES. 611, House Report 105-830.

Historical Impeachment Documents:
Proceedings of the Senate Sitting for the Trial of Andrew Johnson

National Bipartisan Commission on the Future of Medicare.
H.R. 4328 The Omnibus Appropriations Bill for FY 1999.

FEEDBACK   About THOMAS

Library of Congress Links:
LIBRARY of CONGRESS HOME | AMERICAN MEMORY | LC BICENTENNIAL | COPYRIGHT OFFICE | GLOBAL LEGAL
INFORMATION NETWORK | EXHIBITIONS | The LIBRARY TODAY

Library of Congress
101 Independence Ave.S.E.
Washington, D.C. 20540

- Department of State (DOS)
- Department of Transportation (DOT)
- Department of the Treasury
- Department of Veterans Affairs

The list of links then continues to list the independent agencies of the federal government:

- Advisory Council on Historic Preservation (ACHP)
- Central Intelligence Agency (CIA)
- Commodity Futures Trading Commission (CFTC)
- Consumer Product Safety Commission (CPSC)
- Environmental Protection Agency (EPA)
- Equal Employment Opportunity Commission (EEOC)
- Export-Import Bank of the United States
- Farm Credit Administration (FCA)
- Federal Communications Commission (FCC)
- Federal Deposit Insurance Corporation (FDIC)
- Federal Election Commission (FEC)
- Federal Emergency Management Agency (FEMA)
- Federal Energy Regulatory Commission (FERC)
- Federal Labor Relations Authority
- Federal Maritime Commission
- Federal Reserve System (FRS)
  - Board of Governors of the Federal Reserve System
  - Federal Reserve Banks
- Federal Trade Commission (FTC)
- General Services Administration (GSA)
  - Consumer Information Center (Pueblo, CO)
- Merit Systems Protection Board (MSPB)
- National Aeronautics and Space Administration (NASA)
- National Archives and Records Administration (NARA)
- National Commission on Libraries and Information Science (NCLIS)
- National Credit Union Administration (NCUA)
- National Endowment for the Arts (NEA)
- National Endowment for the Humanities (NEH)
- National Mediation Board
- National Railroad Passenger Corporation (AMTRAK)
- National Science Foundation (NSF)
- National Transportation Safety Board (NTSB)
- Nuclear Regulatory Commission (NRC)
- Occupational Safety and Health Administration (OSHA)
- Office of Government Ethics (OGE)
- Office of Personnel Management (OPM)
- Office of Special Counsel (OSC)

- Overseas Private Investment Corporation (OPIC)
- Peace Corps
- Pension Benefit Guaranty Corporation
- Postal Rate Commission
- Railroad Retirement Board (RRB)
- Securities and Exchange Commission (SEC)
- Selective Service System (SSS)
- Small Business Administration (SBA)
- Social Security Administration (SSA)
- Tennessee Valley Authority (TVA)
- Thrift Savings Plan (TSP)
- United States Agency for International Development (USAID)
- United States Arms Control and Disarmament Agency (ACDA)
- United States Information Agency (USIA)
  - United States Information Agency Home Page (USIA)
  - United States Information Agency International Home Page (USIA)
- United States International Trade Commission (USITC)
- United States Postal Service (USPS)
- United States Trade and Development Agency

If we click on any of these links, such as the CIA, we will arrive at that agency's home page, which will then offer us dozens of links to offices within that agency. The CIA home page, for example, offers us the following options:

- About the CIA: All you ever wanted to know about the CIA
- CIA Publications: *World Fact Book, Factbook on Intelligence,* and others
- CIA Public Affairs: Press Releases and Statements, DCI Speeches and Testimony
- Other CIA and Intelligence Community Links: other web sites of interest

Of course, the above sites are only the top of the government web site iceberg. Before concluding this chapter, it will be helpful for you to become aware of some good Internet resources for information about political science. If we return to Thomas and select the link named "Judicial," we find ourselves confronting lists of links that provide a wide array of information about courts, laws, and the legal system. Some of the major topics that are thoroughly covered in this system of links are the following:

- The Constitution of the United States
- The U.S. code and public laws
- State statutes
- Government regulations
- Judicial opinions for federal and state courts

- Court rules
- Controller general decisions
- Executive branch legal materials
- Law journals
- Law-related Internet sites

The second major category of sources of information about politics and government includes universities, interest groups, and private research organizations. Many college political science departments provide Internet sites that feature links to thousands of politics and government sites. The John F. Kennedy School of Government at Harvard University is a good example. The Kennedy School Online Political Information Network (OPIN) (http://www. ksg.harvard.edu/ ~ksgpress/opin/index. html) features the following links, each of which provides a wide variety of further links:

- Elections
- Parties, Candidates
- Federal Government
- State/Local Government
- Think Tanks
- Advocacy
- International
- Academia
- More Politics
- Politics of the Net
- Reporters' Resources
- Good Directories

Public interest groups provide a great deal of information on political issues. As you search these sites you must be aware that these groups are in existence to promote a cause and may or may not provide a balanced view of any particular issue. You can find links to the following interest groups (a selected sample of hundreds of groups) by finding the interest group site at the University of Central Oklahoma (www.ucok.edu) or by typing their names in the search box of any major search engine such as Altavista or Yahoo.

- AFL-CIO
- Alliance for Justice
- American-Arab Anti-Discrimination Committee (ADC)
- American Association for Affirmative Action (AAAA)
- American Association for People with Disabilities (AAPD)
- American Association of Retired Persons (AARP)
- American Association of University Women (AAUW)
- American Bankers Association (ABA)

- American Bar Association (ABA)
- American Civil Liberties Union (ACLU)
- American Chemical Society
- American Conservative Union
- American Farm Bureau Federation
- American Federation of State, County, and Municipal Employees (AFSCME)
- American Federation of Teachers (AFT)
- American Hellenic Educational Progressive Association (AHEPA)
- American Israel Public Affairs Committee
- American Legion
- American Petroleum Institute
- American Postal Workers Union (APWU)
- American Public Welfare Association (APWA)
- Americans Against Political Corruption
- Americans for Democratic Action
- Amnesty International
- Animal Rights Coalition
- Catholics United for Life
- Center for Democracy and Technology
- Center for Public Integrity
- Center for Science in the Public Interest (CSPI)
- Children's Defense Fund
- Child Labor Coalition
- Child Welfare League of America
- Christian Coalition
- Citizens Against Government Waste
- Citizens for Budget Reform (CBR)
- Citizens for Tax Justice
- Communications Workers of America
- ConflictNet
- Concord Coalition
- Congressional Accountability Project
- Contract with America
- Council for Responsible Genetics
- Death Penalty Information Center
- EcoNet
- Electronic Frontier Foundation
- Empower America
- Environmental Defense Fund

- Family Farm Alliance
- Federation For American Immigration Reform (FAIR)
- Feminist Majority Foundation Online
- Friends of the Earth
- Fund for Constitutional Government
- Generation X Coalition
- Government Purchasing Project
- GreenNet (environmental)
- Greenpeace International
- Habitat for Humanity
- International Association of Machinists and Aerospace Workers
- International Brotherhood of Teamsters
- International Union of Bricklayers and Allied Craftworkers
- LaborNet
- League of Conservation Voters
- League of Women Voters' Voter Education Project
- Militia Watchdog
- National Abortion and Reproductive Rights Action League (NARAL)
- National Air Traffic Controllers Association
- National Association for the Advancement of Colored People (NAACP)
- National Association for Public Interest Law
- National Association of Arab Americans
- National Association of Baby Boomers
- National Association of Broadcasters
- National Association of Community Action Agencies
- National Association of Home Builders
- National Association of Manufacturers
- National Coalition for the Homeless
- National Education Association (NEA)
- National Endangered Species Act Reform Coalition
- National Gay and Lesbian Task Force
- National Organization for Women (NOW)
- National Recycling Coalition
- National Resources Defense Council
- National Right to Life
- National Rifle Association
- National Rural Electric Cooperative Association
- National Water Resources Association
- Nuclear Waste Citizens Coalition
- Office and Professional Employees International Union (OPEIU)

- PeaceNet
- People for the American Way
- People for the Ethical Treatment of Animals
- Physicians for a National Health Program
- Planned Parenthood
- Public Citizen
- Public Interest Research Groups
- Service Employees International Union
- Sheet Metal Workers International Association
- Sierra Club
- Society for Electronic Access (SEA)
- Society for Human Resource Management
- Taxpayers Against Fraud
- Teledemocracy Action News + Network
- United Autoworkers Workers (UAW)
- United Food and Commercial Workers (UFCW)
- United Mine Workers of America (UMW)
- United States Space Foundation
- Vietnam Veterans of America
- Women's Legal and Public Policy Information

In addition to the listed public interest groups, there are many "think tanks," or private research organizations, that provide high-quality political, economic, and social analyses. Links to some of these organizations may be found by selecting the "Think Tanks" link at the Kennedy School of Government Online Political Information Network site described previously.

The third major category of Internet resources for government and politics includes hundreds of news organizations around the world. CNN, *U.S. News and World Report,* and dozens of other major journalistic ventures provide enormous amounts of information. The *New York Times,* for example, in addition to all its regular news coverage, features a page entitled "Political Points, A Selective Guide to Political Sites on the Internet" by Rich Meislin (www. nytimes.com/library/politics/polpoints.html). This page contains dozens of links to good sources of information about national, international, state, and local political events, trends, and resources.

8.4 Political Science Resources on the Internet

The first site to visit for political science resources is the home page of the American Political Science Association (APSA), the largest organization of professional political scientists in the world. You will find it at http://www.apsanet.org/. On this page you will find the following helpful links:

- Departments of Political Science
- Journals
- Conferences
- Grants and Fellowships
- Related Organizations
- Civic Education

These links lead to dozens of departments, organizations, conferences, journals, and other information about the discipline of political science. If you proceed to the home page of the Department of Political Science at the University of California at Irvine, for example, you will find dozens of links to information helpful to political scientists. This page, entitled "UCI PS Resources" (http://www.lib.uci.edu/) lists many resources. The following are only a sample:

- Berkeley Digital Library Sunsite
- Economics Resources
- Government and Legal Databases Available through the MELVYL(r) System
- Infomine: Social Sciences and Humanities (UC systemwide project to link such resources)
- National Political Index, links to numerous politics sites in 32 categories
- New Horizons in Scholarly Communication
- New Politics, links to activist groups and parties
- NlightN, a massive Index to periodicals, directories, and web sites; displays brief citations, with complete citations available for a fee
- Political Science Resources on the Web, from University of Michigan Libraries
- Politics USA (*National Journal* and American Political Network site)
- Social Science Databases Available through the MELVYL(r) System
- World Wide Libertarian Pages
- Full-Text Journals and Magazines Available through the MELVYL(r) System
- Full-Text Periodicals on Dialog
- Full-Text *Political Science* and Other Journals
- Political Science Periodicals on the Web via University of Michigan Libraries
- *Western European Politics* (table of contents)
- Budget of the United States
- Catalog of Federal Domestic Assistance
- California's Congressional Delegation
- Federal Grants Home Page Foreign Broadcast Information Service
- Infomine: Government Information (UC systemwide project to link such resources)
- Gallup Organization (Gallup Polls)

- Interuniversity Consortium for Political and Social Research
- Public Opinion Data: A UCI Library Reference Guide
- Public Opinion Item Index, an index to questions in the Carolina Polls, General Social Survey 1972–1993, Latin American Public Opinion, Louis Harris Polls, National Network of State Polls, Southern Polls, *USA Today* Polls and Polls Public Opinion Laboratory (Indiana University's polling institute)
- ACLU
- Amnesty International
- Center for the Study of Democracy (UC-Irvine)
- Democratization Resources on the Web
- Research Paper Series in Empirical Democratic Theory
- Fourth World Documentation Project (indigenous peoples' information)
- Global Democracy Network (from Parliamentary Human Rights Foundation)
- Human Rights Watch
- Lawyers Committee for Human Rights
- Media Research Center
- Rand Corporation
- Stockholm International Peace Research Institute
- Twentieth Century Fund
- UCLA Asian American Studies Center

9

Book Reviews and Article Critiques

9.1 Book Reviews

Successful book reviews answer three questions:

- What did the writer of the book try to communicate?
- How clearly and convincingly did he or she get this message across to the reader?
- Was the message worth reading?

Capable book reviewers of several centuries have answered these three questions well. People who read a book review want to know if a particular book is worth reading, for their own particular purposes, before buying or reading it. These potential readers want to know the book's subject and its strengths and weaknesses, and they want to gain this information as easily and quickly as possible. Your goal in writing a book review, therefore, is to help people efficiently decide whether to buy or read a book. Your immediate objectives may be to please your instructor and get a good grade, but these objectives are most likely to be met if you focus on a book review's audience: people who want help in selecting books to read. In the process of writing a book review that reaches this primary goal, you will also

- Learn about the book you are reviewing.
- Learn about professional standards for book reviews in political science.
- Learn the essential steps of book reviewing that apply to any academic discipline.

This final objective, learning to review a book properly, has more applications than you may at first imagine. First, it helps you to focus quickly on the essential elements of a book, to draw from a book its informational value for yourself and others. Some of the most successful people in government, business, and the professions speed-read several books a week, more for the knowledge they contain than for enjoyment. These readers then apply this knowledge to substantial advantage in their professions. It is normally not wise to speed-read a book you are reviewing because you are unlikely to gain from such a fast reading enough information to evaluate it fairly. Writing book reviews, however, helps you to become proficient in quickly sorting out information that is valuable from material that is not. The ability to make such discriminations is a fundamental ingredient in management and professional success.

In addition, writing book reviews for publication allows you to participate in the discussions of the broader intellectual and professional community of which you are a part. People in law, medicine, teaching, engineering, administration, and other fields are frequently asked to write book reviews to help others assess newly released publications.

Before beginning your book review, read the following sample. It is Gregory M. Scott's review of *Political Islam: Revolution, Radicalism, or Reform?* edited by John L. Esposito (Boulder, CO: Lynne Rienner Publishers. 1997). The review appeared in the *Southeastern Political Review* (26:2, June 1998) and is reprinted here by permission.

> Behold an epitaph for the specter of monolithically autocratic Islam. In its survey of Islamic political movements from Pakistan to Algeria, *Political Islam: Revolution, Radicalism, or Reform?* effectively lays to rest the popular notion that political expressions of Islam are inherently violent and authoritarian. For this accomplishment alone John L. Esposito and company's scholarly anthology merits the attention of serious students of religion and politics, and justifies the book's own claim to making a "seminal contribution." Although it fails to identify how Islam as religious faith and cultural tradition lends Muslim politics a distinctively Islamic flavor, this volume clearly answers the question posed by its title: Yes, political Islam encompasses not only revolution and radicalism, but moderation and reform as well.
>
> Although two of the eleven contributors are historians, *Political Islam* exhibits both the strengths and weaknesses of contemporary political science with respect to religion. It identifies connections between economics and politics, and between culture and politics, much better than it deciphers the nuances of the relationships between politics and religious belief. After a general introduction, the first three articles explore political Islam as illegal opposition, first with a summary of major movements and then with studies of Algeria and the Gulf states. In her chapter entitled "Fulfilling Prophecies: State Policy and Islamist Radicalism," Lisa Anderson sets a methodological guideline for the entire volume when she writes:
>
>> Rather than look to the substance of Islam or the content of putatively Islamic political doctrines for a willingness to embrace violent means to desired ends, we might explore a different perspective and examine the political circumstances, or institutional environment, that breeds political radicalism, extremism, or violence independent of the content of the doctrine (18).
>
> Therefore, rather than assessing how Islam as religion affects Muslim politics, all the subsequent chapters proceed to examine politics, economics, and culture in a variety of Muslim nations. This means that the title of the book is slightly misleading: it discusses Muslim politics rather than political Islam. Esposito

provides the book's conclusion about the effects of Islamic belief on the political process when he maintains that "the appeal to religion is a two-edged sword. . . . it can provide or enhance self-legitimation, but it can also be used as a yardstick for judgment by opposition forces and delegitimation" (70).

The second part of the volume features analyses of the varieties of political processes in Iran, Sudan, Egypt, and Pakistan. These chapters clearly demonstrate not only that Islamic groups may be found in varied positions on normal economic and ideological spectrums, but that Islam is not necessarily opposed to moderate, pluralist politics. The third section of the anthology examines the international relations of Hamas, Afghani Islamists, and Islamic groups involved in the Middle East peace process. These chapters are especially important for American students because they present impressive documentation for the conclusions that the motives and demands of many Islamic groups are considerably more moderate and reasonable than much Western political commentary would suggest.

The volume is essentially well written. All the articles with the exception of chapter two avoid unnecessarily dense political science jargon. As a collection of methodologically sound and analytically astute treatments of Muslim politics, *Political Islam: Revolution, Radicalism, or Reform?* is certainly appropriate for adoption as a supplemental text for courses in religion and politics. By way of noting what it does not cover, readers may consider that although it is sufficient for its purposes as it stands, the volume could be a primary text in a course on Islamic politics if it included four additional chapters:

1. an historical overview of the origins and varieties of Islam as religion
2. a summary of the global Islamic political-ideological spectrum (from liberal to fundamentalist)
3. an overview of the varieties of global Islamic cultures
4. an attempt to describe in what manner, if any, Islam, in all its varieties, gives politics a different flavor from the politics of other major religions.

Elements of a Book Review

Book reviews in political science contain the same essential elements as all book reviews. Because political science is nonfiction, book reviews within the discipline focus less on a work's writing style and more on its content and method than do reviews of fiction. Your book review should generally contain four basic elements, although not always in this order:

1. Enticement
2. Examination
3. Elucidation
4. Evaluation

Enticement

Your first sentence should entice people to read your review. A crisp summary of what the book is about entices your reader because it lets her know that you can quickly and clearly come to the point. She knows that her time and efforts will not be wasted in an attempt to wade through your vague prose in hopes of finding out something about the book. Notice Scott's opening line: "Behold an epitaph for the specter of monolithically autocratic Islam." It is a bit overburdened with large words, but it is engaging, and it precisely sums up the essence of the review. Your opening statement can be engaging and "catchy," but be sure that it provides in one crisp statement an accurate portrayal of the book.

Examination

Your book review should allow the reader to join you in examining the book. Tell the reader what the book is about. One of the greatest strengths of Scott's review is that his first paragraph immediately tells you exactly what he thinks the book accomplishes.

When you review a book, write about what is actually in the book, not what you think is probably there or ought to be there. Do not tell how you would have written the book, but tell instead how the author wrote it. Describe the book in clear, objective terms. Tell enough about the content to identify the author's major points.

Elucidation

Elucidate, or clarify, the book's value and contribution to political science by defining (1) what the author is attempting to do and (2) how the author's work fits within current similar efforts in the discipline of political science or scholarly inquiry in general. Notice how Scott immediately describes what Esposito is trying to do: "This volume clearly answers the question posed by its title." Scott precedes this definition of the author's purpose by placing his work within the context of similar current writing in political science: "For this accomplishment alone John L. Esposito and company's scholarly anthology merits the attention of serious students of religion and politics, and justifies the book's own claim to making a 'seminal contribution.'"

The elucidation portion of book reviews often provides additional information about the author. Scott has not included such information about Esposito in his review, but it would be helpful to know, for example, if Esposito has written other books on the subject, has developed a reputation for exceptional expertise on a certain issue, or is known to have a particular ideological bias. How would your understanding of this book be changed, for example, if you knew that its author was a leader of Hamas or the PLO? Include in your book review information about the author that helps the reader understand how this book fits within the broader concerns of political science.

Evaluation

Once you have explained what the book is attempting to do, you should tell the reader the extent to which the book has succeeded. To evaluate a book effectively, you will need to establish evaluation criteria and then compare the book's content to those criteria. You do not need to define your criteria specifically in your review, but they should be evident to the reader. Your criteria will vary according to the book you are reviewing, and you may discuss them in any order that is helpful to the reader. Consider, however, including the following among the criteria that you establish for your book review:

- How important is the subject to the study of politics and government?
- How complete and thorough is the author's coverage of the subject?
- How carefully is the author's analysis conducted?
- What are the strengths and limitations of the author's methodology?
- What is the quality of the writing? Is it clear, precise, and interesting?
- How does this book compare with others on the subject?
- What contribution does this book make to political science?
- Who will enjoy or benefit from this book?

When giving your evaluations according to these criteria, be specific. If you write, "This is a good book; I liked it very much," you have told the reader nothing of interest or value. Notice, however, how Scott's review helps to clearly define the content and the limitations of the book by contrasting the book's contents to what Scott believes to be an ideal primary text for a course in Islamic politics: "By way of noting what it does not cover, readers may consider that although it is sufficient for its purposes as it stands, the volume could be a primary text in a course on Islamic politics if it included four additional chapters."

Qualities of Effective Political Science Book Reviews

Effective political science book reviews

- Serve the reader.
- Are fair.
- Are concise and specific, not vague and general.

Write your review with the potential reader, not yourself or the book's author, in mind. The person who may read the book is, in a manner of speaking, your client.

Your reader wants a fair review of the book. Do not be overly generous to a book of poor quality, but do not be too critical of an honest effort to tackle a very complex or difficult problem. If you have a bias that may affect your review, let your reader know about it, but do so briefly. Do not shift the focus from the book's ideas to your own. Do not attack a work because of the author's politics. Do not chide the author for not having written a book different from the one he or she has written.

The reader of your book review is not interested in your thoughts about politics or other subjects. Try to appreciate the author's efforts and goals, and sympathize with the author, but remain sufficiently detached to identify errors. Try to show the book's strengths and weaknesses as clearly as possible.

Write a review that is interesting, appealing, and even charming, but not at the expense of accuracy or of the book being reviewed. Be erudite but not prolix. (To be erudite is to display extensive knowledge. To be prolix is to be wordy and vague.) Your goal is to display substantial knowledge of the book's content, strengths, and weaknesses in as few words as possible.

Preliminaries: Before Writing a Book Review

Before sitting down to write your review, make sure you do the following:

- *Get further directions from your instructor.* Ask if there are specific directions beyond those in this manual for the number of pages or the content of the review.
- *Read the book.* Reviewers who skim or merely read a book's jacket do a great disservice to the author. Read the book thoroughly.
- *Respond to the book.* As you read, make notes on your responses to the book. Organize them into the categories of enticement, examination, elucidation, and evaluation.
- *Get to know the subject.* Use the library to find a summary of works on the issue. Such a summary may be found in a review in a journal or in a recent textbook on the subject.
- *Familiarize yourself with other books by the author.* If the author has written other works, learn enough about them to be able to describe them briefly to your readers.
- *Read reviews of other political science books.* Many political science journals have book review sections, usually at the end of the issue. Go to the library and browse through some of the reviews in several journals. Not only will you get to know what is expected from a political science book review, but you will also find many interesting ideas on how books are approached and evaluated.

Format and Content

The directions for writing papers provided in Chapters 1 through 4 apply to book reviews as well. Some further instructions specific to book reviews are needed, however. First, list on the title page, along with the standard information required for political science papers, data on the book being reviewed: title, author, place and name of publisher, date, and number of pages. On the sample that follows, note that the title of the book should be in italics or underlined, but not both:

```
                        A Review of

                      Ties of Common Blood:

A History of Maine's Northeast Boundary Dispute with Great Britain

                            by

                  Geraldine Tidd Scott

          Bowie, Maryland: Heritage Books, Inc.

                  1992. 445 pages.

                      reviewed by

                      Paula Smith

                        POL 213

                  Dr. Benedict Arnold

              Centralsouthwestern University

                  January 1, 2000
```

Reflective or Analytical Book Reviews

Two types of book reviews are normally assigned by instructors in the humanities and social sciences: the *reflective* and the *analytical*. *Ask your instructor which type of book review you are to write.* The purpose of a reflective book review is for the student reviewer to exercise creative analytical judgment without being influenced by the reviews of others. Reflective book reviews contain all the elements covered in this chapter—enticement, examination, elucidation, and evaluation—but they do *not* include the views of others who have also read the book.

Analytical book reviews contain all the information provided by reflective reviews but add an analysis of the comments of other reviewers. The purpose is thus to review not only the book itself but also its reception in the professional community.

To write an analytical book review, insert a review analysis section immediately after your summary of the book. To prepare this section, use the *Book Review Digest* and *Book Review Index* in the library to locate other reviews of the book that have been published in journals and other periodicals. As you read these reviews,

1. List the criticisms (strengths and weaknesses) of the book that are made in the reviews.
2. Develop a concise summary of these criticisms, indicate the overall positive or negative tone of the reviews, and mention some of the most common comments.
3. Evaluate the criticisms found in these reviews. Are they basically accurate in their assessment of the book?

4. Write a review analysis of two pages or less that states and evaluates steps 2 and 3, and place it in your book review immediately after your summary of the book.

Length of a Book Review

Unless your instructor gives you other directions, a reflective book review should be three to five typed pages in length, and an analytical book review should be five to seven pages long. In either case, a brief, specific, concise book review is almost always to be preferred over one of greater length.

9.2 Article Critiques

An *article critique* is a paper that evaluates an article published in an academic journal. A good critique tells the reader what point the article is trying to make and how convincingly it makes this point. Writing an article critique achieves three purposes. First, it provides you with an understanding of the information contained in a scholarly article and a familiarity with other information written on the same topic. Second, it provides an opportunity to apply and develop your critical thinking skills as you attempt to evaluate critically a political scientist's work. Third, it helps you to improve your own writing skills as you attempt to describe the selected article's strengths and weaknesses so that your readers can clearly understand them.

The first step in writing an article critique is to select an appropriate article. Unless your instructor specifies otherwise, select an article from a scholarly journal (such as *American Political Science Review, Journal of Politics,* or *Southeastern Political Science Review*) and not a popular or journalistic publication (such as *Time* or the *National Review*). Chapter 8 of this manual includes a substantial list of academic political science journals, but your instructor may also accept appropriate articles from academic journals in other disciplines, such as history, economics, or sociology.

Choosing an Article

Three other considerations should guide your choice of an article. First, browse article titles until you find a topic that interests you. Writing a critique will be much more satisfying if you have an interest in the topic. Hundreds of interesting journal articles are published every year. The following articles, for example, appeared in the June 1998 (26:2) issue of the *Southeastern Political Review*.

- "Activists, Contributors, and Volunteers: The Participation Puzzle" by Grant Neeley and Anthony J. Nownes
- "Religious Influences on Political Participation" by Adrian S. Clark
- "Determinants of Voter Turnout in Illinois School Referenda" by Corliss Lentz

- "Complexity, Patronage, and the Density of Interest Groups in the American States" by Barbara Morris
- "Rational Choice and Supreme Court Decision Making: A Review Essay" by Saul Brenner
- "Opportunistic Foreign Policy and the Political Management of the News Media Content: The Case of Grenada" by Douglas A. Van Belle
- "The Institutionalization of the Romanian Parliament: A Case Study of the State-Building Process in Eastern Europe" by Steven D. Roper and William Crowther
- "Maintaining Momentum: An Overview of South Africa's Progress toward Democratic Consolidation" by Robert J. Griffiths
- "'Republicanizing' Kant's Republic: Making Politics' Tribute to Morality Count" by Scott Roulier
- "The 'Culture Wars' in the South: Partisanship, Race, and Cultural Conservatism in the 1990 North Carolina U.S. Senate Election" by Kenneth A. Wink and Peter Laroche

The second consideration in selecting an article is your current level of knowledge. Many political science studies, for example, employ sophisticated statistical techniques. You may be better prepared to evaluate them if you have studied statistics.

The third consideration is to select a current article, one written within the twelve months before the time you select your article. Most material in political science is quickly superseded by new studies. Selecting a recent study will help ensure that you will be engaged in an up-to-date discussion of your topic.

Writing the Critique

Once you have selected and carefully read your article, you may begin to write your critique, which will cover five areas:

1. Thesis
2. Methods
3. Evidence of thesis support
4. Contribution to the literature
5. Recommendation

Thesis

Your first task is to find and clearly state the thesis of the article. The thesis is the main point the article is trying to make. In a 1997 article entitled "Unequal Participation: Democracy's Unresolved Dilemma" (*American Political Science Review* 91:1–14), APSA President Arend Lijphart, Research Professor of Political Science, University of California, San Diego, states his thesis very clearly:

> Low voter turnout is a serious democratic problem for five reasons: (1) It means unequal turnout that is systematically biased against less well-to-do

citizens. (2) Unequal turnout spells unequal political influence. (3) U.S. voter turnout is especially low, but, measured as percent of voting-age population, it is also relatively low in most other countries. (4) Turnout in midterm, regional, local, and supranational elections—less salient but by no means unimportant elections—tends to be especially poor. (5) Turnout appears to be declining everywhere.

Many authors, however, do not present their theses this clearly. Do you have to hunt for the thesis of the article? Comment about the clarity of the author's thesis presentation, and state the author's thesis in your own paper. Before proceeding with the remaining elements of your paper, consider the importance of the topic. Has the author of the article written something that is important for us as citizens or political scientists to read?

Methods

What methods did the author use to investigate the topic? In other words, how did the author go about supporting the thesis? In your critique, carefully answer the following two questions. First, were appropriate methods used? In other words, did the author's approach to supporting the thesis make sense? Second, did the author employ the selected methods correctly? Did you discover any errors in the way the author conducted his or her research?

Evidence of Thesis Support

In your critique, answer the following questions: What evidence did the author present in support of the thesis? What are the strengths of the evidence presented by the author? What are the weaknesses of the evidence presented? On balance, how well did the author support the thesis?

Contribution to the Literature

This step will probably require you to undertake some research. Using the research resources discussed in Chapter 8 of this manual, identify articles and books published within the last five years on the subject of your selected article. Browse the titles, and read perhaps half a dozen of the publications that appear to provide the best discussion of the topic. In your critique, list the most important other articles or books that have been published on your topic and then, in view of these publications, evaluate the contribution that your selected article makes to a better understanding of its topic.

Recommendation

In this section, summarize your evaluation of the article. Tell your readers several things. Who will benefit from reading this article? What will the benefit be? How important and extensive is that benefit? Clearly state your evaluation of the article, in the form of a thesis for your own critique. Your thesis might be something like the following:

Arend Lijphart's article entitled "Unequal Participation: Democracy's Unresolved Dilemma" is the most concise and comprehensive discussion of the problem of unequal participation published in recent years. Political scientists should conscientiously confront Lijphart's warning because he conclusively demonstrates that unequal participation presents an imminent threat to American democracy.

When writing this assignment, follow the directions for formats in Chapter 3 of this manual. Ask your instructor for directions concerning the length of the paper, but in the absence of further directions, your paper should not exceed five pages (typed, double-spaced).

10

Traditional Research Papers and Literature Reviews

10.1 Traditional Political Science Research Papers

When Amy Klobuchar began to write her senior essay at Yale College, she probably did not expect it would eventually be published as a book. She was interested in the ten years of political battles that had surrounded the building of the Minneapolis Hubert Humphrey Metrodome, the stadium home of baseball's Minnesota Twins and football's Minnesota Vikings. Klobuchar's essay, which was published in 1982 as *Uncovering the Dome*, describes the interest groups, politicians, government agencies, and state and local legislative processes involved in making the ultimate decision on whether to build the dome. Her purpose in writing her paper was to help her readers understand how local and state politics affected the decision to build the dome and to evaluate the extent to which the public interest was served in the political process that surrounded the decision.

Klobuchar's study is an example of the traditional approach in political science, which is used to write hundreds of books and articles every year. *Uncovering the Dome* is traditional in its approach because it describes

- The history of the previous stadium, including the business community's attempts to encourage business development and keep the two professional sports teams in Minneapolis.
- The structure and operations of Minnesota's local and state governments.
- The personalities and political characters of the elected and appointed officials involved in the Metrodome decision.
- The interests and activities of groups who became politically active in the process of making decisions about the dome.
- The role of the media in the controversy.
- The response and actions of the area's citizens.

After describing the political events and personalities surrounding the building of the dome, Klobuchar draws conclusions about the nature of the political process. She is particularly interested in the extent to which that process served the public interest. She observes that the answer to that question depends on the perspective people bring to the subject. Public opinion about the dome was not favorable, and some critics concluded that in the public's eyes the public interest had not been well served in the decision. If one believes, however, that serving the public interest depends less on the outcome than on having a fair and open decision-making process, then it may be concluded that the public interest was served. Looking back on the process, Klobuchar states the thesis of her book:

> Viewed as a reflection of public opinion, the Minneapolis Metrodome is an uncertain example of a government serving the public's interest. Seen as the result of a fair political process, the government's balancing of diverse wants stands as an arguably good example of how the political process serves the public interest. (Amy Klobuchar. 1982. *Uncovering the Dome*. Prospect Heights, IL: Waveland. 161.)

Traditional studies in political science usually deal with concepts such as the public interest and the values of freedom, equality, equity, justice, and order in society. The history of the development of the traditional approach in political science is summarized in the Introduction to this manual.

Definition: Traditional Studies in Political Science

The word *traditional* does not have a fixed or precise meaning in political science today. When we write traditional papers in political science, however, we normally utilize both

1. The traditional approach to the study of politics (as described in the Introduction to this manual and in this chapter).
2. The traditional format for papers (as described in Chapter 3).

Traditional papers in political science attempt to help readers understand political actors, events, trends, institutions, or movements. They explain the context, precedents, causes, conditions, and outcomes of political activity. They usually focus on one or more aspects of political life:

- History
- Biography, leadership, management, or personality
- Institutions
- Constitutions, laws, and legislation
- Issues
- Philosophies, theories, methods, and concepts like freedom, justice, and equality

It is important to note that what is normally considered "traditional" keeps changing. For example, in the early 1960s, Gabriel Almond's use of the term *political socialization* and David Easton's use of the term *political system* were considered to be departures from "traditional" political science concepts. Today, however, these concepts have been so widely adopted that they and similar terms are used in standard discourse within the traditional approach.

Political histories are among the oldest examples of the use of the traditional approach. They attempt to explain political events by describing the actions, motives, goals, culture, and ideologies of a particular group of people in a particular place at a particular time. One of the most famous political histories is Thucydides' *History of the Peloponnesian War.* Thucydides was a former Athenian general who wanted to describe the events in the long war between Athens and Sparta over control of Greece and the surrounding area. Like all good traditional papers, his *History* states a thesis: "What made war inevitable was the growth of Athenian power and the fear which this caused in Sparta" (Thucydides. 1986. *History of the Peloponnesian War.* Translated by Rex Warner. Harmondsworth: Penguin Books. 49). Thucydides then supports his thesis with evidence, which includes detailed accounts of negotiations and battles between the two city-states.

Many traditional studies in political science focus on the ways that a single individual affects and responds to the political environment. Such works most often take the form of biographies and studies of leadership, management styles, and personalities. Numerous biographies and autobiographies of American presidents are published before, during, and after their terms of office. These studies normally attempt to draw conclusions about the nature of politics, leadership, or power. Reflecting on his own years as president, Jimmy Carter has this to say:

> Although I was surrounded by people eager to help me, my most vivid impression of the Presidency remains the loneliness in which the most difficult decisions had to be made. As a matter of fact, very few easy ones came to my desk. If the answers to a question were obvious, they were provided in a city hall or a state capitol. If they involved national or international affairs and were not particularly controversial, decisions were made at some lower level in government. . . . And I prayed a lot—more than ever before in my life—asking God to give me a clear mind, sound judgment, and wisdom in dealing with affairs that could affect the lives of so many people in our country and around the world. (Jimmy Carter. 1982. *Keeping Faith: Memoirs of a President.* Toronto: Bantam Books. 1982. 61–62.)

Other traditional studies attempt to explain the roles of political institutions. Woodrow Wilson published *Constitutional Government in the United States* in 1908, four years before he became president. His book is an excellent example of a traditional political study in that it describes its subject in an attempt to prove a thesis. Supporting a thesis always requires at least a basic theoretical or analytical framework. A theoretical framework consists of a clearly defined subject and an organized, rational procedure for drawing conclusions about it. Beginning his first chapter, Wilson states:

> My object in the following lectures is to examine the government of the United States as a constitutional system as simply and directly as possible, with an eye to practice, not to theory. And yet at the very outset it is necessary to

pause upon a theory. The government of the United States cannot intelligently be discussed as a constitutional system until we clearly determine what we mean by a "constitutional" government; and the answer to that question is in effect a theory of politics. (Woodrow Wilson. 1961. *Constitutional Government in the United States.* New York: Columbia Univ. Press. 1.)

Regardless of whether traditional studies in political science focus primarily on individuals, institutions, laws, constitutions, or political concepts such as freedom, order, or justice, they almost always describe their subjects within their historical, legal, and political contexts and attempt to evaluate them with the help of values or standards such as "the public interest" or "constitutionality."

An Example of Traditional Political Science: *American Extremists*

Traditional political science can be fascinating reading. An excellent example is *American Extremists: Militias, Supremacists, Klansmen, Communists, and Others* (Amherst, NY: Prometheus Books, 1996) by two of America's foremost experts on extremist groups, John George and Laird Wilcox. George and Wilcox conducted their study not only by reviewing thousands of documents, but by interviewing hundreds of people as well:

> This book discusses American political extremism in some detail with the discussion filtered, naturally, through our experiences with hundreds of people who fall into the extremist "category," such as it is. We have talked with them in their homes and at public meetings, demonstrations, and debates; in restaurants over coffee; in the classroom; and sometimes while just walking along a busy thoroughfare. Some of our contacts have been deep and very personal and have extended over many years, while others were more on the order of single interview situations. Over the years we have encountered approximately six hundred individual extremists between us, and it is from this pool of experience that we draw our conclusions, which are necessarily tentative and subject to further evidence. (8)

According to George and Wilcox, extremism is rooted in insecurity and manifests itself in bias:

> In our study of extremism we have become very aware that all human beings have biases and tend to see events from certain perspectives. We recognize the "Rashomon" principle, whereby individuals tend to interpret, and even distort, events in order to preserve their own integrity and sense of self-esteem. . . . Political extremists tend to be very prone to both conscious and unconscious distortions of various kinds. Simply put, they prefer to believe what they prefer to be true. The extremist tends to be the ideologue in purest form, i.e., the a priori thinker who believes what he "must" believe, regardless of evidence to the contrary. Extremists usually attempt to deduce the facts of an issue from a set of principles, often in the form of a political ideology, rather than determine the facts of an issue and then induce the principles that necessarily derive from them. It is this primacy of belief over knowledge that accounts for the often bizarre and impractical systems they create. (8–9)

Following the methods of traditional political science, George and Wilcox characterize and classify various types of extremists. The bombing of the Murrah Federal Building in Oklahoma City on April 19, 1995, helped militias gain public attention. George and Wilcox provide the following observations about American militias:

> The ideological roots of the militias are somewhat obscured by the highly individualistic nature of their adherents. The movement consists primarily of white males between thirty and sixty, although a surprising number of women are active, too. Several blacks have been identified with militias, along with a few Asians, American Indians, and even some Jews. Most militia activists appear to have roots in their communities, with families, jobs, and children in school.
>
> As far as we can ascertain, most militia members are political neophytes. Those with a political past were active in the so-called patriot movement, which consists of a hodgepodge of small tax protest, parents rights, anti–gun control, constitutionalist, monetary reform, and radical libertarian groups. Some of the modern civilian militias have their roots in the survivalist movement that developed in the late 1970s. A few activists have been members of "hate groups" like the Ku Klux Klan, but these are generally weeded out soon after they're discovered.
>
> If one were to select at random a group of actual members of militias, five categories would probably be represented in the following order of frequency:
>
> 1. People generally conservative in outlook, although not very ideological, who are worried about what they see as a repressive government imposing all manner of strictures on them from unfair taxes to gun control.
> 2. Would-be adventurers—generally nonideological weekend-warrior types who like to wear camouflage and play soldier in the woods. They watch movies with western and military themes and like to hunt and fish.
> 3. Libertarian-conservatives who accept some government on the local or state level, but who oppose federal regulations of almost all kinds.
> 4. Anarcho-libertarians who consider virtually all government as repressive and overbearing. They refer to themselves as "freemen" or "sovereigns."
> 5. Hard-core extremists who harbor an obsessive conviction that the United States, indeed the world, is in the grip of an all-powerful conspiracy. (249)

Perhaps the greatest strength of traditional political analysis is the new perspective on people and politics that we gain from reading it. Good traditional analysis helps us to sort out fact from fallacy and acquire a more accurate understanding of social and political events, and the people who participate in them. Consider the following insight that George and Wilcox, after their far-reaching investigation, have to share:

> A common error in dealing with extremists is to assume that if two or more extremists are alike in some respects, they must be alike in all or at least most

respects. This fallacy of stereotyping is structurally similar to ethnic or religious prejudice, where an observation that "they're all alike" is a recognizable slur. We make the case that extremists only tend to have certain behavioral traits in common, and that these represent relative inclinations. By no means are they absolute criteria. Both of us have found surprising exceptions to virtually any generalization we might make. We have known extremists who were miserable, hateful individuals, who were virtually everything their enemies might say they were, and who would easily fulfill the stereotype of the hate-filled bigot or the wild-eyed revolutionary nihilist. But we have also known extremists who we felt were basically good people struggling with issues and problems, and who, once they were outside their conflict area, were decent and well-meaning. Generalizations may have a certain limited validity, but it must constantly be borne in mind that extremists are individual human beings. (10)

The Audience for the Traditional Paper

One of the fundamental considerations for a writer is the intended audience. In writing policy analysis papers, for example, the author's first consideration is the person or group that has commissioned the study. The question of audience, however, rarely comes up in discussions of the traditional political science paper, perhaps because the audience is assumed. It is unfortunate that this assumption is not often examined.

Who is the audience for most traditional papers? The answer is *students of political science*. This group usually comprises three types of "students": (1) the instructor who assigned the paper and who will read it primarily to evaluate the writer's understanding; (2) college or university students, who will hear the paper discussed in a seminar or may read it for their own research needs; and perhaps even (3) the general public, who will read it to enhance their understanding of a topic they find to be of interest.

The Four Components of Traditional Papers in Political Science

Before writing your traditional paper, be sure to read Chapters 1 and 2. Reading these chapters will save you much time. You will find there is not one set pattern or process for writing papers. Certain basic tasks need to be completed, but you must experiment to find out how you can best accomplish them. Remember that traditional papers are meant to explain some aspect of politics or government, which they do by (1) stating a thesis and (2) supporting that thesis with appropriate documentation. To perform these two tasks, traditional papers normally include four basic types of information:

- A specific *definition* of the topic or subject of the paper
- A description of the historical, legal, and institutional *context* of the subject
- A careful *description* of the subject
- A concluding *evaluation* of the subject

Definition

A precise *definition* of a paper's subject is often the most difficult part to write. Suppose that you are studying the development of presidential power during the twentieth century in order to understand how such power works. You must at some point define presidential power. Is it the expressly granted powers of the Constitution? Is it the power to persuade? Is it the growing bureaucracy over which the president has some control?

Context

The historical, legal, and institutional *context* of the subject of a paper is normally an important part of a traditional study in political science. To continue with our example, the development of presidential power during the twentieth century can be understood only if certain facts influencing its development are also known. What effect did the Great Depression, for example, have on President Roosevelt's ability to change government social welfare policies? What portions of the Constitution allow presidents to assume powers they had not exercised previously? What effect has public media technology had on presidents' ability to influence votes?

Description

The *description* of the subject is the largest component of many traditional studies. A paper on the development of presidential power during the twentieth century would spend considerable time describing the manner in which this power has been expanded, probably giving numerous examples from most if not all of the presidencies of the century.

Evaluation

The *evaluation* is a challenging element of traditional papers. Merely listing facts about presidents and their exercise of power, for example, would normally not be sufficient; you would instead need to show that you are capable of drawing conclusions from the materials you have studied. In what respects has presidential power increased? What factors contributed the most to this increase? In what ways is presidential power more limited now than in 1900?

Evaluation takes place in two steps. The first step is to establish evaluation criteria. Applied to our example, this means that you must identify the phenomena that would indicate the existence and degree of change in presidential power. You might examine the change in public opinion polls before and after presidential addresses, or count the number of presidentially sponsored bills passed by Congress.

The second step is to apply the evaluation criteria that you have selected and draw conclusions from the results. If, for example, you find a greater increase in presidential popularity after the addresses of President Reagan than after those of President Carter, what does this difference mean to your overall assessment of presidential power in this century? The conclusion to your traditional political science paper will normally be your interpretation of the results of your evaluation of your subject. Your conclusion therefore will clearly restate your thesis and the evidence that you have gathered for its support. It should also include any insights that you have gained in the process of writing your paper.

Steps in Writing a Traditional Paper

When writing your traditional political science paper, follow the suggestions in Chapters 1 through 8. Traditional papers may be written on many subjects and may emphasize different aspects of these subjects. *Be sure to ask your instructor to clarify the assignment.* You are most likely to write a good paper if you thoughtfully consider the appropriate role that each of the four basic elements of traditional papers will play: a specific *definition* of the topic; a *discussion* of the historical, legal, and institutional context of the subject; a careful *description* of the subject; and a concluding *evaluation* of the subject.

Finding a Topic for a Traditional Paper

Topics for traditional papers in political science may come from all areas of the discipline. Before beginning your search, read the guidelines for selecting a topic presented in Chapter 1. *Ask your instructor for specific advice on what is appropriate for the course.*

10.2 How to Conduct a Literature Review

Your goal in writing a research paper is to provide for your readers an opportunity to increase their understanding of the subject you are addressing. They will want the most current and precise information available. Whether you are writing a traditional library research paper, conducting an experiment, or preparing an analysis of a policy enforced by a government agency, you must know what has already been learned in order to give your readers comprehensive and up-to-date information or to add something new to what is already known about the subject. If your topic is welfare administration in Tennessee, for example, you will want to find out precisely what national, state, and local government policies currently affect welfare administration in Tennessee, and the important details of how and why these policies came to be adopted. When you seek this information, you will be conducting a *literature review,* which is a thoughtful collection and analysis of available information on the topic you have selected for study. It tells you, before you begin your experiments or analyses, what is already known about the subject.

Why do you need to conduct a literature review? It would be embarrassing to spend a lot of time and effort preparing a study, only to find that the information you are seeking has already been discovered by someone else. Also, a properly conducted literature review will tell you many things about a particular subject. It will tell you the extent of current knowledge, sources of data for your research, examples of what is *not* known about the subject (which generates ideas for formulating hypotheses), methods that have been used for research, and clear definitions of concepts relevant to your own research.

Let us consider an example. Suppose that you have decided to research the question "How are voter attitudes affected by negative advertising?" First, you will need to establish a clear definition of "negative advertising," then you will need to find a way to measure attitudes of voters, and finally you will need to use or develop a method of discerning how attitudes are affected by advertising. Using research techniques explained in this and other chapters of this manual, you will begin your research by looking for studies that address your research question or similar questions at the library, on the Internet, and through other resources. You will discover that many studies have been written on voters' attitudes and the effects of advertising. As you read these studies, certain patterns will appear. Some research methods will appear to have produced better results than others. Some studies will be quoted in others many times—some confirming and others refuting what previous studies have done. You will constantly be making choices as you examine these studies, reading very carefully ones that are highly relevant to your purposes, and skimming those of only marginal interest. As you read, constantly ask yourself the following questions:

- How much is known about this subject?
- What is the best available information, and why is it better than other information?
- What research methods have been used successfully in relevant studies?
- What are the possible sources of data for further investigation of this topic?
- What important information is still not known, in spite of all previous research?
- Of the methods that have been used for research, which are the most effective for making new discoveries? Are new methods needed?
- How can the concepts being researched be more precisely defined?

You will find that this process, like the research process as a whole, is recursive: Insights related to one of the preceding questions will spark new investigations into others, and these investigations will then bring up a new set of questions, and so on.

Your instructor may request that you include a literature review as a section of the paper that you are writing. Your written literature review may be from one to several pages in length, but it should always tell the reader

1. What specific previously compiled or published studies, articles, or other documents provide the best available information on the selected topic.
2. What these studies conclude about the topic.
3. What the apparent methodological strengths and weaknesses of these studies are.

4. What remains to be discovered about the topic.
5. What appear to be, according to these studies, the most effective methods for developing new information on the topic.

Your literature review should consist of a written narrative that answers not necessarily consecutively, the preceding questions. The success of your own research project depends in large part on the extent to which you have carefully and thoughtfully answered these questions.

11

Issue Reaction Papers

11.1 Elements of Issue Reaction Papers

This assignment originated with Professor Stephen Jenks of the University of Central Oklahoma. Its purpose is to develop and sharpen your critical thinking and writing skills. Your objective in writing this assignment is to define an issue clearly and to formulate and clarify your position on that issue by reacting to a controversial statement. Completing this assignment requires accomplishing the following six tasks:

1. Select a suitable reaction statement.
2. Explain your selection.
3. Clearly define the issue addressed in the statement.
4. Clearly state your position on the issue.
5. Defend your position.
6. Conclude concisely.

Select a Suitable Reaction Statement

Your first task is to find or write a statement to which to react. *Reaction statements* are provocative declarations. They are controversial assertions that beg for either a negative or a positive response. Your instructor may assign a reaction statement, you may find one in a newspaper or on the Internet or hear one on television, or you may construct one yourself, depending on your instructor's directions. The following statements may elicit a polite reply but will probably not sir up people's emotions. They are therefore not good reaction statements:

It's cold out today.

Louis XIV grew tired of Paris.

Orange is not green.

Saturday morning is the best time to watch cartoons.

The following statements, however, have the potential to be good reaction statements, because when you hear them you will probably have a distinct opinion about them:

Abortion is murder.

Capital punishment is necessary.

Government is too big.

Such statements are likely to provoke a reaction, either negative or positive depending on the person who is reacting to them. Although they may be incendiary, however, they are also both ordinary and vague. If your instructor assigns you a statement to which to react, you may proceed to the next step. If you are to select your own, select or formulate one that is provocative, imaginative, and appropriate to the course for which you are writing the paper. Professor Jenks, for example, once assigned this question in his political philosophy class:

The best state (government) would be one ruled by a benevolent and wise dictator who is supported by a well-equipped and well-trained staff.

Consider the following examples of reaction statements for other political science classes:

Automatic weapons should be banned.

All endangered species deserve the strongest possible protection.

Criminals should be punished, not rehabilitated.

America should be a Christian nation.

Strengthening democracy in other countries often leads to war.

The form of government a country has is irrelevant. It is the quality of the leadership that counts.

Government agencies ought to be run more like businesses.

The Supreme Court should take an active role in determining social policy.

The Electoral College should be abolished.

Where do you find good reaction statements? A good way is to think about subjects that interest you. When you hear something in class that sparks a reaction because you either agree or disagree with it, you know you are on the right track. Be sure to write your question and ask your instructor for comments on it before beginning your paper. Once you have completed your selection, state it clearly at the beginning of your paper.

Explain Your Selection

After you have written the reaction statement, write a paragraph that explains why it important to you. Be as specific as possible. Writing "I like it" does not tell the reader anything useful, but sentences like the following are informative:

"People are losing their lives in many places in the world in their struggle for democracy. We have a moral duty to help them."

Clearly Define the Issue Addressed in the Statement

Consider the statement assigned by Professor Jenks: "The best state (government) would be one ruled by a benevolent and wise dictator who is supported by a well-equipped and well-trained staff." What is the most important issue addressed in this statement? Is it the efficiency of government? Is it the importance of popular participation in government? Is it the question of whether or not some people are more wise than others? Perhaps some of these aspects of the statement are more important than others. As you define the issue addressed in the statement, you provide yourself with some clarification of the statement that will help you state your position.

Clearly State Your Position on the Issue

In response to Professor Jenks's statement, you might begin by saying, "A benign dictator is an oxymoron (a contradiction in terms). People are too selfish and power hungry to govern in the interest of others. Socrates was definitely wrong when he said that philosopher-kings should rule." The reader of this response will have no doubt about where you stand on this issue.

Defend Your Position

You should make and support several arguments to support your stand on the issue. When evaluating your paper, your instructor will consider the extent to which you

- Identified the most important arguments needed to support your position (When arguing for rule by a dictator, did you mention actual successful benign dictators in history?)
- Provided facts and information, when appropriate. (When arguing that defense expenditures are too high, you should state the actual amounts of recent expenditures and the things that the money was spent on.)
- Introduced new or creative arguments to those traditionally made on this issue. (Have new developments in technology enabled dictatorships to be more or less easy to maintain?)
- Presented your case accurately, coherently, logically, consistently, and clearly.

Conclude Concisely

Your concluding paragraph should sum up your argument clearly, persuasively, and concisely.

When writing this assignment, follow the directions for formats in Chapter 3 of this manual. Ask your instructor for directions concerning the length of the paper, but in the absence of further directions, your paper should not exceed five pages (typed, double-spaced).

11.2 A Sample Reaction Paper

Read the following sample reaction paper and assess its strengths and weaknesses. How well does it meet the criteria by which the paper will be graded?

A Response to a Reaction Statement: "The federal government

spends too much money on education."

by

Jeremy Scott

Cornell College

Education is the cornerstone of our society. The acquisition of knowledge is beneficial not only for the personal satisfaction that comes from learning about yourself and your culture, but for the resulting intellectual contributions to society as well. Statistics show that educated people make better decisions and contribute more to society than uneducated people do.

The effectiveness of an education is shown clearly in national statistics. College graduates have an unemployment rate that is half that of high school graduates, and the median income of a college graduate is $15,000 greater than the income of a high school graduate. Despite the effectiveness of these programs and the stunning statistics they produce, the government insists on cutting back on educational spending.

Parents are aware of the opportunities and insight a good education provides. In a recent poll, 98 percent of parents in America said they wanted their children to attend college. However, it is becoming increasingly difficult for parents to finance that education. Pell grants, which originally funded up to 75 percent of a student's education, now fund only up to 25 percent. Studies show that federal student aid programs have been extremely effective at educating people who otherwise could not have afforded college.

Despite clear evidence that education is a good investment, it is
not high on many legislators' lists of priorities. Funding for public schools and higher education is diminishing in the wake of
excessive spending on other programs. For example, a report
recently issued by the Justice Policy Institute, a research and
advocacy organization in Washington, D.C., reveals that California
and Florida now spend more money on prisons than on higher education. The report also says the average cost to incarcerate a felon
is from $22,000 to $25,000 per year, the same amount charged by
selective liberal arts colleges. If we can pay large sums of money
to keep people from being productive, we should be able to find the
funds to help people lead more productive and fulfilling lives.

Republicans have spearheaded the effort to slash educational
appropriations and cut social programs. Speaker of the House Newt
Gingrich calls his plan the "Job Creation and Wage Enhancement
Act." Gingrich plans on "creating jobs" by eliminating $28 million
in a program that helps homeless and disadvantaged kids enroll in,
attend, and succeed in school. He also intends to eliminate $108
million in federal aid to tech.-prep. programs, cut Title I money
to educate poor children by $105 million, and slash bilingual edu-
cation funds by more than $38 million. According to the United
States Department of the Treasury, 70 percent of the money will be
spent on those individuals who make more than $200,000 a year; the
rest will be spent on defense. Over $240 billion will be spent on
defense in 1997, while only $30 billion will be spent on education
at a time when the annual military budget of the United States
almost matches the military spending of the rest of the world combined.

It is therefore easy to see that the statement "The federal
government spends too much money on education" is easily refuted by
a thoughtful analysis of the benefits of aid to education. The com-
paratively small amount of money set aside for education is a clear
indication of our country's lack of concern for our future. Today
education is more important than ever. Our potential will go unmet
unless we invest it in properly training our minds. Education is
the catalyst of a successful future.

12

Position Papers

The "X" Memorandum

On February 22, 1946, George F. Kennan, career foreign service officer serving as minister-counselor in the U.S. Embassy in Moscow, sent a telegram to Secretary of the Navy James Forrestal. The telegram sparked Forrestal's interest. "The result," wrote Kennan, "was that on January 31, 1947, I sent to him, for his private and personal edification, a paper discussing the nature of Soviet Power as a *problem in policy* for the United States." (George F. Kennan. 1967. *Memoirs.* Boston: Little, Brown. 354. Italics added.)

Kennan's article appeared anonymously in the July 1947 issue of *Foreign Affairs.* The author was listed as "X." The "X Article" became the most famous position paper ever written. In the article, Kennan described the two postwar power centers (Soviet-Communist and Western-Capitalist) and advocated the political "containment" of communism in Eastern Europe within its postwar boundaries, which became the cornerstone of American foreign policy for the remainder of the cold war.

Kennan notes in his memoirs that his statements were misconstrued by Walter Lippmann and others as referring to military as well as political containment. Similar ideas had been discussed by others. The fact remains, however, that Kennan's impressive exposition of the possibilities of American foreign policy remained at the center of the debates that determined the core of American foreign policy for more than three decades. Not all position papers are as influential as this one. They do, however, have a daily, continuing significant effect on the formation of public domestic and foreign policies. Position papers are elementary exercises in policy analysis. As a student of political science you need to understand the techniques necessary for writing effective and influential position papers.

12.1 Definition of a Position Paper

A *position paper* is advice. It is a document written to provide guidance to a decision maker on how to solve a problem. In a position paper, the author takes a position on how to solve a particular problem. Although position papers are not identical in format or style, all successful examples

- Clearly define a specific problem.
- Evaluate alternative approaches or methods for solving the problem.
- Recommend a course of action to solve the problem.

Hundreds of position papers are written in business and government every day. Business managers and public officials (presidents, governors, mayors, city managers, bureau directors) are constantly faced with problems. They usually ask their staff members for information on the problems and for recommendations on how to solve them. Sometimes subordinates write position papers to provide the requested information in a clear, precise, and persuasive manner. Position papers are particularly effective for making presentations to committees and boards of directors.

The Purpose of Position Papers

Successful political science position papers all share the same general purpose and objective: to persuade a public official to take a specific action to resolve a problem.

Public managers are problem solvers. Their primary responsibility is to make decisions that solve problems. The person who helps decision makers make decisions is responsible for presenting appropriate and relevant information that the manager can use. A position paper is therefore an entirely practical exercise. It is neither theoretical nor general in nature. It has a very narrow focus: *to solve one specific problem*. Theoretical treatises and general-subject essays have their place in communication, but not here. The object of the exercise is to persuade a public official to take the course of action that you recommend. You should not recommend an action in which you do not believe, and if you believe it is the best way to solve the problem, you need to persuade the decision maker to implement your recommendation. Otherwise your work is of no value; it is a waste of time and effort.

12.2 Selecting Topics

General Guidelines

Several considerations govern the selection of topics for position papers for courses in political science. First, the topic should be a problem facing a public, or government, official. Although position papers are frequently written for managers

of private concerns, such as businesses or research institutes, such papers in political science should normally deal with problems and policies of public (government) managers.

A second parameter for selecting position paper topics is that such papers
should address current, not historical, problems and issues. When you write a
paper on an issue that has yet to be resolved, you are participating in the political
and governmental environment. A current issue is more likely to be of interest
than one that has already been decided. There is even a possibility that the paper,
if actually submitted to the appropriate government manager, may influence
public policy. Analyses of problems already solved are best placed within the context of a history course.

A third requirement is that position paper topics should have an appropriate scope. A common mistake is for students to choose topics that are too complex or that require special technical knowledge or skills beyond those readily
available. A good general rule for your position paper is to work with the lowest
level of government possible. Even local governments deal with problems that
entail numerous social, economic, and environmental factors. In general, the
higher a level of government is on the federal scale, the more varied are the interests served and the more complex are the issues to be settled. Information from
local sources is often much more easily and quickly obtained than information
from the state capital or Washington. Local government officials are also more
likely to be personally available and thus able to provide you with a direct experience with government. Keep the topic narrowly defined, regardless of the level of
government that is being examined.

Here are some examples of topics. Which are sufficiently narrow to be suitable for position papers courses in American national, state, or local government
or policy analysis? Which are too vague or complex?

1. Equipment Failures at Madison North Fire Station
2. Free Speech
3. The Balanced Budget Amendment
4. Discipline Problems at Vandever High School
5. Inadequate Budget Procedures in Washington County
6. Abortion
7. Inadequate Personal Financial Accountability of Missouri State Legislators
8. Ineffective Affirmative Action Procedures of the Ohio Department of Education

On this list, topics 2, 3, and 6 are too vague or complex.

A fourth guideline for writing position papers is to avoid legal questions.
Remember that the point of the paper is to present sufficient information clearly
enough to allow a public official to make a decision. You are not trying to argue
fundamental principles of law. The moral, ethical, legal, legislative, and historical
facets of abortion, for example, are more appropriately presented in the format
of a legal brief rather than a position paper. Topics in constitutional law are
therefore best reserved for courses in the subject (see Chapter 16). Problems in

judicial administration, however, such as court docket procedures or jail over-crowding, are often very interesting position paper topics.

Personal Interest

There are two general approaches to selecting a topic for a position paper. The first is to select a topic tied to your own interest, perhaps one that relates to your future vocation. Government policy affects every vocation in some way and affects most of them directly. You may find a topic by asking yourself, "What are my career goals and interests? In what way does government affect me?" Many college students, for example, are affected by government student loan policies. Or, if you want to be a teacher, for example, you may want to investigate the quality of schools in your home school district or a specific educational policy or problem of state or national government. If you are an aspiring athlete, you may want to study a particular aspect of U.S. Olympic policy, whereas if medical school is in your plans, you may want to look at problems in medical reimbursement.

Once you have decided on a general topic from personal interest, an excellent way to narrow the topic is to contact a public administrator concerned with that subject and have the person identify a related problem currently facing his or her agency. Remember that the purpose of a policy paper is to define a problem and recommend the best way to solve it. One of the best ways to define a valid problem is to have a public official currently involved in working on a particular problem define that problem for you. For example, if you are interested in aviation, a good first step would be to contact an appropriate government employee in the field. You start by looking in the blue pages of the phone book, which contain entries under the following headings:

Helpful Numbers
Government Offices, City
Government Offices, County
Government Offices, State
Government Offices, United States

You then select an appropriate number and call that office. After identifying yourself, explain that you are writing a paper for a class in political science, and ask for an appointment with the agency's public information officer. If they do not have a person with this title, explain your topic and ask to speak to the person at the agency who knows the most about it. Most public employees will take time to talk to citizens who call to request information. The first official called may refer you to someone else, but continue to follow referrals until you find someone who will give you an interview.

Current Events

If you have no luck finding a topic related to your personal interests, a second approach is to select a current event. Newspapers, television, and radio continually present actual problems currently being faced by decision makers at all levels of government. Investigate the problem by contacting government officials and other individuals identified in the article or on the broadcast.

Newspaper Articles

Every day your local newspaper contains viable topics for position paper topics, and Sunday editions usually discuss a variety of issues in more detail. Sometimes newspapers will highlight community problems and activities on a specific day of the week.

12.3 Conducting Research

Whereas most traditional research projects begin with a trip to the library, position paper research starts with a government official. Because position papers investigate topics of current concern to the government, much of the most pertinent information is not available in libraries. Much of it is in the form of technical reports written by consultants, government employees, or citizen groups interested in specific problems. By first contacting an appropriate official, you may find that agency staff members have collected much of the best available information and will provide it to you upon request. By asking questions, you can identify further sources of information. When speaking to the government employee you have contacted, ask for the names of people and organizations that have a direct interest in the matter under investigation. Call some of these sources and ask for more information.

Interviews

You will usually find it essential to interview public officials, representatives of interest groups, and technical experts to get all the information necessary to write a position paper.

Other Sources of Information

Since the purpose of your paper is to help an actual government decision maker to make a decision, the information you present must be as reliable as possible. Newspaper and news magazine articles (unless used as incidental illustrations) are often inaccurate and therefore unacceptable as primary sources. Also unacceptable as sources for college-level work are encyclopedia articles. Appropriate sources include government documents and reports, academic journal articles, technical reports of private consultants, and direct interviews. The number of sources, of course, varies with the subject, but in general undergraduate papers in political science should cite three sources per page of text. (For more on how to find information for position papers, see Chapters 7 and 8.)

12.4 Format and Contents

The format of a position paper should follow the directions provided in Chapter 3.

NOTE. The directions for position papers are much more specific than those for other paper assignments because position papers have a much more narrow purpose: to help a busy decision maker arrive at the correct decision as quickly as possible. The format for position papers given in Chapter 3 has proved to be effective in telling decision makers precisely what they need to know to make a decision: (1) the nature and extent of a problem; (2) the relative merits of the options available to solve the problem; and (3) the best solution to the problem. A position paper assignment is not intended primarily as an opportunity for a student to express creativity. It is instead an exercise in precision, in problem solving, and in clear, concise communication.

The Contents of a Position Paper

Each position paper contains five basic elements:

1. Title page
2. Outline page that summarizes the paper
3. Text, or body, of the paper
4. References to sources of information
5. Appendixes

The Outline Page

The outline page in a position paper deserves special attention, because the paper's audience is likely to be someone who needs to gain information quickly. A one-page, single-spaced outline immediately follows the title page. An outline page supersedes a table of contents, which is not necessary in a position paper. The outline will be composed of *complete sentences* that express the central concepts to be more fully explained in the text. It will consist of a series of the topic sentences of the first paragraphs of each major section of the text.

The purpose of the outline is to allow the decision maker to understand, in as little time as possible, the major considerations to be discussed in the paper. Each statement must thus be clearly defined and carefully prepared. The decision maker should be able to get a thorough and clear overview of the entire problem, major alternative solutions, and your recommendation by reading nothing but the one-page outline. The content of the outline follows the content of the text of the paper. The outline should thus be written after the text has been completed, and should utilize the topic statements of the text as the sentences in the outline.

The outline (and the text of the position paper) should always begin with the words "The problem is . . ." In addition, every position paper outline should use verbatim the italicized words in the following sample. The number of alternatives, of course, will vary with the particular topic of the paper.

OUTLINE OF CONTENTS

I. *The problem* is that parking, picnic, and restroom facilities at Oak Ridge Community Park have deteriorated and are of inadequate quantity to meet public demand.
   A. The park was established as a public recreation "Class B" facility in 1943. Only one major renovation has occurred, in the summer of 1967,
   B. The Park Department estimates that 10,000 square feet of new parking space, fourteen items of playground equipment, seventeen new picnic tables, and repairs on current facilities would cost about $43,700.
II. *Three possible solutions* have been given extensive consideration:
   A. *One option is to do nothing.* Area residents will use the area less as deterioration continues. No immediate outlay of public funds will be necessary.
   B. *The first alternative solution* is to make all repairs immediately. Area residents will enjoy immediate and increased use of facilities. About $43,700 in funds will be needed. Sources include: (1) Community Development Block Grant funds; (2) raised property taxes; (3) revenue bonds; and (4) general city revenues.
   C. *A second alternative* is to make repairs according to a priority list over a five-year period, using a combination of general city revenues and a $20,000 first-year bond.
III. *The recommendation of this report is that* alternative "C" be adopted by the City Council. The benefit/cost analysis demonstrates that residents will be satisfied if basic improvements are made immediately. The City Council should, during its May 15 meeting: (1) adopt a resolution of intent to commit $5,000 of funds per year for five years from the general revenue fund, dedicated to this purpose; and (2) approve for submission to public vote in the November 1995 election a $20,000 bond issue.

The Text

The text, or body of the paper, should follow the outline that follows. Study it carefully before proceeding; each statement will be fully explained in this chapter.

THE CONTENTS OF A POSITION PAPER

I. A clear, concise definition of the problem
   A. A statement of the background of the problem
   B. A description of the extent of the problem
II. Possible solutions to the problem
   A. The first possible solution is always to take no action
      1. An estimate of the benefits of this alternative
      2. An estimate of the costs of this alternative

B. The first alternative to taking no action
    1. An estimate of the benefits of this alternative
    2. An estimate of the costs of this alternative
C. The second alternative to taking no action
    1. An estimate of the benefits of this alternative
    2. An estimate of the costs of this alternative
III. A precise recommended course of action in two parts:
    A. Policy recommendation
    B. Implementation recommendation

Two general rules govern the amount of information presented in the body of the paper. First, content must be adequate for making a good decision. All the necessary facts must be present. If a critical fact is omitted, a poor decision will likely be made. Never delete important facts simply because they tend to support a recommendation other than your own. Write this paper as if you were a member of the staff of the person to whom you are writing. As a staff member, your role is to inform your superior. The decision is his or her responsibility. It is far better for the decision maker to select an alternative different from your recommendation, based on a review of all the facts, than to make the wrong decision based on inadequate information.

The second guideline for determining the length of a position paper is to omit extraneous material. Include only the information that is helpful in making the particular decision at hand. If the paper addresses the crime rate in Atlanta, Georgia, for example, national crime statistics are of little use unless some direct application to Atlanta's problem is evident. A theoretical discussion about the causes of crime is of no value at all, unless differences in philosophy in the community are contributing to the city's inability to reduce crime.

Describing the Problem

Defining the Problem.   Defining the problem is often the most difficult task in writing a position paper. The problem may be other than what at first appears. When the student writing the paper outlined earlier defined "deterioration of facilities" as the problem at Oak Ridge Community Park, she precluded a number of other possibilities. For example, upon investigation, she might have found that the problem was actually a lack of recreational facilities for a neighborhood population that would actually prefer a different type or location of facilities. In other words, restoring the park might not have solved the problem. Again, suppose that the actual problem was political. Suppose she had discovered that the only reason local residents wanted the park restored was that they had felt left out of past city budget appropriations and wanted some city project as a sort of recognition of their needs. If this is the case, another project might better meet the real need (recognition), and the city could save scarce tax dollars in the process.

A common mistake made by students writing position papers is confusing "needs" with "problems." A need is not a problem but an assumption that a particular good or service will solve a problem. Confusing the need with the problem often leads to the wrong solution. For example, a student may write, "The problem is that Clark County needs a new hospital." If one asks, "Why does Clark County need a new hospital?" the answer might be "Emergency medical services in Clark County are inadequate." In other words, the real problem (inadequate emergency medical services) may not require a new hospital.

Problems most commonly consist of

1. Deprivation: a lack of something necessary to safety, health, or well-being.
2. Obstruction: an impediment to safety, health, or well-being.

A typical conversation that identifies real problems proceeds as follows:

Student Smith: "Officer Jones, what is the greatest problem the police department is currently facing?"
Officer Jones: "We need more officers."

If the student ended her investigation at this point, she would have allowed Officer Jones to define the problem for her. If the problem is the lack of officers, the paper will center on ways the police department can get more officers. The outline of the paper would probably look something like the following:

I. The problem is a shortage of police officers in the City of Springfield.
   A. Since 1993, fourteen vacancies on the police force have been left unfilled because of budget cuts.
   B. In this same period, the crime rate in Springfield has risen 22 percent.
II. The police chief has considered four options.
   A. The first option is to do nothing. The crime rate is likely to continue to rise, leaving citizens with even less protection.
   B. The first alternative solution is to divert $350,000 in funds from other city projects to hire seven new officers. Other city agencies have already faced budget cuts.
   C. The second alternative solution is to increase the property tax by $0.5 million to hire seven new officers. Part of the need would be met.
   D. The third alternative solution is to increase the property tax by $1 million and hire eight to fourteen new officers. The crime rate is expected to decrease. Some adverse effects on the local economy are anticipated.
III. This report recommends that option D be followed. Law enforcement problems in the community are sufficiently severe to merit facing possible adverse economic impacts.

In this outline, the entire inquiry ends when the statement that "The problem is a shortage of police officers" is accepted. Suppose, however, that the student had continued the questioning:

Student Smith: "Why do you need more officers?"
Officer Jones: "Our auto theft rate has increased 50 percent in the past five years, and our current personnel are not sufficient to handle the problem."

Student Smith:	"It would seem, then, that the increased auto theft rate is the real problem."
Officer Jones:	"Yes, that is the case."
Student Smith:	"What are some other ways people have suggested for lowering the auto theft rate?"
Officer Jones:	"Well, since most of the thefts are done by juveniles, some have suggested stronger penalties or a curfew on youths after 10:00 P.M. Others have said that cars are too easy to steal. They suggest that the state legislature pass a law requiring that antitheft devices be installed on all new vehicles sold in the state."

If the conversation had continued in this manner, the real problem would have been identified as an increased auto theft rate, and different solutions would have been presented. The student's outline might then have looked like this:

I. The problem is an increase in auto thefts in Springfield from 11,500 in 1991 to 28,200 in 1997.
   A. Property damage has increased in proportion to the thefts; 93 percent of stolen autos are recovered, and 75 percent of these have had significant damage.
   B. Auto insurance rates have risen 250 percent in Springfield during this period.
II. Four options for solving the problem have been investigated.
   A. The first option is to do nothing. Auto thefts are expected to increase.
   B. The first alternative solution is to hire up to fourteen new police officers, which would cost $700,000 annually.
   C. The second alternative solution is to impose a 10:00 P.M. curfew on juveniles, because 35 percent of vehicle thefts are done by juveniles between 10:00 P.M. and 7:00 A.M. The rights of law-abiding citizens may be infringed by the curfew.
   D. The third alternative solution is to support state legislative action to require antitheft devices on new automobiles. Price increases for new autos would average $100.
III. This report recommends that option D be followed.

A comparison of the two outlines shows that solving the problems facing society depends on defining them correctly. The wrong definition usually leads to the wrong solution.

   The Background of the Problem.   After the problem has been clearly defined, the reader needs to know how the problem arose and how serious it is. If the problem is defined as "increased auto theft in Springfield," the history of auto theft rates in the city should be included. The description should focus on recent developments and time periods in which the problem became more intense. If the rate increase was substantially greater in the years since 1991, for example, that period should be given the most attention.

   Although the cause of a social problem is often difficult to determine, the attempt should be made because the solution may be possible only when the cause is resolved. However, you must use caution and common sense while searching for underlying causes. If auto theft is the problem, the ultimate answer may reside in understanding the psychological bases of human behavior. This vast, complex, and controversial subject is a valid subject for research, but it is not appropriate for a position paper in political science. The *immediate* cause should be determined from the best available studies or opinions of local "experts" (people involved with the problem on a daily basis). In our example, Officer Jones has indicated that juveniles appear to be responsible for much of the increase in auto theft. Perhaps education policies, drug abuse, or other factors are directly involved in the increase. If this is the case, appropriate actions may be included in the list of options.

After describing how the problem arose, explain its extent. If the problem is auto theft, be sure to provide statistics on the number of autos stolen and recovered, as well as other relevant facts, for each year of the period in question. The number of people affected and the extent of the economic impact on each person or on the group as a whole are major factors to be included in almost every position paper.

Formulating Options (Alternatives) for Solving the Problem

As the author of a position paper, you want to be effective in clearly presenting a problem and in assisting a public official in making a decision. To achieve this purpose it is helpful to imagine yourself in that official's position. Begin with the obvious. Public managers at all levels are human. They probably would not have attained a position of authority if they did not have a sense of responsibility and a desire to succeed. They usually want to make the best decision possible, not only for the community, but for themselves as well. Making poor decisions would most likely limit their effectiveness.

Imagine yourself as an effective, motivated public official. When presented with a problem, a certain logical process will automatically begin, having been refined through years of general education, specialized training, and experience. The first thing you will ask yourself is "What exactly is the problem? How did it start? How extensive is it?"

Having received satisfactory answers to these questions, the next question you will ask is "What are my options for solving this problem?" One of the most common mistakes of students who write position papers is to fail to answer this question correctly. To define options is to describe different approaches to solving the problem, not to describe different measures that are all combined in one approach.

A person approaching a wall, for example, has a problem. He or she wants to continue along a path, but the wall is in the way. The first task is to identify the options correctly. There may be several somewhat reasonable alternative courses of action. The first is to do nothing and stay in place. Other options include going around the wall to the right, going around the wall to the left, tunneling under the wall, pole-vaulting over the wall, or destroying some or all of the wall.

Options in position papers are different, mutually exclusive approaches to a problem. If one alternative is selected, the others are rejected. The writer of the paper may incorrectly select all options, repeatedly achieving the same objective. Or the writer may actually examine only one option and mistake a part of it (a step toward a solution) for a complete option in itself—a common error. In the car-theft example, student Smith may list the following alternatives:

> Option A: Do nothing.
> Option B: Draw up antitheft device legislation.
> Option C: Find a legislative sponsor.
> Option D: Initiate a campaign of public support for the legislation.

All four "options" are actually only four steps in carrying out one option: passing antitheft device legislation. Again, steps *toward* a single solution are not options for position papers. Distinct, mutually exclusive (practically and politically) ways of approaching problems are viable options.

Let us assume, for example, that Lisa Smith has defined a problem: the increasing auto theft rate in Springfield. Correctly identifying viable alternatives, Lisa Smith lists the following options:

> Option A: Do nothing.
> Option B: Hire more police officers.
> Option C: Establish a curfew for juveniles.
> Option D: Legislate mandatory auto theft devices.

If she formulates the options correctly, she will select the most appropriate one (which she decides is option D). Student Smith may, however, fall into a common trap for writers of position papers. It is true that options A, B, C, and D are not necessarily *theoretically* exclusive. In other words, a community may adopt three measures (options B, C, and D) simultaneously without having them conflict with each other. If options are correctly formulated, however, each one alone should be sufficient to solve the problem. If this is not the case, specific actions must be combined into single options, or options must be formulated differently so that each alternative is a viable solution by itself.

Reflect, however, on the practical probabilities of public management. Each of the suggested alternatives (including option A) has an immediate and direct cost to the community. Persuading the population to accept any one of them will probably be difficult. Persuading the community to adopt all three will probably be impossible, and in fact would be likely to impair the chance that any one option will be taken seriously.

Comparing Alternatives for Solving the Problem

For each available option you should describe first the benefits and then the costs of taking that particular action. Benefits are the positive outcomes expected. Costs include time, money, and the resources expected to be used, as well as probable or possible negative outcomes (known as "disbenefits"). Both benefits and costs may include economic, social, political, and environmental factors. Benefits of improving the Oak Ridge Community Park may include

1. Improved quality of life for area residents.
2. Increased property value in adjacent neighborhoods.
3. Decreased personal injury liability to the city.
4. Increased political support from area neighborhoods.
5. Reduced environmental damage from proper maintenance procedures.

Costs of improving the park may include

1. $43,700.
2. Fewer resources for other community projects.
3. Political opposition from other areas in the community.

As mentioned, *all* reasonable costs and benefits should be included in the paper. You should never exclude possible costs or benefits of any one option in order to make another option appear more or less attractive. The position paper will be submitted to someone who is responsible for making the proper decision. If an option other than the one recommended is selected and full information has been provided, the writer of the position paper has acted appropriately. Elected and appointed officials may legitimately choose options that are technically not the most cost-effective. But if a policy maker selects the wrong option because of incomplete information in the position paper, the writer is clearly responsible.

Benefit-Cost Analyses.   Lengthy books have been written on how to conduct benefit-cost analyses. Only a simplified (but still very helpful) process will be outlined here.

To analyze benefits and costs *for each option,* first list the benefits and then list costs of that alternative. In the analysis of the Oak Ridge Community Park, conducted by Lisa Smith, the first option is to do nothing. Lisa may list the benefits of doing nothing as follows:

Benefit 1: Saving immediate cash outlay
Benefit 2: Directing staff effort to other projects

The costs of doing nothing may include these:

Cost 1: Deterioration of facilities
Cost 2: Lower local real estate value
Cost 3: Local public discontent

The second step is to assign a monetary value to each cost and benefit based on the advice of experts, who usually include government officials, consultants, or members of private organizations with expertise in the area.

For benefit 1 of doing nothing, for example, Lisa obtained price estimates from engineers in other state agencies, which show that the full project cost would be $43,700. Benefit 1 would thus be an immediate cash saving of this amount.

Benefit 2 of doing nothing can be determined by estimating the number of staff hours to be expended on the project and multiplying that figure by an average cost per hour. After consulting with the Park Department's personnel office, Lisa may estimate that the average cost per employee-hour, including salary benefits and related expenses, would be $22. Estimating that eighty hours of staff time would be used on the project, she concludes that the total benefit of hours saved by not continuing with the project would be $1,760.

Next, the costs of taking no action must be estimated. After discussion with Park Maintenance Department officers, Lisa finds that allowing the equipment in the park to continue to deteriorate (considering expected inflation in replacement costs) would cost an additional $27,000 (above the estimated $43,700 in current costs) at the end of five years. Long-range costs of repairing and replacing equipment, therefore, are $70,700 ($43,700 current plus $27,000 future costs).

Lisa consulted with an experienced real estate assessor who was familiar with the Oak Ridge area. The assessor estimated that fifteen residences in close proximity to the park would each experience a 5 percent value increase if park conditions are improved. The average value of the fifteen houses was $87,500. Lisa then calculated that the cost to neighborhood residents of doing nothing would be $65,625 in lost real estate value ($87,500 × 5% × 15 houses).

The final cost was most difficult to estimate. "Local public discontent" is not easily quantified, yet an attempt may reasonably be made to do so. For the purpose of a position paper, it is acceptable to estimate such intangible variables as high, medium, or low. You should, through asking questions of the people involved, attempt to estimate the general level of discontent with an existing, proposed, or potential policy. Use the term *high, medium,* or *low,* and then explain how you arrived at the designation you selected. Your explanation should reveal to your reader what the designation means in a particular situation. Lisa estimated that local discontent would be "medium" if no action were taken to improve the park's facilities. She reached this conclusion after finding that a few of the local residents—those with young children—felt quite strongly about the need for improvement. In addition, most of the other residents indicated that they had been unhappy with the condition of the park for some time.

A summary of the benefit-cost analysis for all alternatives should be presented in table form, followed by a paragraph or two of explanatory comparisons, in the recommendation section of your paper. The table for Lisa's paper might look like the following:

LISA SMITH'S BENEFIT-COST ANALYSIS SUMMARY

ALTERNATIVE	BENEFIT	COST
Do nothing	Save staff effort ($1,760)	Deterioration ($70,700)
Make repair now	Immediate use of park; avoid inflation	Construction ($43,700)
Make repair gradually	Partial use of park now	Construction ($20,000 now; $27,000 more over 5 years)

Making a Recommendation for Solving a Problem

Your purpose in writing a position paper is to take a position on a policy or course of action. That position should be clear and unambiguous. The paper will be most effective if you arrange the options so that your recommendation is the final one listed. The recommendation should *not* be one that was not previously addressed in the list of options. Instead, it should reiterate the selected option, explaining why it is superior to those that are rejected.

Again, place yourself in the position of the public official who is reading your paper. She has clearly understood the problem. As she reads the options list, she first comes to understand that taking no action is undesirable and that some action is necessary. As she reads each succeeding option, she becomes aware of its costs. By the time she comes to the last alternative, it is (hopefully) obvious that it produces the greatest benefit at the lowest cost. Finally, she reads the recommendation. It confirms in her mind the conclusion she herself has been coming to: The final option is the best course of action. People learn by repetition. As the official reads the comparative benefits of the preferred option in the recommendation section, its advantages and benefits should become more solidly embedded in her mind.

The implementation section of a position paper tells the reader not only what should be done, but it explains, briefly, *how* it should be done. In other words, the writer should detail in a few clear, specific steps the actions that should be taken to implement the recommendation. Continuing the examples of student Smith's study of the Springfield Police Department, the final section of her recommendation (after reiterating her selected option and comparing its benefits to others in a benefit-cost analysis) might be as follows:

```
To implement this recommendation, I recommend that the city
manager take the following series of actions:
   I. Draw up, in consultation with the state attorney, automo-
      bile antitheft device legislation that includes, at a min-
      imum, the following requirements:
      A. That only selected, certified types of devices be eligi-
         ble for consideration
      B. That the selected types of devices be mandatory in all
         new vehicles registered on or after January 1, 1995
      C. That registration be denied to vehicles not meeting these
         requirements
  II. Contact the city's legislative representatives and formu-
      late a plan for the following:
```

```
    A. Finding legislative sponsors for the bill
    B. Promoting support for passage among state legislators
    C. Advocating public awareness and support of the bill
```

Appendixes

Appendixes can provide the reader of position papers with information that supplements the important facts presented in the text. For many local development and public works projects, a map and a diagram are often very helpful appendixes. You should attach them to the end of the paper, after the reference page. You should not append entire government reports, journal articles, or other publications, but selected charts, graphs, or other pages. The source of the information should always be evident on the appended pages.

References

All sources of information in a position paper must be properly cited, following the directions in Chapter 4.

13
Political Analysis Papers

In 1651 the philosopher Thomas Hobbes, contemplating the savagery of the English Civil War of the previous decade, commented:

> Againe, men have no pleasure (but on the contrary a great deale of griefe) in keeping company, where there is no power able to over-awe them all. For every man looketh that his companion should value him, at the same rate he sets upon himself. . . . So that in the nature of man, we find three principal causes of quarrell. First, Competition; Secondly, Diffidence; Thirdly, Glory. (Thomas Hobbes. 1985. *Leviathan*. Harmondsworth: Penguin. 185.)

In his most famous work, *Leviathan,* Hobbes brought to political analysis a new perspective on traditional concepts such as freedom, sovereignty, and justice, proposing a social contract in which people who hold a natural right to acquire what they please would voluntarily relinquish that right to a sovereign ruler in exchange for order and security in society. He knew that to analyze politics one must examine political events and attempt to explain why political life unfolds as it does. From his seventeenth-century perspective, Hobbes looked for the guiding principles of politics in the nature of man. He believed that people share an innate political psychology that is activated by greed, insecurity, and a desire for the esteem of others. Hobbes's contribution to political analysis was to redirect political thought from medieval concepts of divine authority in worldly affairs to modern concerns of the consent of the people to government authority. In a general sense, his philosophical writings constitute political analysis because they attempt to break down the components of political life (law, obligation to authority, rights) and examine them as separate entities and in their relations with one another. Today political scientists use the methods of science to describe political behavior. Political analysis, however, now as in the time of Hobbes, goes beyond description. It attempts to show and explain causal relationships in political activity.

Robert A. Dahl: Polyarchy

One of the most difficult aspects of political analysis is the ambiguity of terms that are normally used to describe political events, movements, behavior, and institutions. In his book *Modern Political Analysis,* Yale University political scientist Robert Dahl examines the two basic concepts of political analysis: power and political systems. Dahl believes that political analysis must focus on political institutions, stating that "among the differences in political systems that make a difference—indeed a crucial difference—are their institutions for sharing and exercising power" (Robert A. Dahl. 1991. *Modern Political Analysis.* 5th ed. Englewood Cliffs, NJ: Prentice Hall. 71). He then attempts to define the institutions of the modern Western democracies and to identify those that appear essential to the vitality of democracy. Finding, however, that the word *democracy* has different meanings for different people, he wants to find a term that will more precisely designate those modern governments that share a number of features often understood to be democratic, while avoiding the arguments of definition that the use of the term *democracy* so often involves. He accordingly invents a new term, *polyarchy,* that becomes his basic unit of political analysis, and formulates a list of seven characteristics of governments whose behavior he wants to compare with one another or examine as a group distinct from governments not having these qualities. The seven characteristics of every polyarchy, as Dahl defines them, are as follows:

1. Control over government decisions about policy is constitutionally vested in elected officials.
2. Elected officials are chosen and peacefully removed in frequent, fair, and free elections in which coercion is absent or quite limited.
3. Virtually all adults have the right to vote.
4. Most adults have the right to run for public office.
5. Citizens possess a right, effectively enforced by judicial and administrative officials, to freedom of expression, including criticism of and opposition to the leaders or party in office.
6. They have access, and an effectively enforced right to gain access, to sources of information that are not monopolized by the government or by any other single group.
7. They possess an effectively enforced right to form and join political organizations, including political parties and interest groups.

13.1 Conducting Political Analysis

Whereas *policy* analysis attempts to explain the relative costs and benefits of different government decisions, *political* analysis examines the substance of the political process itself. Most simply, political analysis examines three basic phenomena:

1. Political *power* (or influence).
2. The political, legal, economic, cultural, and environmental *systems* (broadly speaking, institutions, rules, and environments) in which power is exercised.
3. The relationship between power and the political (and other) systems within which it operates.

Your political analysis paper will have one primary purpose: *to describe the characteristics of political power within a specific political system.* In accomplishing this goal, you may focus on one of several aspects of political systems, such as economics, culture, organizational behavior, or political communication, but your objective will be to explain how your selected topic influences and participates in the overall political process. Like Thomas Hobbes, you will be attempting to understand who governs, why they govern, what impels them to govern, what makes their government accepted and effective, and what limitations their effectiveness and governing capacities have. Like Robert Dahl, you will organize political concepts into a framework that helps you understand the many facets of power and influence that you will study.

When you write a political analysis paper, your *audience* will be (1) your instructor, who wants you to analyze carefully and insightfully and write well, and (2) college students and others who study politics to improve their chances of success in political careers, to better understand the political process in order to affect political events, or to teach political science to others.

13.2 Writing a Political Analysis Paper: An Overview

There are four basic steps in writing a political analysis paper. You should use these steps as a general guideline, but they need not necessarily be followed consecutively:

1. Selecting a political system
2. Selecting an analytical framework
3. Collecting and analyzing the data
4. Writing the paper

Selecting a Political System

Political analysis is an endeavor as broad and expansive as politics itself. It is not always conducted with specific reference to a political system. For your paper to have manageable content and a focus amenable to analysis, however, you will need to select a specific political system to analyze. This limitation is not very restrictive because you may choose from a virtually infinite number of systems. For our definition of political system we turn again to David Easton, who described politics as the "authoritative allocation of values," and a system as "any set of variables regardless of the degree of interrelationship among them" (David Easton. 1966. "Categories for the Systems Analysis of Politics." In David Easton, ed. *Varieties of Political Theory.* Englewood Cliffs, NJ: Prentice Hall. 143–54). Following this definition, a political system is the set of variables that authoritatively allocate values. This means that any set of variables (people, institutions, groups) capable of making decisions about values may be called a political system. Under this definition, a political system may be, for example,

- Your family.
- A Methodist church.
- A local school board in Montana.
- The voters of Colorado.
- A city council in Florida.
- A regional planning commission in Maine.
- A state health board in Arizona.
- The Congress of the United States.
- The U.S. Department of Labor or any of its bureaus.
- The United Nations.
- The informal unwritten agreements among the world's most powerful nations.

Ask your instructor what kind of political system is appropriate for a paper in your course. Remember that a system's complexity is normally in direct, if not exponential, relation to its size. In other words, the larger the system you select, the less specific your paper will be about the interactions of the variables in the system.

Selecting an Analytical Framework

After you have selected a political system, you must select an analytical framework for examining the system. An analytical framework is a set of principles that organizes an investigation. It tells you what aspects of your subject to look at and what criteria to use to evaluate them. The scientific method, for example, is an analytical framework. It is a set of rules for observing and describing physical (and social) phenomena. The American legal system operates under a very complex analytical framework, which is the combination of laws, regulations, and court decisions that determine what events are legal questions, what evidence is allowed in the courts, and what procedures must be used to settle disputes or to determine guilt or innocence.

This manual presents four examples of what may be called, for the purposes of this assignment, analytical frameworks, each of which presents a different approach to the study of political systems:

- Systems analysis
- Structural-functional analysis
- Analysis of the state
- Decision-making analysis, including game theory and cybernetics

These four are not the only frameworks that are available, but, as some of the most widely used and accepted methods, they have been chosen to assist you in making a selection. You will find an expanded description of each of these alternatives in the next section of this chapter.

Collecting and Analyzing the Data

The data collection and analysis methods that you use will depend on the analytical framework that you select. You may collect documents, conduct interviews or surveys, or use a combination of several methods. The descriptions of the analytical frameworks in the next section of this chapter will indicate appropriate data collection and analysis methods, and other chapters of this manual will briefly explain these methods.

Writing the Paper

When writing a political analysis paper, your primary goals will be accuracy and clarity in communication. Read Chapters 1 and 2 before proceeding with your paper.

13.3 The Format of a Political Analysis Paper

Political analysis papers all have the following six components:

1. Title page
2. Abstract *or* executive summary
3. Table of contents *or* outline page
4. Text, or body, of the paper
5. Source citations and reference page
6. Appendixes

Chapter 3 describes in detail how these six components should be written. *Ask your instructor if you should provide an abstract or an executive summary, and a table of contents or an outline page. Also ask your instructor about the length of the paper.*

13.4 Analytical Frameworks for Political Analysis

In this section the analytical frameworks are described in only enough detail to provide you with directions for writing political analysis papers. For many other assignments you will have to consult other texts to understand fully the concepts and terms used in these directions. This manual is not a textbook on political analysis. It does not offer complete descriptions of political analysis techniques. It does, however, provide what most texts do not: explicit directions on the appropriate content of political analysis and other political science papers.

Systems Analysis

A primary advantage of systems analysis is that it provides categories that help you to describe a political system as a whole and then to discuss its component parts in terms of certain standard roles played by actors in every political system. The primary tasks of your analysis are to

- Define the major elements of the system.
- Describe their major characteristics.
- Describe the relationships among them in systems theory terms.
- Explain how the system works.

Definition and Description

In the process of completing the primary tasks of your analysis, first identify and briefly describe at least the following systems elements:

- The people, groups, or populations who are parts of the system.
- The gatekeepers who set the agenda for making decisions.
- The authorities who speak for the system.
- Inputs (including demands for actions and services) and supports that help maintain and strengthen the system.
- Outputs (decisions made by the system).
- The intrasocietal (inside the system) and extrasocietal (outside the system) environments of the system.
- Disturbances that cause stress in the system.

Flow Model

Next draw a *flow model,* a diagram that illustrates the relationships among the elements of the system. Your flow model should contain the systems elements in the preceding list. In addition, it should show major *transactions* (one-way actions) and *exchanges* (two-way interactions) with other internal and external systems of the environment, including

- The feedback loop, or how outputs return to the system as new inputs.
- The covariance, or how changes in some elements in the system act in response to changes in other elements in the system.
- The interdependence of elements of the system.

Evaluation

As the final step in your systems analysis, you should evaluate how the political system you have selected operates. Your evaluation should include at least the following considerations:

- The current level of stress in the system; the way the system handles stress; the critical range, or limits, of the system's ability to handle stress.
- The system's openness to change and to adapt to new demands, stresses, and conditions.
- The effectiveness and efficiency of the system in converting inputs to outputs and the effectiveness and efficiency of the outputs.
- The objectives of the system, and its potential for and limitations in respect to fulfilling its objectives.
- Suggestions for improving the system.

If the system you have selected is accessible, such as a city council, you will find your information primarily through collecting documents like minutes of meetings and the city charter and by conducting interviews. You may well find that formal rules determine a part of the system's process but that informal power structures and influences play an even greater role. In many communities, for example, a few influential people who do not hold office are able to assure the success or failure of proposals that come before the government institutions. Use systems analysis as a tool to find out how the system really works!

Structural-Functional Analysis

To write a structural-functional analysis, you must first select a political system to analyze. Structural-functional analysis, like systems analysis, may be conducted on systems of any size but is particularly appropriate for a large political system, such as a nation-state, or for a comparison of two or more nation-states. It is appropriate for such purposes because, as Gabriel Almond and James Coleman point out, although political structures are very different from place to place, their basic political functions are the same. (Gabriel A. Almond and James S. Coleman, eds. 1960. *The Politics of the Developing Areas.* Princeton, NJ: Princeton University Press.) Every political structure, for example, makes rules for its community to follow. From the Boy Scouts to the United Nations, political systems have some way of making rules under which the system operates. The directions for this paper assignment are written to utilize structural-functional analysis in that area of political science in which its methods are of the greatest benefit: comparative politics. It was

Almond who introduced structural-functional analysis to the study of comparative government. Many of his concepts are employed in the following discussion.

You should begin your structural-functional analysis by selecting two nation-states to compare. The nations you choose will determine the emphasis of your analyses. Select two nations that have some characteristics in common and others that are different. This approach will allow you to hold certain variables constant while examining the effects of differences in other variables. Russia and Ukraine, for example, share a common recent history as former members of the Soviet Union and adjacent geographic territories. Finding such commonalities facilitates comparison. It will be more difficult to make meaningful comparison of two nations as different as Japan and Uganda.

Your structural-functional analysis paper should include the following basic elements:

- A structural-functional analysis of the first nation you have selected.
- A structural-functional analysis of the second nation you have selected.
- A comparison of the structural-functional analyses of the two nations.

For each country that you have selected, your structural-functional analysis should

- Briefly describe the nation's major political structures.
- Describe the nation's major input functions.
- Describe the nation's major output functions.

Political Structures

The political structures of the nation include political and legal institutions, such as executive, legislative, and judicial agencies, and the rules, such as the constitution and principal laws under which the institutions operate. If you were to describe the political structures of the United States, for example, you would summarize the main elements of the Constitution. You would then explain how the Constitution establishes a federal system in which national, state, and local governments operate. You would next briefly describe the national government's institutions, including the presidency, Congress, the Supreme Court and other federal courts, and the federal departments and other national agencies. Your structural analysis would then examine the organization of the government, including the organizational principles under which it operates. In the United States, these include checks and balances such as the president's veto power and judicial review.

Input Functions

Your next task will be to describe the four input functions of the nation you have selected:

1. Political socialization
2. Interest articulation

3. Interest aggregation
4. Political communication

1. *Political socialization* is the manner in which people learn the political values of their culture. Describing the political socialization process requires finding the answers to many questions. Through what mediating institutions do people learn their political values—families, schools, churches, private clubs? Which mediating institutions have the greatest impact within the political culture? What effects do these influences have on politics in these nations?

2. *Interest articulation* includes the ways in which interests may be expressed. Are some organizations or ideologies more effective at expressing their views than others? If so, which organizations? Why are they more effective? Do unwritten rules of expression exist? Do some groups have no voice in the politics of the society? What are the patterns of interest articulation in the nation you have selected? How open or closed are they? Must one follow a rigid social code to have one's views heard? Can all members of society (for example, women and minorities) contribute to the discussion?

In the 1840s the French aristocrat Alexis de Tocqueville came to America and made some interesting observations about American politics. Tocqueville said that he found less freedom in American democracy than in the monarchies of Europe, because in America certain values were held so strongly by such a large majority that freedom of speech on these issues was effectively precluded. He noted, for example, that a man who was called as a witness in a court in New York was not allowed to testify because he stated that he did not believe in the existence of God, and the judge had said that his testimony would therefore not be considered credible. Tocqueville noted that the newspapers reported what had happened without commenting further on the judge's action. He described such attitudes as forming what he called the "tyranny of the majority."

3. *Interest aggregation* is the process by which interests compete, cooperate, and compromise to distribute the resources and make the rules of society. In the United States much interest aggregation is done by political parties before the elections. Presidential candidates, for example, need to receive the votes of a broad spectrum of the electorate in order to get the 270 electoral college votes necessary for election. During the nominating process they must get the support of many groups, such as Hispanics, labor union members, small business operators, and fundamentalists, aggregating the various interests into a winning electoral coalition. In contrast, in parliamentary systems like Great Britain's, much interest aggregation is done *after* elections. Prime ministers are not elected on a separate ballot. After the members of Parliament are elected, they elect the prime minister from among their membership. Often in parliamentary systems no political party elects a majority. They must then make bargains with other parties and form coalitions that have enough votes to elect a prime minister. Interest aggregation takes place as parties agree to support each other's interests in the process of forming a majority coalition.

4. *Political communication* is the means by which political values in society are communicated. The main focus of your efforts in understanding the commu-

nication function should be to determine how open political communication in your selected nation actually is. The first question to ask is, "Is there freedom of the press?"—but do not stop here. In the United States we enjoy freedom of the press, but some commentators say that our abilities to influence opinion are far from equal. They point out that the major media organizations, such as newspapers, television, and radio, are in the hands of a few powerful people, and that certain individual citizens, such as Ross Perot, may have a substantial effect on a presidential election. Is such access available only to the wealthy?

Output Functions

Output functions are more easily understood than input functions, perhaps because more is said in the daily news about them. Three output functions should be addressed in your paper:

1. Rule making
2. Rule application
3. Rule adjudication

1. *Rule making* is primarily a legislative function. In the United States rules are made by parents, teachers, religious leaders, coaches, city councils, state legislatures, Congress, and many other organizations in authority. The people who make the rules, the manner in which they are selected, the amount of authority they have, and the extent of bargaining and compromise they must do are very different from one country to another. Rule makers face different challenges in Puerto Rico, a democratic commonwealth of the United States, than in Cuba, a communist dictatorship. When writing your structural-functional analysis paper, describe the primary rule makers in each country you have selected in sufficient detail to understand how and why rule making in the two nations is both similar and different.

2. *Rule application* is normally an executive function. The first function of any bureaucracy is to apply general rules to specific circumstances. The Department of the Interior, for example, makes regulations to apply the laws that Congress has passed to govern the management of public lands. In your structural-functional analysis paper, begin your discussion of rule application by listing the primary types of rule application structures, such as government departments and regulatory agencies (e.g., the United States Environmental Protection Agency) in the nations you have selected. Do not, however, end your examination here. Attempt to describe how a nation's customs and political culture affect the rule application process. In some authoritarian regimes, for example, public administrators act as though it is the privilege, not the right, of the public to receive their services, and they exhibit little need to respond to citizen complaints. In other regimes, people at all levels of the bureaucracy depend on bribes as a normally expected part of their income for their services.

Rule application is not as simple as it seems. In many countries, local religious beliefs impede the delivery of health care services. In the recent crisis in

Somalia, the devastating effects of a drought were magnified many times by relief agencies' inability to deliver food supplies due to theft by armed bands controlled by local warlords.

3. *Rule adjudication* is primarily a judicial function. In examining rule adjudication in the nation you have selected, first describe the court system and then examine who settles disputes. Ask questions about the process. Does the judicial system enjoy the respect of the people? Are most disputes settled formally, through the courts, or in other settings? Why, for example, does the United States have many more lawyers for its population than any other nation in the world?

Analysis of the State

In recent years, some political scientists making comparative studies have given new attention to the state as a unit of analysis. They believe that systems analysis and structural-functional analysis reduce political societies to so many parts that it is difficult to understand the unity of political systems. The state, they claim, is more than just a government; it is a cohesive set of systems that determine political life. The state is not merely an institution that responds to other forces in society, but is rather a creative and vital source of important initiatives. The political and economic elites that direct states are substantially autonomous, and studying these elites will help explain domestic and international political events. Bob Jessup identifies "six crucial factors about the state or state system" that are most often examined by "state-centered theorists" (Bob Jessup. 1990. "Putting States in Their Place: State Systems and State Theory." In *New Developments in Political Science*. Edited by Adrian Leftwich. Aldershot: Edward Elgar. 43–60). When writing your analysis of a state, an effective approach is first to select a specific state system of interest to you and then to examine these six factors as they are found in that state:

1. Geopolitical position
2. Role of the military
3. Internal powers
4. External powers
5. State managers
6. Pathologies

1. Describe first the *geopolitical position* of the state and the implications of that position both in history and at the current time. The development of the great trading centers of the Middle Ages, for example, was a primary factor in ending the feudal system. One after another, Venice, Holland, Spain, Portugal, France, and England took turns, using the geopolitical advantages of their location, to develop commercial empires. Geopolitical power can change over time. Panama, for example, will always have at least some importance to world trade, but its location was more important at the turn of the twentieth century than at the turn of the twenty-first. Why, for example, did the United States intervene quickly and forcefully to save Kuwait from Iraqi domination, but fail to use deci-

sive force to save people caught in the civil war in the Congo? The answer probably has much to do with the geopolitical positions of the two countries.

2. The *role of the military* is more important in many countries than it is in the United States, but even here defense issues consume many hours of public debate, and defense expenditures continue to be a significant part of the budget. The role of the military is especially important in South American countries, where regimes change by military coup with relative frequency. Some of the factors to investigate in regard to the military are direct influences, such as the number of military leaders in civilian positions and the likelihood of a military coup if policies unfavorable to the military are adopted; and indirect influences, such as the social prestige of a military career and the threat of human rights violations by members of military units.

3. The *internal powers* of the state are used to organize society. They include the threat of force by military and police, the support of the people who believe that the state's laws are legitimate, and the sense of political obligation that is the norm in a particular political culture. What types of powers are most frequently used to organize society by the state you have selected for study? Some dictators use secret police to effectively control opposition forces, for example, whereas presidents and prime ministers in democracies are likely to make substantial use of television and other news media.

4. The *external powers* of the state are revealed in its role in the international arena. The power of a state in international relations is based on much more than its geopolitical position. For example, the economic strength of the United States was a primary factor in its dominance of the post–World War II era. Castro's alliance with the Soviet Union gave Cuba exceptional influence in the events of the Cold War. The support of the Jewish community around the world has given Israel influence that it would not otherwise enjoy. Explore such factors that determine the extent of external power that the state you have selected enjoys.

5. Analysts of the state place substantial emphasis on the people who manage a state. These elites, the *state managers,* may not all hold government positions. Some of them may enjoy immense wealth or have a popular following. When analyzing elites, first identify the key actors in the state's decision-making process. Then describe how they have gained their positions of influence and how they relate to one another to form a power structure that guides the society as a whole. In South Africa, for example, tribal leaders gain influence partly by appealing to loyalties based on ancient customs and traditions. In attaining a substantial voice in South Africa's political process, they have become members of the country's political elite.

6. Finally, examine the *pathologies of* the state system and its government structures. What elements of the system seem to cause trouble or not to work well? If a state suffers continual revolutions, what are the basic causes? If corruption is widespread, does the state system combat or encourage it? If a society appears to be stable, is there unrest among groups who are excluded from the governing process? The avenues to explore are as numerous as states that you may examine.

Decision-Making Analysis

Game Theory

Politics is not a game like Monopoly, played for fun without serious consequences, nor is it like professional football, in which the objective is merely to prove who has the better team. Politics is, however, a contest with rules. It has winners and losers, tactics and strategies. Politics, as viewed by game theorists, is perhaps similar to poker. How you play the hand you hold is usually more important than the hand itself, and winning depends on your ability to assess what others are likely to do. According to Thomas Schelling, "Game theory is the formal study of the rational, consistent expectations that participants can have about each other's choices" (*Strategy of Conflict*, 1966. New York: Free Press. 75–97). Political science borrowed game theory from economics, where it was used to understand fluctuations in market conditions.

Game theory's contribution to political science is its value in analyzing decisions. The foundation of game theory is rationality. Game theory assumes that people are rational creatures, who will make rational decisions most of the time, and provides a systematic way to understand the options available to someone who needs to make a decision. Most decisions, especially those in international politics, are made without full knowledge of how another nation may respond. Let us consider an example of a decision-making situation to which game theory may apply.

Suppose that France captures an Algerian suspected of being a terrorist and proceeds to place him on trial. Algeria responds by saying that France has no grounds for such actions and threatens to retaliate against French citizens in Algeria if France proceeds with the trial. France has two choices: to place the suspected terrorist on trial or to drop the charges. Algeria has two choices: to take action against French citizens or to take no action. A diagram of these choices may look like the following:

	Algeria's Choices	
	Retaliate	Do Not Retaliate
Try Terrorist	A 0 0	B −1 +1
Do Not Try Terrorist	C 0 −1	D +1 −1

France's Choices

The numbers in the boxes refer to the consequences of the decisions. France's gains and losses are represented by numbers in the lower left of the boxes, and Algeria's gains and losses are represented by numbers in the upper right. The scenario portrayed in box B is that France tries the suspected terrorist, but Algeria does not retaliate. If this happens, France will gain its objective, which is to try the terrorist without suffering retaliation. France's gain is represented by a +1 in the lower left of box B. In this situation, Algeria fails in its objective (to keep the terrorist from being tried) and fails to make good on its threat, so Algeria's failures are represented in box B as a -1. Looking at all boxes one at a time, the whole pattern of likely choices and consequences becomes clear.

Our example of a hypothetical dispute between France and Algeria is rather simple, much more so than actual decisions in international relations. Surprisingly, though, it is for this reason that game theory may be especially helpful in solving problems. Let us suppose that, instead of two viable options, each side to the dispute has five viable options. The game theory matrix would now have twenty-five boxes (5 × 5) instead of four (2 × 2). Many more combinations of results are now possible. Game theory helps analysts in situations like these to thoughtfully, systematically, and thoroughly examine all the combinations of possibilities that they may imagine.

Let us take this analysis one step further. We will label the type of game we are playing a *zero-sum* game, in which there is always a winner and a loser. If two people toss a coin to see who keeps the coin, the results will be heads or tails—one wins and one loses.

In a *zero-difference* game, the parties succeed or fail together. Suppose, for example, that, as Mary and Jane share a ride home from work, they discuss having a picnic lunch in the park the next day. They propose that one of them will bring some sandwich meat and the other will bring a loaf of bread. Mary is in a hurry to pick up her daughter from the day-care center, and as they discuss who will bring the meat and who will bring the bread, they are interrupted. That evening each goes to a different grocery store and realizes that she cannot remember what she is supposed to buy. If Mary buys meat and Jane buys bread, they both "win" the game. If Jane buys meat and Mary buys bread, again they both win. However, if both buy either meat or bread, both lose.

A third type of game is an *inefficient* game. Suppose that, on a hot afternoon, John is driving an air-conditioned taxi that has no radio. Jim's cab has a radio but no air conditioning. John wants to keep driving in his air-conditioned cab except from 1:30 to 2:30, when his favorite jazz program comes on the radio. Jim would like to drive John's air-conditioned cab all the time if he could. If John keeps his air-conditioned cab all afternoon, he will not get to listen to the radio program. If he gives up his air-conditioned cab to listen to the radio, he may not get it back until the next day. If Jim and John can reach an agreement whereby they trade cabs for one hour, both will gain from the exchange. This situation is an inefficient game, however, because the lack of agreement between the two players will definitely result in an inefficient solution, that is, one in which neither gains from the situation.

To write a political analysis paper based on game theory, you will need to know much more about the theory than is presented in this manual. There are several basic steps, however, that may be taken to write an informative game theory paper. The first is to select a decision dilemma in contemporary politics. These dilemmas may be found in your daily newspaper. Not long ago, for example, Ukraine was being pressured to give up its nuclear arms. Its leaders wanted good relations with and economic support from the United States and Russia, which could be gained by giving up those weapons. Many people in Ukraine, however, were distrustful of the Russians and wanted to keep the arms. In this situation, Ukraine had two choices: keep or destroy its weapons. The United States and Russia also had two choices: provide or deny aid. The game diagram for this situation would look like this:

```
                              Choices of
                               Ukraine

                        Keep            Destroy
                       Weapons          Weapons

                     ┌──────────────┬──────────────┐
                     │ A        +2  │ B         +1 │
         Provide     │              │              │
           Aid       │              │              │
                     │              │              │
Choices of the       │ 0            │ +1           │
United States     ───┼──────────────┼──────────────┤
  and Russia         │ C         0  │ D         0  │
                     │              │              │
          Deny       │              │              │
           Aid       │              │              │
                     │ 0            │ +2           │
                     └──────────────┴──────────────┘
```

It is apparent that, in this example, conflict between Ukraine on the one side and the United States and Russia on the other is an inefficient game. If no agreement can be reached, the result will be an inefficient outcome for both sides. Each may win some benefit, however, if some agreement can be reached. After selecting a situation, describe it and its historical development in detail. Then carefully define the options available to each side. Your next step is to construct a game diagram or decision matrix in which each option for one side is compared to each option for the other. From this diagram, draw conclusions about the best and worst choices for both sides. Your final step is to label the games—zero-sum, zero-difference, or inefficient—and explain your classification as well as any insights about the politics that you have gained.

Cybernetics

Cybernetics is the systematic study of human communication. According to Karl Deutsch, the political system is a "self-conscious network" that is continuously self-responsive (Karl W. Deutsch. 1966. *The Nerves of Government.* New York: Free Press. 78). Being self-responsive means that changes in one part of a system lead to adjustments in other parts of the system and to the system as a whole. The key to politics, therefore, is communication. Deutsch compares communications systems in politics to the nervous system in the human body. The communications network within which political decisions are made functions like the eyes, ears, and nose of the corporate political body. Deutsch sees a political system as a "self-modifying communications network," or a "learning net," which he defines as "any system characterized by a relevant degree of organization, communication, and control, regardless of the particular processes by which its messages are transmitted and its functions carried out (78)." Politics cannot be understood by examining only individual human beings and their actions. A nation is most clearly seen as an information network. Information, and not power, as is commonly understood, is thus the essence of politics. Power is an implement of last resort, not an ongoing function of political systems.

What really counts, according to cybernetics, is the process of making, not implementing, decisions, because the relatively small amounts of information utilized in decision making keep massive establishments moving by providing the direction they need. Deutsch compares government to a ship. The decision-making process is like the ship's steering mechanism, which determines the direction the vessel will take. When President Bush and a small group of advisers made decisions during Operation Desert Storm, for example, the three million members of the military and its related civilian agencies moved quickly to carry them out. Messages are the basic units of cybernetic analysis. Political systems often suffer from a kind of selective deafness to messages, caused by excessively rigid ideologies, which are patterns of thinking that exclude certain types of information even though it may be accurate and valid. One of the most famous examples of the effects of rigid ideologies occurred in World War II, when German Chancellor Adolph Hitler, believing that his Aryan armies were inherently superior to Allied forces, commanded his troops to take actions that his generals knew would fail.

The viability of a political system, according to cybernetics, depends on the system's ability to

- Absorb information.
- Process it expeditiously.
- Respond appropriately.
- Evaluate its own response.

Your cybernetics paper should focus on these four variables. In writing your paper, complete the following tasks. First, select a political system to analyze. The system should be one that is primarily responsible for making decisions, and its offices should be directly accessible. A school board, city council, or state legislature, for example, would be an appropriate system. Your second task is to collect information on how the selected organization makes decisions. This will require a series of interviews with the people who work in the organization. As you conduct your interviews, ask questions that will allow you to describe

- The individuals who are responsible for making decisions, including their positions and responsibilities.

- The laws, regulations, and rules that govern making decisions.
- The steps in the normal process through which the organization's decisions are made.
- Three or four actual decisions made by the organization's leadership and the manner in which they were made.

Suppose that the system you select is a city council in a mayor-council form of municipal government. The mayor and members of the council will be the key decision makers, but others, such as the public works director, city clerk, and tax assessor, may also be influential in a broad range of decisions. Following this example, you should examine the city charter, state laws governing municipalities, federal laws and regulations that apply to cities, agreements between the city and other regional governments, such as regional planning commissions, and finally city ordinances. In describing the decision-making process, examine the manner in which issues come before the city council. How are these issues handled once they are made known? What process must they go through to be accepted and acted upon or rejected? How are decisions carried out? Using the types of information described in this example of a cybernetic analysis of a city council, write a description of the decision-making process in the organization you have selected. Your next task is to evaluate the manner in which the institution absorbs, processes, and responds to information, and how it evaluates its own response. Refer to the actual decisions that you described earlier. Examine issues such as the following:

- The thoroughness and efficiency of the process by which information was collected.
- The leadership's openness to information that is relevant to decisions.
- The sufficiency of the information available for making decisions.
- Ideological outlooks among decision makers that may have excluded relevant information.
- The extent of participation in the decision-making process.
- The efficiency of the decision-making process.
- Patterns of influence among decision makers.
- The existence and effectiveness of procedures through which the organization evaluates its own decision-making process.

Having examined these issues, your final step is to draw conclusions about (1) the effectiveness and efficiency of the institution's decision-making process and (2) the strengths and weaknesses (based on your study) of cybernetics as an analytical tool for understanding politics, government, and administration.

14

Policy Analysis Papers

14.1 The Basics of Policy Analysis

What Is Policy Analysis?

Policy analysis is the examination of the components of a decision to enable one to act according to a set principle or rule in a given set of circumstances (a policy). This analysis is conducted at the local, state, national, and international levels of government. The most publicized reports tend, naturally, to be the reports of presidential commissions. Presidents create commissions to do policy analysis: The president appoints a group of people to study possible government policies on a certain topic or problem, and report their findings and recommendations.

Policy Analysis in Action: The Brownlow Commission Report (1937)

Numerous presidential commissions have studied a wide range of subjects, including crime, poverty, and violence. One of the most famous, and one that had far-reaching effects, was the President's Committee on Administrative Management of 1937, known as the Brownlow Commission for one of its three primary authors, Louis Brownlow.

President Roosevelt appointed the Brownlow Commission to find ways to make the operation of the bureaucracy more efficient. The commission found "in the American government at the present time that the effectiveness of the chief executive is limited and restricted; . . . that the work of the executive branch is badly organized; that the managerial agencies are weak and out of date." In response to these problems, the commission made the following five recommendations to the president:

1. To deal with the greatly increased duties of executive management falling on the president, the White House staff should be expanded.
2. The managerial agencies of the government, particularly those dealing with the budget, efficiency research, personnel, and planning, should be greatly strengthened and developed as arms of the chief executive.
3. The merit system should be extended upward, outward, and downward to cover all nonpolicy-determining posts; the civil service system should be reorganized; and opportunities established for a career system attractive to the best talent in the nation.
4. The whole executive branch of the government should be overhauled and the present 100 agencies reorganized under a few large departments in which every executive activity would find its place.
5. The fiscal system should be extensively revised in light of the best governmental and private practice, particularly with reference to financial records, audit, and accountability of the executive to Congress. (President's Committee on Administrative Management, *Administrative Management in the Government of the United States,* January 8, 1937. Washington, D.C.: Government Printing Office. 4.)

14.2 Prelude to Policy Analysis: Policy Analysis Research Proposals

This chapter includes directions for two types of paper assignments: a policy analysis research *proposal* and a policy analysis research *paper.* The proposal is a description of the research that will be conducted during the writing of the research paper. This assignment is included here because students who hope to become policy analysts will find that, when working in or consulting to government organizations, they will almost always be required to submit a proposal explaining and justifying the research that they expect to do before they are commissioned or funded to conduct the research itself.

The Purpose of Research Proposals

Research proposals are sales jobs. Their purpose is to "sell" the belief that a research study needs to be done. Before conducting a policy analysis research study for a government agency, you will need to convince someone in authority that

- The study needs to be written.
- The study will provide helpful information.
- The study will be properly conducted.
- You are qualified to conduct the study.
- The cost of the study will be reasonable in comparison to its benefits.

As part of this "selling" process, you will have to submit a policy analysis research proposal designed to accomplish the following seven tasks:

1. Prove that the study is necessary.
2. Describe the objectives of the study.
3. Explain how the study will be done.
4. Describe the resources (time, people, equipment, facilities, etc.) that will be needed to do the job.
5. Construct a schedule that states when the project will begin and end, and gives important dates in between.
6. Prepare a project budget that specifies the financial costs and the amount to be billed (if any) to the government agency.
7. Carefully define what the research project will produce, what kind of study will be conducted, how long it will be, and what it will contain.

The Content of Research Proposals

An Overview

In form, policy analysis research proposals contain the following four parts:

1. Title page (You may follow the format prescribed by your instructor or institution, or use the format shown in Chapter 3.)
2. Outline page (This is very important and must be done correctly. For directions and an example, see Chapter 3.)
3. Text
4. Reference page

An outline of the content of policy analysis proposals follows:

I. Need for a policy analysis study
   A. An initial description of the current policy problem
      1. A definition of the deficiency in or problem with the current policy
      2. A brief history of the policy problem
      3. The legal framework and institutional setting of the policy problem
      4. The character of the policy problem, including its size, extent, and importance
   B. Policy analysis imperatives
      1. The probable costs of taking no action
      2. The expected benefits of a policy analysis study

  II. Objectives of the proposed policy analysis study
      A. Clarification of the current policy problem
          1. A better problem definition
          2. A better estimate of the quality and quantity of the problem
          3. A more accurate projection of policy problem development
      B. An accurate evaluation of current relevant public policy
          1. An evaluation of the primary current applicable public policy
              a. A clarification of the primary policy
              b. A clarification of the legal foundation of the primary policy
              c. A clarification of the historical development of the policy
              d. A clarification of the environment of the policy
              e. A description of current policy implementation
              f. An evaluation of the effectiveness and efficiency of the policy
          2. An evaluation of secondary applicable public policies
      C. An evaluation of alternatives to present policies
          1. A presentation of possible alternative policies
          2. A comparative evaluation of the expected costs and benefits of the present and alternative policies
 III. Methodology of the proposed policy analysis study
      A. Project management methods to be used
      B. Research methods to be used
      C. Data analysis methods to be used
  IV. Resources necessary to conduct the study
      A. Material resources
      B. Human resources
      C. Financial resources
   V. Schedule for the policy analysis study
  VI. Budget for the policy analysis study
 VII. Product of the policy analysis study

The Text of Research Proposals

    The text of a policy analysis research proposal contains the following seven elements:

    1. An explanation of the need for the study
    2. A description of the objectives of the study
    3. An explanation of the methods that will be used to conduct the study
    4. A list of the human, material, and financial resources needed to conduct the study
    5. A project schedule
    6. A project budget
    7. A description of the anticipated product of the study

    An Explanation of the Need for the Study.   Have you ever listened to an automobile salesperson who is trying to sell a car to someone? The first thing the salesperson will usually ask a customer, after getting the customer's name, is

"What kind of a vehicle do you *need*?" Perhaps she will follow up that question with "How many people are in your family?" and then say something like "It seems that you *need* a large vehicle." The good salesperson will not stop this line of questioning until she finds that the customer has agreed on some statement of need. The first objective of a research proposal involves a similar tactic: to demonstrate that the person for whom it will be written needs the information that the policy analysis will contain because he is faced with one or more problems that his present policies are inadequate to handle. Start your proposal, therefore, with a clearly written statement of need. Suppose that you believe, for example, that the current policy of the Springfield Board of Education is inadequate for visually impaired children. Your statement of need might be constructed like this:

> According to reports from school administrators, the Springfield Board of Education's policy on provision of supplemental services for the visually impaired (a policy that provides only for minimal services) leaves some district children without sufficient resources to complete their secondary education.

This statement clearly indicates a need for review of the district's policy. Your need statement should be comprehensive enough and clear enough to impress people immediately that a definite need exists.

The Policy Problem and the Policy Deficiency.   Statements of need in policy analysis proposals should clearly identify both a specific *policy problem* and a specific *policy deficiency*. A policy problem is a problem that a public policy is supposed to solve. A policy problem occurs when there is a deficiency in a public policy that is caused by a problem independent of that policy. The policy of the Springfield Board of Education (minimal services) is deficient because it does not solve a *problem* (some children are visually impaired). In this case, the policy did not create the problem. The policy is deficient, however, because it does not solve the actual problem. The *policy problem* is the visual impairment of some of the students. The *policy deficiency* is the fact that the current policy does not solve the problem of visual impairment, which in turn means that the district's goal of providing a secondary education to all district children cannot be achieved.

Research Imperatives.   If a study is *imperative,* it must be done. Not every need that an organization has will be called an imperative, because there are always more needs than can be met. Every successful organization, however, meets those needs that are imperative and leaves some of the ones that are not imperative unfulfilled, at least temporarily. If your proposal merely states a need, the people to whom you are writing may decide that meeting the need you have identified is not imperative and thus may choose not to proceed with the study. A good proposal therefore includes a statement of research imperatives to impress people with the necessity of the proposed study.

To continue our example, policy imperatives for the problem of visual impairment may include the argument that the school district, if it does not change its policy, may

- Fail to meet its fundamental obligation to the children involved.
- Fail to meet the community's need for educated, self-sufficient citizens.
- Fail to meet state and federal standards for education.

When formulating a statement of policy imperatives, it is vital to follow two principles:

1. Make a strong case that the research is imperative.
2. Be completely accurate and honest: Do not overstate your case.

A Description of the Objectives of the Study.   Think about the person for whom you are writing your research proposal. As we have noted, the first question this person will ask when presented with a proposal for a full research study is "Why do I need this study?" After you have answered this question, the person will ask, "What will this study do for me?" In your answer you should state, in general terms, that the proposed study will

1. More clearly define the problem.
2. Identify deficiencies in the present policy.
3. Examine different ways of overcoming these deficiencies.
4. Recommend the most promising solution.

Problem Clarification.   Your policy analysis research proposal will include an initial definition and explanation of the problem, but because you have not yet investigated the policy problem in detail, it will not provide a sufficiently clear picture of its character and extent. Your proposal should therefore explain that the policy analysis study will further clarify and examine the nature and size of the problem. In our continuing example, your proposal should state something like the following:

> The proposed policy analysis research study will clarify and quantify the policy problem: visual impairment among district schoolchildren. The study will (1) determine the exact number of children in the district who experience some form of visual impairment and (2) determine the form and extent of impairment that each of these children has.

Your proposal should now briefly explain how these tasks will be carried out. Using the above example, you will want to explain whether the children will be tested for degree of visual impairment or whether you will rely on school records to determine the status of each child.

Evaluation of Current Policy.   Your proposal will then tell its readers that your study will thoroughly examine current relevant policy. For our Springfield Board of Education example, you should write something like the following:

> The proposed policy analysis research study will evaluate the extent to which the Springfield District's current policy meets and fails to meet the needs of children with visual impairment.

You must now explain how you will carry out this task, giving a general idea of the criteria you will use to evaluate the current policy.

Comparative Evaluation of Political Alternatives.   The major purpose of a policy research study is to examine ways of solving a current policy problem. If the present policy does not work, what others might do a better job? Your proposal will promise to conduct an evaluation of alternative policies. Following our example, you might say something like this:

> The proposed policy analysis research study will identify and evaluate alternatives to the present policy. It will list the comparative advantages and disadvantages of each policy option.

Follow this statement with a brief description of some of the alternatives that you may evaluate in the actual policy analysis study.

Presentation of Recommendations.   Your policy analysis study may or may not actually recommend a specific solution to the problem. You should determine whether to include a policy recommendation by asking the person to whom the proposal is being submitted, before it is submitted, if she wants a recommendation included. Her answer will depend on a number of political considerations specific to her particular circumstances. Many public policy issues are decided not on the basis of the technical merits but on political motives. The decision of whether to build a stadium for sporting events or an auditorium for theater and ballet, for example, will probably depend more on who supports sports and who supports ballet than on the technical advantages of one facility over the other. *Do not assume that you know whether a recommendation should be included.* Always ask. If the answer is affirmative, you may state something like this:

> Based on an examination of the comparative advantages and disadvantages of each option, the proposed study will recommend the adoption of a specific policy.

An Explanation of the Methods of the Study.   By this time, the person to whom you are submitting your proposal may be impressed with the precision, if not the length, of your answers. She will still want to know, however, "How do you propose to do all this?" At this point you explain your methodology—the steps you will take in conducting your analysis. They will include, as a minimum, collecting and analyzing information and presenting it in a form that people can understand.

Research Process and Methods.   Your research proposal will briefly describe the steps you will take to find, evaluate, and draw conclusions from the information that is pertinent to your study. The research process normally proceeds in three steps:

1. Data (information) collection: gathering the appropriate information.
2. Data analysis: organizing the data and determining its meaning or implications.
3. Data evaluation: determining what conclusions may be drawn from the data.

In your proposal you should (1) state that you intend to carry out these three steps and (2) explain briefly how you intend to do them. Returning to our Springfield Board of Education example, your research proposal will say something like this:

The proposed policy analysis research study will (1) review the visual test records of the district's children, (2) using standards set by the American Optometric Association, determine from these records how many children experience visual impairment and to what extent they are impaired, and (3) using standards recommended by the American Optometric Association, determine the materials and equipment necessary to educate each child.

Quality Control.   Quality control is a formal procedure to ensure that a product meets all relevant standards and is free of defects. It is an important part of the development of any product, including a policy analysis report. In policy analysis, quality control is normally provided by experts, that is, people who have years of experience in dealing with the problem at hand. Your proposal should (1) state that quality control will be provided for the study and (2) explain how it will be provided. Following our example, a proposal might say something like this:

> Dr. William Wareham of Northeast Central University and Dr. Lila Gray of the American Optometric Association will provide quality control for the proposed study by reviewing the methods and results of the research.

A List of Resources Needed to Conduct the Study.   Finally, the person who has commissioned your study will want to know how much money, time, and other resources it will demand. This section of a proposal is most important in scientific or engineering studies, where extensive experimentation or design work is carried out. For most policy analysis studies, this section may be brief, although it should describe the material and human resources that will be necessary to conduct the study. Following our Springfield example, your proposal may say,

> Conducting the proposed study will require the use of a computer with an integrated word processing data management software program. Paper for report production and reproduction equipment for making copies of the report will also be needed. The principal investigator possesses the necessary computer equipment and will contract for copy services.

The study will require the following human resources:

- A principal investigator familiar with policy and data analysis techniques.
- Two quality control advisers, one of whom is familiar with the standards of the American Optometric Association and another who is familiar with policy analysis research methods.
- A research assistant who is capable of entering data from school forms into the computer.

A Project Schedule.   You should include in the proposal a research schedule that states the following:

- When the project will begin
- When the major phases of the project will begin and end

- When any preliminary, interim, or final reports will be issued
- When any special events in the research or analysis process will occur
- When the project will end

   A Project Budget.   A project budget is the next section to be included in a research proposal. The budget will normally be divided into the following categories:

- Materials (paper, computer disks, supplies, etc.)
- Facilities (conference rooms, places with special capabilities, etc.)
- Equipment (laboratory supplies, copy machines, computers, etc.)
- Travel
- Personnel

For each category, list the items needed and their cost. In the personnel section you should list each person or position separately, the rate of pay, and the total cost per person.

   A Description of the Anticipated Product of the Study.   In the final section of the proposal, you will describe the anticipated product of your study. In other words, you will tell the persons for whom you are writing the proposal exactly what they will receive when the project is done. If you are writing this paper for a class in public policy analysis, you will probably write something like the following:

> The final product will be a policy analysis research study from twenty-five to thirty pages in length that will provide an analysis of the policy problem and an evaluation of alternative new policies that may solve the problem.

14.3 Policy Analysis Papers

Definition: A Policy Analysis Paper

   A policy analysis paper evaluates a decision by reviewing current and potential government policies. It is a document written to help decision makers select the best policy for solving a particular problem. In writing a policy analysis paper, you should

1. Select and clearly define a specific government policy.
2. Carefully define the social, governmental, economic, or other problem the policy is designed to solve.
3. Describe the economic, social, and political environments in which the problem arose and in which the existing policy for solving the problem was developed.
4. Evaluate the effectiveness of the current policy or lack of policy in dealing with the problem.

5. Identify alternative policies that could be adopted to solve the selected problem, and estimate the economic, social, environmental, and political cost and benefits of each alternative.
6. Provide a summary comparison of all policies examined.

Policy analysis papers are written every day at all levels of government. Public officials are constantly challenged to initiate new policies or change old ones. They want to know how effective their current policy is, if they have a formal policy at all. They then want to know what options are available to them, what changes they might make to improve current policy, and what the consequences of those changes will be. Policies are reviewed under a number of circumstances. Policy analyses are sometimes conducted as part of the normal agency budgeting processes. They help decision makers decide what policies should be continued or discontinued. They may be very narrow in scope, such as deciding the hours of operation of facilities at city parks. Or they may be very broad, such as deciding how the nation will provide health care or defense for its citizens.

The Purpose of Policy Analysis Papers

Successful policy analysis papers all share the same general purpose and the same general objective. The objective of a policy analysis paper is to inform policy makers about how public policy in a specific area may be improved.

Elected officials are employed full time in the business of making public policy. Legislators at the state and national levels hire staff people who continually investigate public policy issues and seek ways to improve legislated policy. At the national level, the Congressional Research Service continually finds information for representatives and senators. Each committee of Congress employs staff members who help it review current laws and define options for making new ones. State legislatures also employ their own research agencies and committee staff. Legislators and other policy makers are also given policy information by hundreds of public interest groups and research organizations.

A policy analysis paper, like a position paper, is an entirely practical exercise. It is neither theoretical nor general. Its objective is to identify and evaluate the policy options that are available for a specific topic.

The Contents of a Policy Analysis Paper

Summary of the Contents

Policy analysis papers contain six basic elements:

1. Title page
2. Executive summary
3. Table of contents, including a list of tables and illustrations
4. Text (or body)

5. References to sources of information
6. Appendixes

Parameters of the Text

Ask your instructor for the number of pages required for the policy analysis paper assigned for your course. Such papers at the undergraduate level often range from twenty to fifty pages (double-spaced, typed) in length.

Two general rules govern the amount of information presented in the body of the paper. First, content must be adequate to make a good policy evaluation. All the facts necessary to understand the significant strengths and weaknesses of a policy and its alternatives must be included in the paper. If your paper omits a fact that is critical to the decision, a poor decision will likely be made.

Never omit important facts merely because they tend to support a perspective other than your own. It is your responsibility to present the facts as clearly as possible, not to bias the evaluation in a particular direction.

The second guideline for determining the length of a policy analysis paper is to omit extraneous material. Include only the information that is helpful in making the particular decision at hand.

The Format of a Policy Analysis Paper

Title Page

The title page for a policy analysis paper should follow the format provided in Chapter 3.

Executive Summary

A one-page, single-spaced executive summary immediately follows the title page. An executive summary is composed of carefully written sentences expressing the central concepts that are more fully explained in the text of the paper. The purpose of the summary is to allow the decision maker to understand, as quickly as possible, the major considerations to be discussed. Each statement must be clearly defined and carefully prepared. The decision maker should be able to get a thorough and clear overview of the entire policy problem and the value and costs of available policy options by reading nothing but the one-page summary.

Table of Contents

The table of contents of a policy analysis paper must follow the organization of the paper's text and should conform to the format shown in Chapter 3.

The Text of a Policy Analysis Paper

An Overview

The text, or body, of the paper should contain five kinds of information:

1. A description of the policy to be analyzed.
2. A description of the social, physical, economic, and political (including legal and institutional) environments in which the policy has been or will be developed.
3. An evaluation of the effectiveness and efficiency of the current policy.
4. An evaluation of alternatives to the current policy.
5. A summary comparison of policy options.

A policy analysis paper should follow this outline:

I. Policy description
   A. A clear, concise statement of the policy
   B. A brief history of the policy
   C. A description of the problem the policy was aimed at resolving, including an estimate of its extent and importance
II. Policy environment
   A. A description of the social and physical factors affecting the origin, development, and implementation of the policy
   B. A description of the economic factors affecting the origin, development, and implementation of the policy
   C. A description of the political factors affecting the origin, development, and implementation of the policy
III. Effectiveness and efficiency of the current policy
   A. How well the existing policy does what it was designed to do
   B. How well the policy performs in relation to the effort and resources committed to it
IV. Policy alternatives
   A. Possible alterations of the present policy, with the estimated costs and benefits of each
   B. Alternatives to the present policy, with the estimated costs and benefits of each
V. Summary comparison of policy options

Policy Description

The first task of a policy paper is to describe the policy that currently exists to allow the reader to understand the present situation and how it developed. Policy descriptions contain three basic elements. The first is a clear and concise statement of the policy selected. You may find that there is no written policy on the subject under consideration. If this is the case, you should first state the lack of a written policy on the subject, and then list and describe any policies that may indirectly affect the problem. For example, a school district may have no policy that explicitly addresses destructive gang activities, but it may have policies on acceptable attire in school, rules of order in the classroom, and so on.

When written formal policies exist, quote them directly from the documents that state them, and provide the source of the quotation. If the policy is established under the authority of more general legislation, quote and cite the legislation also. For example, an Indiana law may state that "school districts may establish appropriate rules of behavior and guidelines for suspension or expulsion for violations of these rules." The public schools of the city of Indianapolis, then, may have a regulation that says that "students shall not wear clothing that unduly distracts or offends other students." Further, a particular school principal may have a policy that "shirts without sleeves shall not be worn in class during school hours except when participating in athletic activities." In these three examples we find three levels of public policy, all leading to a specific guideline applied in a specific school. Preparing a complete description of the policy at hand is very important if your analysis of the problem is to be accurate and beneficial.

The second part of this section of your policy analysis paper should include a brief history of the policy. Several basic questions should be answered here:

- When was the existing policy initiated?
- How did it come about?
- In response to what problem or need did it come about?
- What effects did the policy have?

The third part of this section is a careful description of the problem the policy was aimed at resolving, including an estimate of its extent and importance. If the policy being examined is a school's dress code, estimate the number of students who have violated the code and the seriousness of the violations. These estimates are crucial for proper policy formulation. For example, suppose that a school district has 18,000 students. If six students at one high school are wearing fluorescent shorts, then the problem is relatively minor. But if 200 students come to school wearing neo-Nazi insignia, a vastly more difficult problem has arisen. You need to provide the reader with an accurate assessment of the extent of the problem.

Policy Environment

No policy exists in a vacuum. Legislators, governors, and presidents do not sit in ivory towers cut off from the real world, and if they act as if they do, they are likely to pay a heavy political price. Policies almost always arise from genuine needs, but they often reflect the needs of one part of the population more than those of others. Policy is formulated within a number of environments, the most important of which are the following:

- The social environment: the cultural, ethnic, religious, and other habits, practices, expectations, and patterns of relating to one another that every society establishes.

- The physical environment: the climate, architecture, topography, natural resources, and other physical features that shape the patterns of life in a society.

- The economic environment: the content and vitality of a society's economic life, including the type of industry and commerce, the relative wealth or poverty of the area affected by the policy, the unemployment rate, the rate of economic growth, and so on.

- The political environment: the government structures, applicable laws, political parties, prevalent ideologies, and salient issues of the day.

The policy paper should include separate discussions of the social, physical, economic, and political environments affecting policy development, giving different amounts of attention to each one according to its relative importance to the policy being discussed. A school dress code policy, for example, may be much more responsive to the social and economic environments than to the physical or political environments in a community. A dress code will probably be influenced by the ethnic diversity or homogeneity of the neighborhood around the school.

Policy Effectiveness

An evaluation of policy effectiveness should tell the reader how well a specific policy does what it is intended to do. There are many methods for evaluating effectiveness and many factors that could be used in the analysis. This chapter will not explain these methods, but they may be found in any basic text on policy analysis. Instead of explaining the wide array of policy evaluation methods, this chapter will describe the basic steps that must be taken to complete any evaluation. *Ask your instructor for specific directions or methods for policy evaluation in your course.* The general explanation provided here may not be sufficient for the analysis paper that you are assigned.

The evaluation of policy effectiveness proceeds in three steps:

1. Constructing an evaluation framework
2. Applying the framework to the policy being examined
3. Drawing conclusions from your application

The first step in policy evaluation is to establish an evaluation framework, which starts with a clearly defined policy to be evaluated. The framework then adds to the policy definition lists of (1) the general goals the policy is designed to meet, (2) the specific objectives that lead to achievement of the goals, (3) criteria for judging the extent to which the objectives are met, and (4) specific measurements for quantifying the fulfillment of the criteria.

To construct an evaluation framework,

- Define the general goals for which the policy was made. The goal of a policy limiting the number of continuous hours that may be flown by an airline pilot, for example, is to keep air travel safe for passengers. Sometimes goals have been defined by the policy-making body that issues the policy. If not, attempt to determine the goals through other means, such as interviews or research.

- Define specific objectives, or steps, that indicate partial accomplishment of the goals. If the goal of the Federal Aviation Administration is to make air travel safe for passengers, for example, an objective might be to improve landing and takeoff conditions at major airports.

- Define specific criteria for determining the extent to which the objectives are met, If the objective is to improve landing and takeoff conditions at major airports, then criteria for determining the quality of these conditions need to be determined. Such criteria might be the surface condition of runways, air traffic congestion, and the capacity and accuracy of air traffic control equipment. Establishing the proper evaluation criteria is one of the most difficult and important tasks in writing a policy analysis paper. *Ask the instructor to help you determine the evaluation criteria for your policy analysis paper.*

- Define specific measurements for applying the criteria to the objectives. If a criterion for good landing and takeoff conditions is the amount of air traffic congestion, then valid measurements might include the number of (1) flights per hour, (2) potential collision incidents, and (3) landing or takeoff delays.

After establishing your framework, use the measurements you have designed to make as many quantitative evaluations as the subject will allow. You may also need to make qualitative evaluations for those criteria that you could find no way to quantify.

You may now take your final step: drawing conclusions from your measurements. A good general practice is to be conservative, interpreting the data to indicate only what they clearly demonstrate—not tendencies or implications that still need more proof.

Policy Efficiency

Efficiency goes a step beyond effectiveness. Efficiency relates cost to accomplishment; it is concerned not only with how well a job is done, but also with the amount of resources committed to getting the job done. In other words, when one inquires about the efficiency of a policy, one is asking, "How well did the policy perform in relation to the effort and resources committed to it?" A program to reduce the number of potential air collisions may require the expenditure of $2 million. If it reduces the number of potential collisions by one thousand, then the efficiency of the program may be expressed in terms of the cost-per-potential-collision ratio, or $2,000 per potential collision.

Evaluating efficiency is often more difficult than it appears. The most important factor in producing a valid efficiency evaluation is selecting the proper factors to place in the ratio. For example, to evaluate the efficiency of a school arts program, one may divide the number of dollars in the annual budget (perhaps $10 million) by the number of students who complete the program (perhaps 5,000). The resulting figure would be $2,000 per student. This figure does not, however, provide any information about the quality of education that the students received. It is therefore a limited measure of efficiency. When writing your policy analysis paper, try to construct an efficiency ratio for the measurements you have made. Be very careful, however, to point out the limitations of the ratio you construct.

Policy Alternatives

As the author of a policy analysis paper, you want to be effective in clearly analyzing a policy and in assisting a public official in improving it. Having clearly defined the deficiencies in the present policy, the next question you will ask is "What can be done about them?" One of the most common mistakes of students who write policy analysis papers is their failure to answer this question correctly. To define options is to describe different approaches to solving the problem, *not* to describe several measures that are all combined in one approach. *Options in policy analysis papers are different, mutually exclusive approaches to a problem. If one alternative is selected, the others are rejected.* Sometimes students mistake the steps necessary to complete one course of action for distinct, separate approaches to the problem. If student Jones is studying urban transportation policy, she may list the following alternatives:

Option A: Demonstrate present traffic congestion.
Option B: Draw up plans for a new subway system.
Option C: Generate funds and state legislative support for the subway system.
Option D: Construct the subway system in five phases over a ten-year period.

All four "options" are actually only four steps in carrying out one option (building a subway). Again, *steps toward a single solution are not options.* An actual set of options for solving the problem of traffic congestion might be

Option A: Continue present policy of encouraging car pooling.
Option B: Plan and construct a new subway system.
Option C: Expand bus service.
Option D: Build additional freeways.

Conducting a Simplified Benefit-Cost Analysis. For each available option, you should first describe its benefits and then its costs. Benefits are the positive outcomes expected. Costs include the time, money, and resources to be spent and the probable or possible negative outcomes (known as "disbenefits"). Both benefits and costs may include economic, social, political, and environmental factors. Benefits of improving the public transportation system may include, for example,

1. Less traffic congestion.
2. Safety.
3. Decreased air pollution.
4. Increased economic development.
5. Increased convenience.

Costs of improving the transportation system may include

1. Construction costs of many millions of dollars.
2. Fewer resources for other community projects.
3. Political opposition from areas in the community not benefited directly.

As mentioned, all reasonable costs and benefits should be included in the paper. Never exclude possible costs or benefits of any one option in order to make another appear more or less attractive. Remember that the policy analysis paper will be submitted to someone who is responsible for making the proper decision. If an option other than the one recommended is selected and full information has been provided, the writer of the paper has acted appropriately. Elected and appointed officials may legitimately choose options that are technically not the most cost-effective. But if a policy maker selects the wrong option based on incomplete information in the policy analysis paper, the writer of the paper is clearly responsible.

Lengthy books have been written on how to conduct benefit-cost analyses. Only a simplified (but still very helpful) process will be outlined here. To analyze benefits and costs, always use the same set of steps for each option. First, list the benefits and then the costs of that option. Next, assign a monetary value to each cost and benefit. Such estimates should be made according to the advice of experts, who usually include government officials, engineers, consultants, or members of private organizations with expertise in the area. Price estimates for construction costs, for example, may be obtained from engineers in local, state, or national government agencies. Personnel cost estimates may be determined by multiplying the number of person-hours or -days by the cost per hour or day for the services desired.

Some costs are more difficult to estimate. Intangible items such as "political discontent" are not easily quantified, yet an attempt may reasonably be made to do so. Public policy analysts call such estimates *compensating variations*. A compensating variation allows analysts to place a dollar value on intangible factors for comparison purposes. The dollar value of an intangible cost is the amount that the average person would normally accept as fair compensation for having paid a particular cost or endured a particular disbenefit.

An example is in order. Suppose that Mrs. Williams lives in a quiet residential neighborhood. A shopping center is planned at the end of her street, which will increase the traffic and noise near her home. Mrs. Williams is unhappy about the proposed shopping center. If asked whether she would prefer that it not be built, she would answer affirmatively. But suppose that Mrs. Williams were offered this choice: (1) no shopping center will be built; or (2) the shopping center will be built, and Mrs. Williams will be paid $100. Mrs. Williams may still prefer alternative 1. Suppose now that the offer is increased to $1,000. Mrs. Williams might then choose to have the money and the shopping center rather than have neither the money nor the shopping center. The compensating variation in this case would be the amount that Mrs. Williams would be willing to accept as fair compensation for the distress caused her by the shopping center. The social cost of building the shopping center may then be calculated as the sum of the compensating variations of the residents to be adversely affected by the project.

Remember that all such estimates can be placed before the judgment of the people who will read the paper. Estimates need be neither exact nor perfect. It is important to realize that someone must make a policy decision, and that a reasonable estimate of its costs and benefits is more helpful than no estimate at all.

Economists and urban planners have long known that attitudes affect development potential. Beliefs about the strength of the economy, for example, have a direct, daily effect on stock exchanges. Popular discontent makes it less likely that people will find a neighborhood a desirable place to live. To estimate discontent as a compensating variation in a decision to make improvements in a community park, a brief survey of popular attitudes would be necessary. Telephone calls to the fifteen homes closest to the park would yield several interviews with homeowners. Asking a few simple, open-ended questions would make it possible to estimate the strength of sentiment about the park. It makes a major difference to the study whether one or two people are mildly concerned or whether fifteen families are planning to move immediately if the park improvements are not made. Mild discontent might be assigned no economic value ($0), whereas widespread strong feelings might make the neighborhood so undesirable that property values would decline by 25 percent (a total of $328,125) if improvements are not made. Both extremes are unlikely, but one can see that it is possible to put a rough value estimate on popular discontent.

In the recommendation section of your paper, a summary of benefit-cost analyses for all alternatives should be presented in table form, followed by a paragraph or two of explanatory comparisons. The table for student Jones's paper on urban transportation policy might look like this:

BENEFIT-COST ANALYSIS SUMMARY

ALTERNATIVE	BENEFIT	COST
Car pooling	Low disruption ($.5 million)	Publicity ($4,000)
Subway	Convenience, economic development ($8 billion over 20 years)	Construction ($4.5 billion)
More buses	Quick installation ($2 million)	Purchase ($3.2 million)
Freeways	Popular ($100 million)	Construction ($750 million)

References

All sources of information in a policy analysis paper must be properly cited, following the directions in Chapter 4.

Appendixes

Appendixes can provide the reader of policy analysis papers with information that supplements the important facts contained in the text. For many local development and public works projects, a map and a diagram are often very helpful appendixes. You should attach them to the end of the paper, after the reference page. You should not append entire government reports, journal articles, or other publications, but selected charts, graphs, or other pages may be included. The source of the information should always be evident on the appended pages.

15

Administrative Case Studies

When Yale University political scientist Herbert Kaufman wrote his preface to *The Forest Ranger: A Study in Administrative Behavior* in June 1959, it is unlikely that he expected his volume to set the standard for case studies in public administration for decades to come. Even forty years later, after the study of administration has incorporated many insights from economics, psychology, sociology, and other fields, Kaufman's work has much to tell us about the dynamics of public organizations and about how a case study should be written. He wanted to know more about bureaucracy, the institutions that carry out the policies formulated by the president and Congress. He wanted to know more about how public agencies work and what makes them effective or ineffective. He believed that a better understanding of the practice of administration would lead to more effective and efficient administrative practices. He selected the U.S. Forest Service to study in depth because of its reputation for effectiveness and efficiency. He set out to find out if the reputation was warranted and, if so, why. In his preface, Kaufman says:

> It is the reader curious about the often neglected relationship between the broad pronouncements at the top levels and the day-to-day activities of those who perform the physical tasks of an agency for whom this volume may hold some interest. Field compliance in the Forest Service is not total, naturally, but it is so high, despite powerful factors tending to reduce compliance, that it cries out for study. The effort to describe the way it is obtained is essentially an effort to capture that elusive phenomenon, "what actually happens in an organization." . . . The Rangers at the base of the administrative pyramid are subjected to influences pulling and pushing them in many different directions, yet they are held together; the restricted but difficult goal of this report is to explain this integration by identifying and describing the factors at work and the interplay among these factors. (Herbert Kaufman. 1960. *The Forest Ranger: A Study in Administrative Behavior.* Baltimore: Johns Hopkins. xi–xii, 6.)

Kaufman had two goals in writing *The Forest Ranger.* The first was to understand in general terms how public organizations work. The second was to find out more specifically why the Forest Rangers, who are dispersed geographically and seem to enjoy much more independence than other government employees, appear to follow administrative direction from their superiors more carefully and willingly than workers in other agencies. In pursuit of these objectives, Kaufman studied the Forest Service from top to bottom—its structure, rules, procedures, and personnel. He reviewed many documents and conducted numerous interviews. The insights he gained helped him to come to some interesting conclusions. For example, Kaufman notes that

> one of the most striking conclusions about the Forest Service is the degree of similarity among the men in it—their love of outdoor life; their pride in the Forest Service; their habit of taking the long view of things; their patience; their acknowledgment of their obligations to the local users of the national forests, and . . . the national interest as against local or special interest; their enjoyment of the variety in Ranger district administration as compared with the narrower scope of industrial forestry; their willingness to do more than is legally required of them in order to get their jobs done. (206–207)

In his case study of the Forest Service, Kaufman

- Selects a particular agency to study.
- Formulates a general goal: to better understand how government works.
- Selects a specific objective: to explain the apparent paradox of the agency's cohesion in the face of many forces working toward fragmentation.
- Describes in general terms the Forest Service and how it operates, and the job of the Forest Ranger.
- Identifies tendencies toward fragmentation in the Service.
- Identifies the techniques of integration used to overcome the tendencies toward fragmentation.
- Draws conclusions about his findings that help to explain how government agencies in general and the Forest Service in particular work.

In your administrative case study, you will perform the same basic tasks that Kaufman completed so well in *The Forest Ranger.*

15.1 The Definition and Purpose of Administrative Case Studies

Definition

An administrative case study is a written description and explanation of some aspect of a government agency's operation. It does not attempt to explain everything there is to know about a government organization. *The Forest Ranger* examined in detail only the fragmenting and unifying tendencies of the Forest Service, and yet Kaufman's book had 259 pages. Case studies may focus on a policy, person, problem, tendency, or characteristic of a public organization.

Case studies have long been used in law schools, where the development of the law is learned through reading the decisions in many court cases. Business schools began to develop administrative case studies to help students understand actual management situations. Courses in public administration adopt the case study method as a primary teaching tool less often than business or law schools, although it has become more common.

Case studies are often found in one of two forms. The first might be called a *didactic* case study, for it is written for use in a classroom. It describes a situation or problem in an administrative setting, but performs no analysis and draws no conclusions. Instead of providing an analysis, it normally lists questions for the student to consider and then answer either individually or in class discussion. This sort of case study allows for teacher evaluation of student analysis skills and, if it is discussed in class, provides students with an opportunity to compare their ideas with those of other students.

The second type, an *analytical* case study, is like *The Forest Ranger*. It provides not only a case description but an analysis as well. The paper that you will write for a political science class will be an analytical administrative case study. This case study, in which you will both describe and analyze an actual administrative case, should have the following features:

- A general goal of contributing to an understanding of how government works.
- An audience focus, in which your paper will be clearly directed toward those for whom it is written. When writing administrative case studies, your audience consists of

    1. The course instructor, who wants you to analyze carefully and insightfully and to write well.
    2. College students who study administration to improve their chances of success in careers in public administration.
    3. Others who are interested in improving their understanding of administration in order to become better administrators.

- An agency focus and a general description of the agency selected for study, which may be local, intrastate regional, state, interstate regional, national, or international. Regardless of the agency chosen, make sure that its personnel are directly accessible to you for interviews.
- A topic focus and a description of how it has developed within the selected agency. If your topic focus is recruitment problems and your agency focus is a municipal police department, for example, you will describe how the recruitment problems evolved within the overall operations of the police department.
- An analysis of the causes of the topic focus within the agency in which it occurs.
- Conclusions about your analysis, including the implications of your study for public administration in general.

Purpose

Case studies fulfill many objectives in public administration education. As a student in a political science course, you will write a case study to improve your ability to

- Analyze information carefully and objectively.
- Solve problems effectively.
- Present your ideas in clear, written form, directed to a specific audience.

In addition, the experience you gain in investigating the case study will allow you to see some of the problems you will face if you become a public administrator and help you to understand

- Some of the possibilities and problems of administration in general.
- The operation of a particular government agency, including problems peculiar to public agencies as opposed to business.
- The development of a particular problem within a government agency.
- The interrelationships of people, structures, rules, politics, administrative styles, and many other factors within a particular setting.

15.2 Limitations of the Case Study Method

Before writing a case study, it is helpful to be aware of the limitations of the methods you will be using in order to avoid drawing conclusions that are not justified by the knowledge you will acquire. First, you should note that case studies are relatively subjective exercises. When you write a case study, you select the facts and arrange them into patterns from which you may draw conclusions. The quality of the case study will depend in large part on the quality of the facts you select and the way you interpret them. Second, every case study, no matter how well written, is in some sense an oversimplification of the events that are described and the environment within which they take place. To simplify an event or series of events at once makes it easier to understand and distorts its effect and importance. Finally, interpretations that are constructed during classroom discussion, no matter how astute or sincere, may not be applicable to an actual administrative situation.

15.3 Writing an Administrative Case Study

Overview

Writing an administrative case study in political science entails a small number of basic tasks, but each one requires considerable work and thought. The three basic tasks are

- Selecting a focus.
- Conducting interviews and collecting documents.
- Writing.

These three activities are not sequential, however. In fact, you may find yourself doing all three simultaneously. While you are conducting interviews you will be refining your topic focus, and when you are taking notes during the interview you will have begun the writing process.

Selecting a Topic

You should have a personal interest in the agency and the subject that you study. In selecting a topic, you are looking for a situation that is likely to provide some interesting insights about public administration. There are two ways to begin your search. The first is to contact a government agency involved with a matter that interests you and then inquire about recent events. If, for example, you are interested in the environment, you could contact a local office of the Environmental Protection Agency or another national, state, or local environmental agency. Tell the person who answers the phone that you are a student who wants to write a course paper about that agency and ask to talk to someone who can explain the organization's current programs. Ask for an appointment for an interview with the person to whom you are referred. When you arrive for the interview, tell the agency official that you are interested in doing a case study on some aspect of the agency's operations and that your purpose is to better understand how government agencies operate. Then ask a series of questions designed to help you find a topic to pursue. These questions might include the following:

> What recent successes has your agency had?
> What is the greatest challenge facing your agency at the moment?
> What are some of the agency's goals for this year?
> What are some of the obstacles to meeting these goals?

You should keep asking questions until you identify a situation in the agency that appears to be appropriate. Consider the following possibilities:

- A social service agency faces budget cuts, and the director may decide among competing political pressures which services to recommend to the governor for reduction.

- A transportation agency faces a reorganization.
- A business regulatory commission receives criticism from utilities for denying a rate increase.
- A school superintendent initiates a strict disciplinary policy.

Another way to select a topic is to find an article of interest in your local newspaper. Hardly a day goes by that a suitable topic does not appear. The successes, failures, challenges, and mistakes of government agencies are always in the news. The benefit of finding a topic in the newspaper is that, when you contact the agency involved, you will already have a subject to discuss. The disadvantage is that, on some publicized topics, government officials may be reluctant to provide detailed information.

The Importance of Interviews

The goal of your first interview is to obtain enough information to request a series of other interviews in which you will ask questions that will allow you to understand the course of events and the agency interactions that resulted in the situation you are studying. Remember that you are writing a story that must be accurate and factual. Do not accept the first version of a course of events that you hear. Ask several qualified people the same basic questions. Take notes constantly. Do not use a tape recorder, because it will tend to inhibit people from giving as much information as they would without a recorder present. At every interview ask about documents relevant to the case, such as committee reports, meeting minutes, letters, and organizational rules and procedures. Sort fact from appearance. When the facts are straight, you will be ready to organize your thoughts first into an outline and then into a first draft of your paper.

15.4 Elements of an Administrative Case Study Paper

Contents

Your administrative case study will consist of four basic parts:

1. Title page
2. Executive summary
3. Text
4. Reference page

The text, executive summary, and reference page should all conform to the directions in Chapter 3.

Text

The text of an administrative case study includes the following elements:

- The facts of the case
- The environment, context, and participants of the case
- Topic analysis
- Conclusions

The various elements should appear with some attention to this order, but to a certain extent they will overlap. *Ask your instructor for the assigned length of the paper.* In general, case studies should be brief and concise. They may include information from numerous interviews and documents, but only use the material essential to understand the case. A case study can be any length, but a paper of about fifteen double-spaced pages should be adequate to describe and analyze a case situation accurately.

The Facts

Write the facts of the case in story-narrative form. Accuracy is the most important quality of a case study, but writing style will determine in large part the benefit the reader receives from reading it. The facts of the case include a description of the events, the major actors, and their relationships with one another. Your opening paragraph may appear as something like the following:

> Jim Smith found himself alone in a hotel bar far from home on his fortieth birthday. He had entered law school as a career change in his early thirties, graduated in the top fifth of his class, and risen quickly to assistant director of research in the Department of Labor's Division of Legal Research. Last year, on his thirty-ninth birthday, he was happily at home in suburban Alexandria, basking in the glow of his latest promotion, expecting to rise to a senior departmental position in the Washington office and then retire. Now, peering out into Duluth's evening snow, he tried to untangle the series of events that had led him to champion the cause of labor regulation reform, popular with the previous administration but anathema to the political appointees of the latest election.

The Environment, Context, and Participants

The facts that you will reveal in your story will also include the external and internal agency environments within which the events of the situation developed. You should consider the following aspects of a situation and relate those items that are relevant to the case:

- Political and economic factors of the agency's external environment, such as political parties, interest groups, ideologies, and economic interests.
- Political and economic factors of the agency's internal environment, such as power and influence, budget constraints, agency structure, rules, role, and mission.

- Factors of the agency's internal administrative environment, such as administrative style, tone, preferences, and procedures.

Make your story's actors anonymous. Without altering the essential facts of the course of events, alter or delete the names of the actors and the agencies for which they work. Accuracy of facts in a case study is for the purpose of correct interpretation. The actual identities of the individuals involved is irrelevant, and people may want their privacy protected. Any change of facts for this purpose should be done in a manner that does not alter the content of the story.

A well-written case study will reveal much about how public administration is conducted in the agency in particular and in the United States in general. Public administrators face many of the same problems as businesses. They must recruit personnel, establish goals and objectives, account for expenditures, and abide by hundreds of rules and regulations. Public agencies are also, however, very different from businesses in several important respects. A public administrator will often serve several bosses (governor, legislators) and have several competing clienteles (interest groups, the general public). Public officials are more susceptible than people in private business to changes in political administrations. They face more legal constraints and are held accountable to higher ethical standards. In addition, public administrators are more likely to face public surveillance and, finally, they are held accountable to a different "bottom line."

The goal of most businesses is, first and foremost, to earn profits for their owners. The amount of these profits is normally easy to quantify. The success of public agencies is, however, hard to measure. Criteria used to evaluate public programs, such as effectiveness and efficiency, often contradict one another. The United States space program has accomplished some remarkable achievements, but not many people acclaim its economic efficiency. Some of these and similar aspects of public administration will hopefully become evident in your case study.

Topic Analysis

Your analysis should explore and explain the events in your selected situation. It should concentrate on the administrative strategies and practices used by the primary actors, answering such questions as the following:

- How did the situation or problem arise?
- What were the important external and internal factors that directed what transpired?
- What were the major sources of power and influence in the situation, and how were they used?
- What administrative styles and practices were employed, and were they effective and appropriate within the situation?
- How did relationships within the organization affect the conduct of public programs?

Conclusions

In your conclusion you should address, to the extent possible, your explanation of what happened. You should identify the causes and effects of the major events and critically apply your knowledge of public administration to evaluate the actions of the administrators involved. A major benefit of writing and reading administrative case studies is to learn from the successes and mistakes of others. In your conclusion, tell the reader what you have learned from this situation, what you would imitate, and what you would do differently if you found yourself in a similar situation.

16

Case Briefs in Constitutional and International Law

16.1 *Amicus Curiae* Briefs for the United States Supreme Court

When people are parties to disputes before the United States Supreme Court, the attorneys representing each side prepare written documents called *briefs on the merit*, which explain the nature of the dispute and present an argument for the side the attorney represents. The justices read the briefs, hear oral arguments, hold conferences to discuss the case, and then write opinions to announce both the Court's decision and the views of justices who disagree in whole or in part with that decision. Cases that come before the Supreme Court are usually important to many people who are not actually parties to the specific case being presented, because the Court's decisions contain principles and guidelines that all lower courts must follow in deciding similar cases. *Roe v. Wade,* for example, did not become famous because it allowed one person to have an abortion free from the constraints of the laws of Texas, but because it set forth the principle that state law may not restrict abortions in the first three months of pregnancy to protect the fetus.

Because Supreme Court cases are important to people other than those directly involved in the case, sometimes groups and individuals outside the proceedings of a specific case want their views on cases to be heard by the Court before it makes a decision. It is not proper, however, to go to the justices directly and try to influence them to decide a case in a particular way. Influencing government officials directly through visits, phone calls, or letters is called *lobbying*. When people want to influence the way Congress handles a law, they lobby their representative by writing letters or talking to them personally. The lobbying of Supreme Court justices, however, is considered improper because the Court is supposed to make decisions based on the content of the Constitution and not on the political preferences of one or more groups in society.

There is a way, however, for outsiders to submit their views to the Supreme Court. The Court invites interested parties, most often organizations, to submit *amicus curiae* briefs (*amicus curiae* means "friend of the court"). A party that submits an amicus curiae brief becomes a friend of the Court by giving it information that it may find helpful in making a decision. As the Court explains, "an amicus curiae brief which brings relevant matter to the attention of the Court that has not already been brought to its attention by the parties is of considerable help to the Court. An amicus brief which does not serve this purpose simply burdens the staff and facilities of the Court and its filing is not favored" (*Rules of the Supreme Court of the United States.* Effective January 1, 1990. Washington, D.C.: Government Printing Office. 45).

In the summer of 1971 the Supreme Court began its review of *Roe v. Wade.* Roe, who was arrested for violating a Texas law forbidding abortions except to save the mother's life, argued that the Texas law was a governmental violation of the right to privacy guaranteed to her by the Constitution. Many national organizations filed amicus curiae briefs. Acting as attorneys on behalf of the National Legal Program on Health Problems of the Poor, the National Welfare Rights Organization, and the American Public Health Association, Alan F. Charles and Susan Grossman Alexander filed an amicus curiae brief in support of the right to an abortion. The Summary of Argument that Charles and Alexander included in that brief is presented here as an example to assist you in writing your own amicus curiae brief:

Brief of Amici Curiae
Summary of Argument

A woman who seeks an abortion is asserting certain fundamental rights which are protected by the Constitution. Among these are rights to marital and family privacy, to individual and sexual privacy; in sum, the right to choose whether to bear children or not. These rights are abridged by the state's restriction of abortions to saving the mother's life. To justify such an abridgment, the state must demonstrate a compelling interest; no such compelling interest exists to save the Texas abortion law.

The state's interest in protecting the woman's health no longer supports restrictions on abortion. Medical science now performs abortions more safely than it brings a woman through pregnancy and childbirth. Any state interest in discouraging non-marital sexual relationships must be served by laws penalizing these relationships, and not by an indirect, overly broad prohibition on abortion. There is no evidence, in any case, that abortion laws deter such relationships. The state's purported interest in expanding the population lacks any viability today; government policy in every other area is now squarely against it. And any purported interest in permitting all embryos to develop and be born is not supported anywhere in the Constitution or any other body of law.

Because of its restriction, the Texas statute denies to poor and non-white women equal access to legal abortions. It is an undeniable fact that abortion in Texas and in virtually every other state in the United States is far more readily available to the white, paying patient than to the poor and non-white. Studies by physicians, sociologists, public health experts, and lawyers all reach this same conclusion. The reasons for it are not purely economic, i.e., that because abortion is an expensive commodity to obtain on the medical marketplace, it is therefore to be expected that the rich will have greater access to it. It is also because in the facilities which provide health care to the poor, abortion is simply not made available to the poor and non-white on the same conditions as it is to paying patients. As a result, the poor resort to criminal abortion, with its high toll of infection and death, in vastly disproportionate numbers.

Largely to blame are restrictive abortion laws, such as the Texas statute, in which the legislature has made lay judgments about what conditions must exist before abortions can be legally performed, and has delegated the authority to make such decisions to physicians and committees of physicians with the threat of felony punishment if they err on the side of granting an abortion. Unlike more privileged women, poor and non-white women are unable to shop for physicians and hospitals sympathetic to their applications, cannot afford the necessary consultations to establish that their conditions qualify them for treatment, and must largely depend upon public hospitals and physicians with whom they have no personal relationship, and who operate under the government's eye, for the relief they seek. The resulting discrimination is easily demonstrated.

Restricting abortion only to treatment necessary to save the mother's life irrationally excludes those classes of women for whom abortion is necessary for the protection of health, or because they will bear a deformed fetus, or who are pregnant due to sexual assault, or who are financially, socially or emotionally incapable of raising a child or whose families would be seriously disrupted by the birth of another child, and these exclusions bear most heavily on the poor and non-white.

In the absence of any compelling state interest, the harsh discriminatory effect on the poor and the non-white resulting from the operation of the Texas abortion law denies to poor and non-white women the equal protection of the laws in violation of the Equal Protection Clause of the Fourteenth Amendment. (Alan F. Charles. 1971. *Motion for Leave to File Brief Amici Curiae in Support of Appellants and Briefs Amici Curiae. Roe v. Wade.* U.S. 70–18. 5–7.)

Scope and Purpose

Your task in this chapter is to write an amicus curiae brief for a case that is being considered by the United States Supreme Court. You will write your own brief, making your own argument about how the case should be decided. Of course, you do not have to be entirely original. You will examine the arguments used in others' briefs, add new arguments of your own, and write the entire brief in your own carefully chosen words. In completing this assignment you will also be meeting five more personal learning objectives:

1. You will become familiar with the source, form, and content of legal documents.
2. You will become acquainted with the procedures of brief preparation.
3. You will become familiar with the details of a selected case currently before the Court. As you follow the news reports on this case, you will eventually learn the Court's decision.
4. You will come to understand a Supreme Court case in sufficient depth to be able to integrate the arguments of actual amicus curiae briefs into your own argument.
5. You will learn how to write a clear, logical, effective, persuasive argument.

Remember that your goal is to *persuade* the Supreme Court to make a certain decision. Before you begin, reread the first part of this manual, especially the sections on how to write clearly and persuasively.

General Considerations and Format

Briefs provide the Court with the facts in a particular case and make arguments about how the case should be decided. The *Rules* of the Court state that "a brief must be compact, logically arranged with proper headings, concise, and free from burdensome, irrelevant, immaterial and scandalous matter. A brief not complying with this paragraph may be disregarded and stricken by the Court" (28). The Court also requires those who submit an amicus curiae brief to provide a statement of permission, which may be either (1) evidence that permission to submit the amicus curiae brief has been granted by both parties to the dispute; or if the permission of both parties has not been granted, (2) the reason for the denial and the reason that the Court should consider the amicus brief in spite of the absence of permission of the parties.

Of course, as a student writing an amicus brief for a class in political science, you will not actually submit your brief to the Supreme Court, so you will not need to write a statement of permission. Information on such statements is provided here so that you will understand their purpose when you encounter them in your research.

Ask your instructor about the page limit for your assignment. The Supreme Court's limit for the actual text of amicus curiae briefs (exclusive of questions presented page, subject index, table of authorities, and appendix) is thirty pages, single-spaced. Your brief, however, will be double-spaced for the convenience of your instructor and as few as fifteen pages, depending on your instructor's requirements. Your brief will be shorter because a central purpose of this assignment is for you to understand the arguments to be made in the case, whereas actual amicus briefs submitted to the Court require much more detail than you will need to know. As you read actual amicus briefs, use your own judgment to select the material that you believe is most important for the Court to understand, and include this information, in your own words, in your brief.

The proper presentation of briefs is essential. Briefs to the Supreme Court are normally professionally printed, and the *Rules* include directions for this process. The Court does, however, also accept typed briefs, and your amicus curiae brief will conform to the Court's instructions for typed briefs in most respects, with modifications to allow your instructor sufficient space to write comments. You must therefore prepare your amicus curiae brief according to the following specifications:

- Black type on white paper, 8½ by 11 inches, double-spaced, printed on one side only
- Text and footnotes in 12-point type
- A typeface as close as possible to that used in actual briefs
- Margins of 1½ inches on the left and 1 inch on all other sides
- A binding that meets your instructor's requirements

You will submit one copy of your brief to your instructor. It is always wise, when submitting any paper, to retain a copy for yourself in case the original is lost. (The Supreme Court requires that sixty copies of a brief be submitted for a case coming to it directly under its original jurisdiction, and forty copies for cases coming to it under appellate jurisdiction from lower courts.)

Resources for Writing an Amicus Curiae Brief

You will find resources for amicus curiae briefs in the library and on the Internet. When you conduct your research in the library, you will need access to two periodicals that may be found in some college and in most if not all law school libraries:

- *Preview of United States Supreme Court Cases,* a publication of the American Bar Association's Public Education Division
- *The United States Law Week,* published by The Bureau of National Affairs, Inc.

If they are not available in your college library, you may request copies through interlibrary loan or ask your instructor to request that the department or library order them.

Preview of United States Supreme Court Cases contains a summary of the following information about cases that have been filed with but not yet decided by the Court:

- Title
- Docket number
- Date of oral argument (when lawyers present their arguments before the justices in the courtroom)
- Issue discussed
- Facts
- Background and significance
- Arguments for each side
- Counsels of record for each side
- Names of groups submitting amicus curiae briefs in support of each side

The United States Law Week lists the following information relevant to cases at all stages of development before the Court:

- Oral arguments, with names of presenters and dates
- Name
- Docket number
- Subject summary

Internet Resources for Writing an Amicus Curiae Brief

Chapter 8 of this manual provides an introduction to the Internet. If you are not familiar with the Internet or with political science resources on the Internet, you may want to read its directions before proceeding. The Internet provides a wealth of material related to constitutional and international law.

To find cases on the Internet that are currently before the Supreme Court but not yet decided, the best place to start is at the U.S. government's page entitled U.S. Judicial Branch Resources (http://lcweb.loc.gov/global/judiciary.html). At this site you will be informed that "This page contains links to U.S. Judicial Branch Resources as well as other Web sites specializing in legal information." Here you will find links to a wealth of information about statutes, regulations, and judicial opinions. Under the title JUDICIAL OPINIONS on this page you will find this statement: "The following are Judicial Opinions available on the Internet. The Internet should not be considered a comprehensive source for caselaw." This announcement is followed by a list of links to the many types of information, including the following:

Federal Courts

- U.S. Federal Courts Home Page
  - U.S. Federal Judiciary Home Page
    The purpose of this site is to function as a clearinghouse for information from and about the Judicial Branch of the U.S. Government.

- Supreme Court of the United States
  - Supreme Court Opinions (Cornell Law School)

    Includes Supreme Court Opinions from 1990 to current, and selected pre-1990 opinions. The version of Supreme Court Opinions available on the Internet may not be the final version.
- Supreme Court Order Lists and Per Curiam Opinions (Cornell Law School)

  Current Supreme Court Term
- Search Historic Supreme Court Opinions
- Supreme Court Opinions, 1937–1975:

  By case name (FedWorld/FLITE)

  By keyword (FedWorld/FLITE)

  By U.S. Reports volume number (Villanova Law School) Click on volume number, then scroll down list by title
- Leading Supreme Court Opinions, 1793–1966 (via USSC+)
- Comprehensive Supreme Court Opinions, 1945–present (USSC+)

Circuit Courts of Appeal

- Search All Circuit Court Opinions Available on the Internet (via Cornell Law School)

If you click on the link entitled "Supreme Court Opinions (Cornell Law School)" you will find a page maintained by Cornell University Law School (http://supct.law.cornell. edu/supct/), which is offered by the Legal Information Institute under the auspices of Project Hermes. This site contains links to many Court decisions available on the Internet, as well as a link entitled "Schedule of Oral Arguments." If you click on this link, you will come to a page listing the current cases for which oral arguments are scheduled (http://supct.law. cornell.edu/supct/argcal98_1.html). Some of the case names on the list are links to briefs that have been written either for the Supreme Court or for lower courts. If you find a reference in one of these links to a circuit or district court, you can return to the U.S. Judicial Branch Resources page, which provides links to briefs prepared for those courts. By following these links, you will find much of the material you need (for the most important cases currently before the Court).

Steps in Writing an Amicus Curiae Brief

Select a Case and a Side

Using the most recent issues of *Preview of United States Supreme Court Cases, The United States Law Week,* or the appropriate Internet sites, select a case and decide which side of the argument you support. The case you choose must fulfill the following two requirements:

1. It must be of personal interest to you.
2. It must be a case that has not yet been decided by the Court.

Obtain Copies of the Amicus Briefs

Your next step is to obtain copies of the briefs on the merits of the appellant and the respondent and any available amicus briefs on the side of the case that you support and one amicus brief on the opposing side. There are three ways to obtain amicus briefs. You may obtain them by going in person to the Office of the Clerk of the United States Supreme Court at the following address, where you will be allowed to photocopy the briefs (the clerk will not send copies of the briefs in the mail):

> Office of the Clerk
> Supreme Court of the United States
> 1 First Street, N.E.
> Washington, D.C. 20543
> Telephone: (202) 479–3000

The second way to obtain the briefs is to request them from the attorneys of record for the organizations that are filing the briefs; *Preview of United States Supreme Court Cases* lists their names, addresses, and telephone numbers. *The United States Law Week* provides this information for some cases and not for others. If this information is not given in either of these publications, you may request it by mail or telephone from the Clerk of the Supreme Court at the address we have given. Be sure to provide the name and the docket number of the case in which you are interested.

When you contact the attorneys of record, tell them

> Your name and address.
> The college or university you attend.
> The nature of your assignment.
> The name and docket number of the case in which you are interested.
> Your interest in obtaining a copy of their amicus brief.
> Your appreciation for their assistance.

The third way to obtain the briefs, when they are available, is to print or download them from the appropriate sources on the Internet.

Write an Argument Outline

Read the arguments in the briefs you have collected, and then construct an outline of an argument that makes the points you believe are most important. Your outline should normally have from two to six main points. *Follow the directions for constructing outlines that you find in Chapter 1 and read Chapter 6 of this manual very carefully.* Submit your outline to your instructor for advice before continuing.

Write the Argument

Following the outline you have constructed, write your argument. Your writing needs to be clear and sharply focused. Follow the directions for writing in the first part of this manual. The first sentence of each paragraph should state its main point.

The *Rules* of the Court state that the argument of a brief must exhibit "clearly the points of fact and of law being presented and citing the authorities and statutes relied upon" (27). The Court also wants to read briefs that are "as short as possible" (27). In addition to conforming to page limitations set by your instructor, the length of your argument should be guided by two considerations. First, content must be of adequate length to help the Court make a good decision. All the arguments necessary to making a decision must be present. Write this paper as if you are an officer of the Court. Under no circumstances should you make a false or misleading statement. Be persuasive, but be truthful. You do not need to make the opponents' argument for them, but the facts that you present must be accurate to the best of your knowledge.

The second guideline for determining the length of your argument is to omit extraneous material. Include only the information that is helpful to the Court in making the decision at hand.

The *Rules* of the Court require that an amicus brief include a "conclusion, specifying with particularity the relief which the party seeks." Read the conclusions of the briefs you collect, and then write your own, retaining the same format but combining the arguments for the groups you are representing, and limiting your conclusion to two pages.

Write the Argument Summary

After you have written the argument itself, write the summary, which should be a clearly written series of paragraphs that include all the main points. It should be brief (not more than three double-spaced typed pages). The Summary of Argument written for *Roe v. Wade* that is included at the beginning of this chapter provides an example.

According to the *Rules* of the Court, briefs should contain a "summary of the argument, suitably paragraphed, which should be a succinct, but accurate and clear, condensation of the argument actually made in the body of the brief. A mere repetition of the headings under which the argument is arranged is not sufficient" (27).

The summary of your argument may be easily assembled by taking the topic sentences from each paragraph and forming them into new paragraphs. The topic sentences contain more information than your subject headings. As complete sentences arranged in logical order, they provide an excellent synopsis of the contents of your brief. Your argument summary should not exceed two pages, double-spaced.

16.2 Interventions for Cases in International Law

Students in courses in international law may be interested in writing a brief for the International Court of Justice, which was established under Article 7 of the United Nations Charter. The International Court meets at The Hague in the Netherlands to arbitrate disputes between nations that have submitted them for resolution. The Court has fifteen judges, no two of whom are from the same country, elected for nine-year terms by the U.N. General Assembly. Five of the judges are elected every three years.

Guidelines for Writing an Intervention

The rules for submitting briefs to the International Court of Justice are not as precise as those that govern submissions to the Supreme Court of the United States. Cases presented before the International Court have two opposing sides: the applicant's and the respondent's. The brief of the applicant is known as the *memorial.* The brief of the respondent is known as the *counter-memorial.* The Court may also receive a *reply* or a *rejoinder* to the memorial or counter-memorial, but only at the invitation of the Court.

1. A Memorial shall contain a statement of the relevant facts, a statement of law, and the submissions.
2. A Counter-Memorial shall contain: an admission or denial of the facts stated in the Memorial; any additional facts, if necessary; observations concerning the statement of law in the Memorial; a statement of law in answer thereto; and the submissions.
3. The Reply and Rejoinder, whenever authorized by the Court, shall not merely repeat the parties' contentions, but shall be directed to bring out the issues that still divide them.
4. Every pleading shall set out the party's submissions at the relevant stage of the case, distinctly from the arguments presented, or shall confirm the submissions previously made. (Kwniko Matsuura et al. 1992. *Chronology and Factbook of the United Nations: 1941–1991.* Dobbs Ferry, NY: Oceana Publications. 555-56.)

The International Court and the Iranian Hostage Crisis

In November 1979 the staff of the United States Embassy in Tehran, Iran, was taken hostage by followers of the Ayatollah Khomeini. On November 29, U.S. Secretary of State Cyrus Vance wrote the following letter to Sir Humphrey Waldock, president of the International Court of Justice:

Dear Sir Humphrey:
    The Government of the United States is today filing with the Court an Application and a Request for Interim measures of

Protection in a case against the Government of Iran for the seizure, and holding as hostages, of members of the United States Embassy in Tehran. As you are aware, at least fifty United States nationals are being subjected to prolonged and inhumane detention. They have already been held hostage for more than three weeks, and threats have been made that they may be placed on trial.

In view of the extraordinary urgency of this case, which is unlike any before submitted to this Court, I respectfully suggest that you, as President of the Court, urge the Government of Iran to act immediately to appoint its Agent in the case. I further urge that the Court in any event hold any hearing on the request for Interim Measures as soon as it has a quorum. My government earnestly hopes that the Court will issue an Order indicating appropriate Interim Measures within days. As the Secretary-General of the United Nations has informed the Security Council, the present crisis constitutes a serious threat to international peace and security.

May I further respectfully request that you, as President of the Court, immediately request the Government of Iran to ensure that no steps are taken to inflame opinion against the hostages, to heighten the danger to which they are exposed, or to place them on trial.

I have designated the Legal Advisor of the United States Department of State, the Honorable Robert B. Owen, as Agent of the United States in this case. (United States Department of State Bureau of Public Affairs. *Selected Documents No. 14. Iran: U.S. Hostage Case to World Court. November 29, 1979.* Washington, D.C.: Government Printing Office. 1.)

In response to the application of the United States, the International Court heard oral arguments on December 10, and on December 15 issued an order that stated, in part,

THE COURT, unanimously,

1. Indicates, pending its final decision . . . [that] the Government of the Islamic Republic of Iran should immediately ensure that the premises of the United States Embassy, Chancery and Consulates be restored to the possession of the United States authorities under their exclusive control, and should ensure their inviolability and effective protection as provided for by the treaties in force between the two States, and by general international law. (United States Department of State Bureau of Public Affairs. *Selected Documents No. 15. World Court Rules on Hostage Case. December 1979.* Washington, D.C.: Government Printing Office. 1.)

This order was ignored by Iran, and the hostage crisis continued. Orders such as these may affirm the principles of international law, but the International Court of Justice has no means with which to enforce them.

Submissions to the International Court are to be made in one of its two official languages—English or French—and relevant documents may be amended to
the submissions. Submissions must be dated and printed, but no further directions are offered because the Court is responsive to the variety of styles and legal
traditions that exist in different countries.

The International Court does not provide for the submission of amicus
curiae briefs, but it does allow for something similar, because states that are not a
party to but are interested in a dispute may be permitted to intervene. The rules
for intervention appear in Article 81 of the *Rules of Court*.

1. An application for permission to intervene . . . shall be filed as soon as possible
   [and requires the signature of a diplomatic representative of the intervening
   country], and not later than the closure of the written proceedings. In exceptional circumstances, an application submitted at a later stage may however be
   admitted.
2. The application shall state the name of the agent. It shall specify the case to
   which it relates, and shall set out:
   (a) the interest of a legal nature which the state applying to intervene considers
       may be affected by the decision in that case;
   (b) the precise object of the intervention;
   (c) any basis of jurisdiction which is claimed to exist as between the state apply-
       ing to intervene and the parties to the case.
3. The application shall contain a list of the documents in support, which documents shall be attached. (Matsuura. *Chronology and Factbook*. 567.)

Steps in Writing an Intervention

To write an intervention for a course in international law, international
organization, or international relations, first you must obtain the memorial and
counter-memorial for a case currently or recently before the International Court
of Justice. Because information on current cases may be relatively difficult to
obtain, it is not necessary to select a case that is currently before the Court. A case
that has already been decided may provide an opportunity to learn much about
the Court and the details of a specific international conflict.

Materials released by the Court may be found at the libraries of the United
Nations in New York and Geneva and in certain United Nations Information centers. Many law and other major libraries, however, also have collections of memo-
rials, counter-memorials, and past decisions of the International Court. For
information on United Nations publications, contact

United Nations Publications
Room 1059
New York, NY 10017
Telephone: (212) 963–1234

After you have selected a case and have read the memorial and counter-
memorial, select a third country that you believe might have reason to have an
interest in the case. Contact officials in the United Nations, at the U.S. Depart-

ment of State, or at an embassy or consulate of the country you have selected, tell them about your assignment, and ask them for information that will assist you in writing your intervention. You may proceed with writing your own intervention even if the representatives of the country you have selected have not intervened and do not intend to intervene.

Your final step is to write the intervention. Your objectives are to

- Become familiar with the source, form, and content of documents used in the international legal system.
- Become acquainted with the procedures of intervention preparation.
- Become familiar with the details of a selected International Court case.
- Become capable of understanding an International Court case between two countries in sufficient depth to be able to extrapolate the arguments that a third party might make when intervening in the case.
- Learn how to write a clear, logical, effective, *persuasive* argument.

With these objectives in mind, write your intervention to conform to the following guidelines:

- Follow the style and format of the memorial for the case you have selected, although your instructor will probably want your paper double-spaced.
- Include the materials requested by the International Court in Article 81 of its *Procedure.*
- Ask your instructor for more specific guidelines and for a page minimum or limit.

The instructions provided here for writing an intervention are less specific than those for any other paper described in this manual. Much more freedom is allowed for constructing and presenting the paper, for two primary reasons. First, this assignment conforms to the policies of the International Court of Justice itself, which are not as rigid as those of certain other legal bodies. Second, this assignment is likely to be given only in upper-level undergraduate or graduate courses with more experienced students. It is a relatively difficult and challenging assignment and requires an unusual amount of creativity. When writing the intervention, the student will need to learn much about the foreign policy of the country selected. The political culture of that society should also be reflected in the submission. The student presented with such a challenge needs the relative freedom that creativity demands.

16.3 How to Read Supreme Court Decisions

When courts in the United States decide a particular case that is brought before them, they state the reasons for whatever they decide in a document known as a *decision.* They publish their decisions in bound volumes known as reporters. The decisions of the United States Supreme Court, for example, are published in the *Supreme Court Reporter.* The first and last pages of a sample decision follow. The boxed numbers in the same pages refer to the numbers at the beginning of each of the following paragraphs.

1. The name of the case is composed of the name of the party who initiates the action, followed by "*v.*" (meaning "versus"), followed by the name of the party against which the action is brought.

2. West Publishing provides the correct citation for the case: "Cite as 117 S.Ct. 1573 (1997)." This citation means that this case appears in volume 117 of the *Supreme Court Reporter* on page 1573, published in 1997.

3. Jon E. Edmond is a *Petitioner.* This means that Edmond has petitioned the Court, asking the justices to review his case. You may also see in this space the word *Plaintiff,* meaning the party that seeks a redress of a grievance, or *Appellant,* the party who appeals the case from a lower court.

4. UNITED STATES, meaning the government of the United States, is the party against whom the action is being brought. In some cases, such as *ACLU v. Reno,* the government official who represents the United States is named instead of the government itself. This party may also be called *Defendant, Appellee,* or *Respondent.*

5. The number 96–262 represents the Court's docket or calendar number. This number means that this was the 262nd case listed on the Court's docket in 1996.

6. The date the case was orally presented before the Court by attorneys representing each side is listed, followed by the date the Court announced its decision. Other dates may be listed in this space, such as the date the case was granted appeal.

7. This paragraph summarizes the actions taken in the case.

8. The judgment of the Court, with respect to the lower court's judgment, is listed. In this case, *Affirmed* means that the decision of the Court of Appeals for the Armed Forces (that the Secretary of Transportation and not the Judge Advocate General has authority to appoint judges to military courts of appeal) was upheld by the Supreme Court.

9. The Supreme Court's decision is based on an agreement of a majority of the nine justices. Justices who disagree with the decision may file a *dissent,* which explains their reason for disagreeing. Justices who agree with a decision, but who have a different basis for reaching that decision, may state their reasons in a *concurring opinion.*

10. Next appear constitutional provisions and laws relevant to the case.

11. The West Publishing Company inserts a topic (in this case *Armed Services*) followed by a key symbol (⌦). The key symbol is an indexing tool. It means that in this or other volumes that West publishes, information relevant to this topic may be found under the heading *Armed Services.*

12. The information listed here includes general principles of law that would normally be applicable to the case.

13, 14, and 15. There is a hierarchy of constitutional law. The Constitution is the supreme law of the land, followed by treaties, acts of Congress and federal regulations, followed next by state and then local law. Any provision of a lower level, such as local ordinances, that conflicts with higher level laws (such as state statutes), is invalid with respect to the inconsistency between them.

16. The Supreme Court frequently refers to statutes and judgments of lower courts. A court may make several judgments about several different issues in a single case. This citation means that the Supreme Court is referring to the second, third, fifth, and sixth judgments in cases in military justice (MJ) cited as *45 M.J. 19* and *44 M.J. 273*.

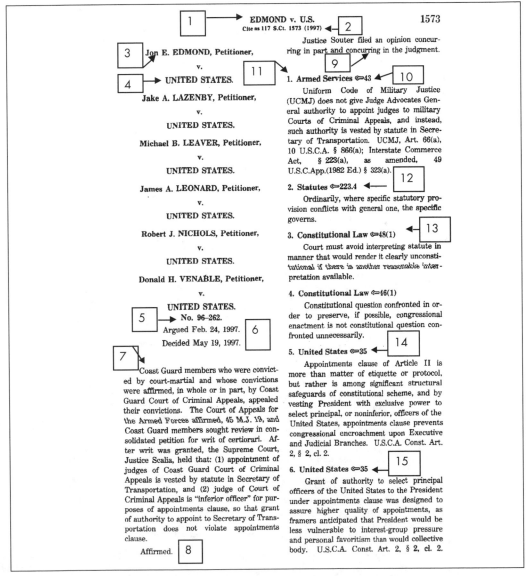

17. In Supreme Court cases, one justice is selected to write the opinion, although she or he may ask the advice of the others. Justice Scalia wrote this unanimously approved decision, and Justice Souter filed a concurring opinion.

16

1576   **117 SUPREME COURT REPORTER**   22

45 M.J. 19 (first judgment), 44 M.J. 273 (second, third, fifth, and sixth judgments), and 44 M.J. 272 (fourth judgment), affirmed.

SCALIA, J., delivered the opinion of the Court, in which REHNQUIST, C. J., and STEVENS, O'CONNOR, KENNEDY, THOMAS, GINSBURG, and BREYER, JJ., joined, and in which SOUTER, J., joined as to Parts I and II. SOUTER, J., filed an opinion concurring in part and concurring in the judgment.

17

Alan B. Morrison, Washington, DC, for petitioners.

Malcolm L. Stewart, Washington, DC, for respondent.

For U.S. Supreme Court briefs, see: 18
    1996 WL 739245 (Pet.Brief).
    1997 WL 33018 (Resp.Brief).   19
    1997 WL 63403 (Reply.Brief).

Justice SCALIA delivered the opinion of the Court.

We must determine in this case whether Congress has authorized the Secretary of Transportation to appoint civilian members of the Coast Guard Court of Criminal Appeals, and if so, whether this authorization is constitutional under the Appointments Clause of Article II.

21   I   20

The Coast Guard Court of Criminal Appeals (formerly known as the Coast Guard Court of Military Review) is an intermediate court within the military justice system. It is one of four military Courts of Criminal Appeals; others exist for the Army, the Air Force, and the Navy–Marine Corps. The Coast Guard Court of Criminal Appeals hears appeals from the decisions of courts-martial, and its decisions are subject to review by the United States Court of Appeals for the Armed Forces (formerly known as the United States Court of Military Appeals).[1]

Appellate military judges who are assigned to a Court of Criminal Appeals must be members of the bar, but may be commissioned officers or civilians. Art. 66(a), Uniform Code of Military Justice (UCMJ), 10 U.S.C. § 866(a). During the times relevant to this case, the Coast Guard Court of Criminal Appeals has had two civilian members, Chief Judge Joseph H. Baum and Associate Judge Alfred F. Bridgman, Jr. These judges were originally assigned to serve on the court by the General Counsel of the Department of Transportation, who is, ex officio, the Judge Advocate General of the Coast Guard, Art. 1(1), UCMJ, 10 U.S.C. § 801(1). Subsequent events, however, called into question the validity of these assignments.

In *Weiss v. United States*, 510 U.S. 163, 114 S.Ct. 752, 127 L.Ed.2d 1 (1994), we considered whether the assignment of commissioned military officers to serve as military judges without reappointment under the Appointments Clause was constitutional. We held that military trial and appellate judges are officers of the United States and must be appointed pursuant to the Appointments Clause. *Id.*, at 170, 114 S.Ct., at 757. We upheld the judicial assignments at issue in *Weiss* because each of the military judges had been previously appointed by the President as a commissioned military officer, and was serving on active duty under that commission at the time he was assigned to a military court. We noted, however, that "allowing civilians to be assigned to Courts of Military Review, without being appointed pursuant to the Appointments Clause, obviously presents a quite different question." *Id.*, at 170, n. 4, 114 S.Ct., at 757, n. 4.

In anticipation of our decision in *Weiss*, Chief Judge Baum sent a memorandum to the Chief Counsel of the Coast Guard requesting that the Secretary, in his capacity as a department head, reappoint the judges so the court would be constitutionally valid beyond any doubt. See *United States v. Senior*, 36 M.J. 1016, 1018 (C.G.C.M.R.1993). On January 15, 1993, the Secretary of Transportation issued a memorandum "adopting"

---

1. The names of the Courts of Military Review and of the United States Court of Military Appeals were changed, effective October 5, 1994, by Pub.L. 103–337, § 924, 108 Stat. 2831.

Reprinted by permission of West Publishing Co.

18 and 19. The attorneys representing each side in the case are listed next, along with the city in which their law practice is based. The numbers assigned by the Court to the briefs (written arguments) submitted to the Court by the attorneys on each side are listed.

20 and 21. Justice Scalia begins his decision by referring to the constitutional principle at issue in the case, and then proceeds to describe the circumstances under which the case arose.

22. The justice who writes the decision normally reviews the major factors in deciding the case, including relevant sections of the Constitution, the facts of the dispute, the strengths and weaknesses of arguments on both sides, and the reasons for which the Court has come to a particular decision. In stating its reasons, the Court will cite its previous decisions, writings of the authors of the Constitution, current social conditions, and many other factors.

17
Public Opinion Survey Papers

Public opinion polls are the barometers of democracy. They describe and sometimes accurately forecast the political climate. If, in a representative democracy, the people hold the ultimate responsibility for determining the content of law and the course of public policy, then opinion polls, to the extent that they accurately express public sentiments, are invaluable guides for heads of state, legislators, and jurists. The results of one or more polls appear in virtually every issue of all national newsmagazines.

Every election year, journalists and political analysts debate the effects of polls on voters' decisions in elections. Much controversy centers on the extent to which voters change their votes according to what they see in the polls. Conventional political wisdom says candidates who appear to have a greater chance to win the election attract more votes than candidates who seem to have little chance to win. This phenomenon increases the importance of the primaries in presidential election years. The winners of the Iowa caucuses and the New Hampshire primary, even though these races are held in states with small numbers of delegates, are able to demonstrate that they can attract voters. These winners then gain momentum to proceed to the other states. Winners attract campaign contributions as well as votes.

On the other hand, voters sometimes vote only for a candidate who seems to have no chance of winning an election. American voters choose this course when they want to protest the choices provided by the Democratic and Republican parties. Third-party candidates often gain enormous numbers of supporters early in their campaigns, when their ratings in the polls are low, but when the polls indicate that they may actually be elected, their support falls off. Their genuinely committed supporters continue to vote for them, but those who wish merely to register a complaint against the two dominant parties usually either switch to other candidates or abstain if the third-party candidate seems to have a genuine chance to win.

There is little doubt that the skillful use of polls can help candidates win elections. Networks have been criticized for predicting the results of elections before all polling places in the United States have closed, because the results may discourage people from voting, thus changing the final result. Campaign consultants now earn large fees by producing accurate information on voter sentiments. Candidates, using privately conducted polls, can find out what issues concern different types of voters (for example, men, women, whites, blacks, wealthy, poor) and then use that information to make their stands on those issues more attractive to the voters. With the information provided by polls, candidates can discover, before announcing a policy position, who will like it and who will not. They can then avoid unpopular positions and take strong stands on issues that are likely to gain them votes. They also can direct their media advertising budgets to selected populations, emphasizing themes specifically tailored to appeal to different interest groups.

Not all polls accurately reflect public opinion, however, and in fact they can mispredict elections. In 1948, for example, Thomas Dewey was declared the winner of the presidential election by the *Chicago Tribune,* but Harry Truman actually won the election. Polls may also be conducted in such a way as to deliberately mislead people about public opinion. If a poll asks, for example, "Do you believe in abortion?" a substantial majority of the American population will answer, "No." But if a poll asks, "Do you believe in criminal penalties for abortion?" a majority of Americans will also answer, "No." If only one of these questions is asked, the results will provide an incomplete picture of American opinion on abortion that can be used to the advantage of one side or another in the pro-life/pro-choice controversy. Students must be aware, therefore, that a poll's validity and accuracy are determined by the manner in which it is constructed, conducted, and interpreted.

17.1 The Scope and Purpose
of a Public Opinion Survey Paper

A *poll,* most simply, is a device for counting preferences. When we go to the polls on election day, the polling officials count the preferences for candidates (and sometimes laws or other issues) that are produced when people mark their ballots. The officers then transmit these results to local, state, or national officials. A *survey* is a series of statements or questions that define a set of preferences to be polled. If a poll is conducted on the subject of national welfare programs, for example, a survey will be constructed consisting of a series of questions, such as "Do you think that welfare benefits ought to be increased or reduced?" or "Do you believe there is a lot of fraud in the welfare system?"

Writing your own public opinion survey paper will serve two purposes. First, you will learn how to construct, conduct, and interpret a public opinion poll, the means by which much research is done within the discipline. You will thus begin to learn a skill that you may actually use in your professional life. Large and small public and private organizations often conduct polls on the public's needs and preferences in order to make their services more effective and desirable. Second, writing a survey paper will help you to understand how to evaluate polls thoughtfully and critically because you will become familiar with the strengths and weaknesses of the polling process.

In this chapter you will learn how to construct and conduct a simple public opinion poll and how to apply some elementary data analysis and evaluation techniques to your poll results. Your instructor may want to add supplemental tasks, such as other statistical procedures, and your text in political science methods will tell you much more about the process of public opinion research. The following set of directions, however, will provide the information you will need to create and interpret a public opinion poll.

17.2 Steps in Writing a Public Opinion Survey Paper

Focus on a Specific Topic

The first step in writing a public opinion survey paper is to select a topic that is focused on one specific issue. Although nationally conducted polls sometimes cover a broad variety of topics, confining your inquiry to one narrowly defined issue will allow you to gain an appreciation for even a single topic's complexity and the difficulties inherent in clearly identifying opinions. Precision is important in clearly understanding public opinion.

Public opinion surveys are conducted on topics pertaining to local, state, national, or international politics, topics nearly as numerous as the titles of articles in a daily newspaper. You will usually increase the interest of the audience of your paper if you select an issue that is currently widely discussed in the news.

Formulate a Research Question and a Research Hypothesis

Once you have selected a topic, your task is to determine what you want to know about people's opinions concerning that topic. If you choose the environment, for example, you may want to know the extent to which people are concerned about environmental quality. You need to phrase your questions carefully. If you ask simply, "Are you concerned about the quality of the environment?" you will probably receive a positive reply from a substantial majority of your respondents. But what does this actually tell you? Does it reveal the depth and strength of people's concern about the environment? Do you know how the respondents will vote on any particular environmental issue? Do people have different attitudes toward air pollution, water quality, and land use? To find out, you will need to design more specific questions. The following sections of this chapter will help you to do so.

To create these specific questions, however, you will first need to formulate a research question and a research hypothesis. Before continuing, read the section in the introduction to this manual on formulating and testing research hypotheses.

A research question asks exactly what the researcher wants to know. Research questions posed by national polls include the following:

- If an election were held today, who would win: Gore or Bush?
- What types of voters are likely to favor free trade agreements?
- What is the social issue about which Americans are most concerned?

Research questions for papers for political science classes, however, should be more specific and confined to a narrowly defined topic. Consider the following:

- Is the population to be surveyed in favor of universal handgun registration legislation?
- To what extent do the people polled believe that their own personal political actions, such as voting or writing to a representative, will actually make a difference in the political process?
- What are the attitudes of the selected population toward legislation that promotes gay rights?

Select a Sample

Surveys of public opinion are usually conducted to find out what large groups of people, such as American voters, members of labor unions, or religious fundamentalists, think about a particular problem. It is normally unnecessary and too costly to obtain the views of everyone in these groups. Most surveys therefore question a small but representative percentage of the group that is being studied. The *elements* of surveys are the individual units being studied. Elements might be interest groups, corporations, or church denominations, but they are most often individual voters. The *population* is the total number of elements covered by the research question. If the research question is "Are voters in Calaveras County in favor of a 1 percent sales tax to pay for highway improvements?" then the population is the voters of Calaveras County. The *sample* is the part of the population that is selected to respond to the survey. A *representative sample* includes numbers of elements in the same proportions as they occur in the general population. In other words, if the population of Calaveras County is 14 percent Hispanic and 52 percent female, a representative sample will also be 14 percent Hispanic and 52 percent female. A *nonrepresentative sample* does not include numbers of elements in the same proportions as they occur in the general population.

All samples are drawn from a *sampling frame,* which is the part of the population being surveyed. To represent the population accurately, a sampling frame should include all types of elements (for example, youth, women, Hispanics) of interest to the research question. If the population is the voters of Calaveras County, a sampling frame might be the parents of children in an elementary school who are registered to vote. *Strata* are groups of similar elements within a population. Strata of the voters of Calaveras County may include voters under thirty, women, labor union members, or Hispanics. *Stratified samples* include numbers of respondents in different strata that are not in proportion to the general population. For example, a stratified sample of the population of Calaveras

County might purposely include a disproportionally large number of Hispanic women if the purpose of the survey is to determine the views of this group.

A survey research design of the Calaveras County issue would thus be constructed as follows:

Research question: Are voters in Calaveras County in favor of a 1 percent sales tax to pay for highway improvements?

Research hypothesis: Fifty-five percent of the voters in Calaveras County will favor a 1 percent sales tax to pay for highway improvements.

Elements: Individual registered voters

Population: Registered voters in Calaveras County

Sampling frame: Five hundred registered voters in Calaveras County selected at random from voter registration lists

Sample: Of the five hundred registered voters in Calaveras County selected at random from voter registration lists, those who answer the survey questions when called on the telephone

How large must a sample be in order to represent the population accurately? This question is difficult to answer, but two general principles apply. First, a large sample is more likely, simply by chance, to be more representative of a population than a small sample. Second, the goal is to obtain a sample that includes representatives of all of the strata within the whole population.

You will find it most convenient if you use as your sample the class for which you are writing your survey paper. The disadvantage of this sample selection is that your class may not be representative of the college or university in which your survey is conducted. Even if this is the case, however, you will still be learning the procedures for conducting a survey, which is the primary objective of this exercise.

NOTE. Public opinion surveys ask people for their opinions. The people whose opinions are sought are known as human subjects of the research. Most colleges and universities have policies concerning research with human subjects. Sometimes administrative offices known as *institutional review boards* are established to review research proposals, to ensure that the rights of human subjects are protected. It may be necessary for you to obtain permission from such a board or from your college to conduct your survey. *Be sure to comply with all policies of your university with respect to research with human subjects.*

Construct the Survey Questionnaire

Your research question will be your primary guide for constructing your survey questions. As you begin to write your questions, ask yourself what it is that you really want to know about the topic. Suppose that your research question is "What are the views of political science students regarding the role of the government in regulating abortions?" If you ask, for example, "Are you for abortion?" you may get a negative answer from 70 percent of the respondents. If you then ask, "Are you for making abortion illegal?" you may get a negative answer from 81 percent of your respondents. These answers seem to contradict each other. By asking additional questions you may determine that, whereas a majority of the respondents finds abortion regrettable, only a minority wants to make it illegal. But even this information may not be sufficient to provide a clear picture of people's opinions. The portion of the population that wants to make abortion illegal may be greater or smaller according to the strength of the legal penalty to be applied. In addition, some of the students who want no legal penalty for having an abortion may want strict medical requirements imposed on abortion clinics, and others may not. You will need to design additional specific questions in order to accurately determine respondents' views on these issues.

The number of questions to include in your questionnaire is a matter to be carefully considered. The first general rule, as mentioned earlier, is to ask a sufficient number of questions to find out precisely what it is you want to know. A second principle, however, conflicts with this first rule. This principle, which may not be a problem in your political science class, is that people in general do not like to fill out surveys. Survey information can be very valuable, and pollsters are found on street corners, in airports, and on the telephone. Short surveys with a small number of questions are more likely to be answered completely than long questionnaires. The questionnaire for your paper in survey research methods should normally contain between ten and twenty-five questions.

Surveys consist of two types of questions, closed and open. Closed questions restrict the response of the respondent to a specific set of answers. Many types of closed questions are used in public opinion surveys, but they may be grouped into three categories:

- Two-choice
- Three-choice
- Multiple-choice

Two-choice questions may ask for a simple preference between candidates, such as

If the election were held today, for whom would you vote: Al Gore or George W. Bush?

Issue-centered two-choice questions offer respondents a choice of one of two answers, most often "yes" and "no," or "agree" and "disagree," as follows:

Is a mandatory five-day waiting period for the purchase of a handgun desirable?

Yes   No

A balanced budget amendment to the Constitution should be passed.

Agree   Disagree

Two-choice questions ask respondents to choose between two statements, neither of which they may entirely support. To find out how many people are ambivalent on these issues, three-choice questions are often asked, giving respondents a third selection, which is most often "undecided," "no opinion," "uncertain," "do not know," "does not apply," or "not sure":

> The political party that does the most for Hispanic people is
>
>   Republican   Democratic   Uncertain

Simple multiple-choice questions are sometimes constructed to provide a wider range of choices, such as in the following:

> If the Republican primary election were held today, for whom would you vote: George W. Bush, Dan Quayle, Pat Buchanan, or Elizabeth Dole?

Just as often, however, multiple-choice questions are constructed to discriminate more clearly between positions in a range of attitudes. For example, *Likert scale multiple-choice questions* are used to distinguish among degrees of agreement on a range of possible views on an issue. A Likert scale question might be stated like this:

> "American military expenditures should be reduced by an additional 10 percent to provide funds for domestic programs." Select one of the following responses to this statement:
>
> Strongly agree   Agree   Not sure   Disagree   Strongly disagree

Guttmann scale multiple-choice questions allow discrimination among a range of answers by creating a series of statements with which it is increasingly difficult to agree or disagree. A respondent who selects one item on the scale of questions is also likely to agree with the items higher on the scale. Consider this example:

> Select the answer with which you agree most completely:
>
> 1. Citizen ownership of military weapons such as rocket launchers should be restricted.
> 2. Citizen ownership of fully automatic weapons such as machine guns should be restricted.
> 3. Citizen ownership of semiautomatic weapons should be restricted.
> 4. Citizen ownership of handguns and concealed weapons should be restricted.
> 5. Citizen ownership of hunting rifles should be restricted.

Closed questions have the advantage that they are easy to quantify. A number value can be assigned to each answer, and totals can be made of answers of different types.

By contrast, *open questions,* or *open-ended questions,* are not easy to quantify. In open questions, respondents are not provided a fixed list of choices but may answer anything they want. The advantage of using open questions is that your survey may discover ideas or attitudes of which you were unaware. Suppose, for example, that you ask the following question and give space for respondents to write their answers:

What should be done about gun control?

You might, for example, get a response like the following:

> All firearms should be restricted to law enforcement agencies in populated areas. Special, privately owned depositories should be established for hunters to store their rifles for use in target practice or during hunting season.

Open questions call for a more active and thoughtful response than do closed questions. The fact that more time and effort are required may be a disadvantage, because in general the more time and effort a survey demands, the fewer responses it is likely to get. Despite this disadvantage, open questions are to be preferred to closed questions when you want to expand the range of possible answers in order to find out how much diversity there is among opinions on an issue. For practice working with open questions, you should include at least one in your survey questionnaire.

Perhaps the greatest difficulty with open questions is that of quantifying the results. The researcher must examine each answer and then group the responses according to their content. For example, responses clearly in favor, clearly opposed, and ambivalent to gun control might be differentiated. Open questions are of particular value to researchers who are doing continuing research over time. The responses they obtain help them to create better questions for their next survey.

In addition to the regular open and closed questions on your survey questionnaire, you will want to add *identifiers,* which ask for personal information about the respondents, such as gender, age, political party, religion, income level, or other items that may be relevant to the particular topic of your survey. If you ask questions about gun control, for example, you may want to know if men respond differently than women, if Democrats respond differently than Republicans, or if young people respond differently than older people.

Once you have written the survey questionnaire, you need to conduct the survey. You will need to distribute it to the class or other group of respondents. Be sure to provide on the survey form clear directions for filling out the questionnaire. If the students are to complete the survey in class, read the directions out loud and ask if there are any questions before they begin.

Collect the Data

If your sample is only the size of a small political science class, you will be able to tabulate the answers to the questions directly from the survey form. If you have a larger sample, however, you may want to use data collection forms such as those from the Scantron Corporation. You may be using such forms, on which respondents use a number 2 pencil to mark answers, when you take multiple-choice tests in some of your classes now. The advantage of Scantron forms is that they are processed through computers that tabulate the results and sometimes provide some statistical measurements. If you use Scantron sheets, you will need access to computers that process the results, and you may need someone to program the computer to provide the specific statistical data that you need.

Analyze the Data

Once you have collected the completed survey forms, you will need to analyze the data that they provide. Statistical procedures are helpful here to perform three tasks:

1. Describe the data.
2. Compare components of the data.
3. Evaluate the data.

There are many statistical procedures especially designed to carry out each of these tasks. This chapter provides only a few examples of the methods that may be used in each category. Consult your instructor or a survey research methods textbook to learn about other types of statistical measurement tools.

Statistics designed to describe data may be very simple. We will start our discussion with two example questions, both employing the Likert scale:

QUESTION 1

"American military expenditures should be reduced by an additional 10 percent to provide funds for domestic programs." Select one of the following responses to this statement:

Strongly agree   Agree   Not sure   Disagree   Strongly disagree

QUESTION 2

"Congress should provide the Department of Defense with more funding for research into germ warfare techniques." Select one of the following responses to this statement:

Strongly agree   Agree   Not sure   Disagree   Strongly disagree

Our objective in describing the data is to see how our hypothetical respondent sample of forty-two students, as a group, answered these questions. The first step is to assign a numerical value to each answer, as follows:

ANSWER	POINTS
Strongly agree	1
Agree	2
Not sure	3
Disagree	4
Strongly disagree	5

Our next step is to count our survey totals to see how many respondents in our hypothetical sample marked each answer to each question:

ANSWER	POINTS	Q1 RESPONSES	Q2 RESPONSES
Strongly agree	1	8	13
Agree	2	16	10
Not sure	3	12	1
Disagree	4	4	12
Strongly disagree	5	2	6

We may now calculate the mean (numerical average) of responses by performing the following operations for *each* question:

1. Multiply the point value by the number of responses to determine the number of value points.
2. Add the total value points for each answer.
3. Divide the total value points by the number of respondents (42 in this case).

To see how this procedure is done, examine the following table, which analyzes the responses to question 1. Notice that column 1 contains the answer choices provided to the respondents; column 2 contains the point value assigned to each choice; column 3 contains the number of respondents who selected each answer; and column 4 contains the value points assigned for each answer choice multiplied by the number of responses.

VALUE POINTS

ANSWER CHOICES	ASSIGNED POINT VALUE	NUMBER OF RESPONSES	(POINT VALUE × NUMBER OF RESPONSES)
Strongly agree	1	8	8
Agree	2	16	32
Not sure	3	12	36
Disagree	4	4	16
Strongly disagree	5	2	10
Total	42	102	
Mean			2.43

We can see that there are 42 total responses and 102 total value points. Dividing the number of value points (102) by the total number of responses (42), we get a mean of 2.43.

If we conduct the same operation for the responses to question 2 in our survey, we get the following results:

VALUE POINTS

ANSWER CHOICES	ASSIGNED POINT VALUE	NUMBER OF RESPONSES	(POINT VALUE × NUMBER OF RESPONSES)
Strongly agree	1	13	13
Agree	2	10	20
Not sure	3	1	3
Disagree	4	12	48
Strongly disagree	5	6	30
Total		42	114
Mean			2.71

We see from this table that the mean of the responses for question 2 is 2.71. Comparing the means of the two questions, we find that the mean for question 1 (2.43) is lower than the mean for question 2. Because the lowest value (1 point) is assigned to a response of "Strongly agree," and the highest value (5 points) is assigned for a response of "Strongly disagree," we know that a high mean score indicates that the sample surveyed tends to disagree with the statement made in the survey question. It is possible to conclude, therefore, that there is slightly more agreement with the statement in question 1 than with the statement in question 2. Comparing the mean values in this fashion allows us to easily compare the amount of agreement and disagreement on different questions among the people surveyed.

Another frequently used statistical measure is the standard deviation, which provides a single number that indicates how dispersed the responses to the question are. It tells you, in other words, the extent to which the answers are grouped together at the middle ("Agree," "Disagree," "Not sure") or are dispersed to the extreme answers ("Strongly agree," "Strongly disagree"). To calculate the standard deviation (S) for question 1, we will follow these steps:

Step 1: Assign a value to each response and the frequency of each response.
Step 2: Find the mean for the question.

Step 3: Subtract the value from the mean.
Step 4: Square the results of step 3.
Step 5: Multiply the results of step 4 by the frequency of each value.
Step 6: Sum the values in step 5.
Step 7: Divide the values in step 6 by the number of respondents.
Step 8: Find the square root of the value in step 7, which is the standard deviation.

Our calculation of the standard deviation of question 1 therefore looks like this:

STEP 1	STEP 2	STEP 3	STEP 4	STEP 5	STEP 6	STEP 7	STEP 8
Value (V) and frequency (F)	Mean	Mean minus value	Step 3 squared	Step 4 times the frequency	Sum of values in step 5	Step 6 divided by no. of respondents	Square root of step 7: standard deviation
$V = 1, F = 8$	2.43	1.43	2.04	16.32			
$V = 2, F = 16$	2.43	.43	.18	2.88			
$V = 3, F = 12$	2.43	− .57	.32	3.84			
$V = 4, F = 4$	2.43	−1.57	2.46	9.84			
$V = 5, F = 2$	2.43	−2.57	6.6	13.2			
					46.08	1.10	1.05

The standard deviation of question 1 is 1.05. To understand its significance, we need to know that public opinion samples usually correspond to what is known as a *normal distribution.* In a normal distribution, 68.26 percent of the responses will fall between (1) the mean minus one standard deviation (2.43 − 1.05, or 1.38, in question 1) and (2) the mean plus one standard deviation (2.43 + 1.05, or 3.48, in question 1). In other words, in a normal distribution, about two-thirds of the respondents to question 1 will express an opinion that is between 1.38 and 3.48 on the scale of assigned point values. Another one-third of the respondents will score less than 1.38 or more than 3.48.

For convenience, we will call the responses "Strongly agree" and "Strongly disagree" *extreme responses,* and we will designate "Agree," "Not sure," and "Disagree" as *moderate responses.* We see that a score of 1.38 is closest to our first extreme, "Strongly agree." A score of 3.48 inclines to "Disagree" but is "Not sure." We may conclude that a substantial portion of the respondents (about one-third) tend to give extreme answers to question 1. We may also notice that the score 1.38, which indicates strong agreement, is closer to its absolute extreme (1.38 is only .38 away from its absolute extreme of 1.0) than is the score 3.48 (which is 1.52 points from its absolute extreme of 5). These results means that the responses are slightly more tightly packed toward the extreme of strong agreement. We may conclude that extreme respondents are more likely to strongly agree than to strongly disagree with the statement in question 1. We can now see more completely the degree of extremism in the population of respondents. Standard deviations become more helpful as the number of the questions in a survey increases, because they allow us to compare quickly and easily the extent of extremism in answers. You will find other measures of dispersion in addition to the standard deviation in your statistical methods textbooks.

After finding the amount of dispersion in responses to a question, you may want to see if different types of respondents answered the question in different ways; that is, you may want to measure relationships in the data. For example, from examining our political party identifier, we find, among our respondents to question 1, 15 Democrats, 14 Republicans, and 13 independents. To compare their responses, we need to construct a *correlation matrix* that groups responses by identifier:

ANSWER	DEMOCRAT RESPONSES	REPUBLICAN RESPONSES	INDEPENDENT RESPONSES	TOTAL (FREQUENCY)
Strongly agree	4	2	2	8
Agree	8	4	4	16
Not sure	3	5	4	12
Disagree	0	2	2	4
Strongly disagree	0	1	1	2

Each number of responses in the matrix is found in a location known as a *response cell*. The numbers in the Total (Frequency) column are known as *response total cells*. From this matrix, it appears that Democrats are more likely to agree with the question 1 statement than are either Republicans or independents. If this is true for the sample population, there is a *correlation* between party affiliation and opinion on the issue.

17.3 Elements of a Public Opinion Survey Paper

A public opinion survey paper is composed of five essential parts:

1. Title page
2. Abstract

3. Text
4. Reference page
5. Appendixes

Title Page

The title page should follow the directions in Chapter 3. The title of a public opinion survey paper should provide the reader with two types of information: the subject of the survey and the population being polled. Examples of titles for papers based on in-class surveys are "University of South Carolina Student Opinions on Welfare Reform," "Wesleyan Student Attitudes about Sexual Harassment," and "The 1994 Gubernatorial Election and the Student Vote."

Abstract

Abstracts for a public opinion survey paper should follow the directions in Chapter 3. In approximately one hundred words, the abstract should summarize the subject, methodology, and results of the survey. An abstract for the example used in this chapter might appear something like this:

A survey of attitudes of college students toward the amount of U.S. military expenditures was undertaken in October 1997 at Western State University. The sample was composed of forty-two students in a political science research methods class. The purpose of the survey was to determine the extent to which students are aware of and concerned about recent defense expenditure reductions, including those directly affecting the Seventh Congressional District, in which the university is located, and to determine student attitudes on related defense questions, such as germ warfare. The results indicate a weak correlation between political party affiliation and attitude toward expenditures, with Democrats favoring reductions more than Republicans.

Text

The text of the paper should include five sections:

1. Introduction
2. Literature review
3. Methodology
4. Results
5. Discussion

Introduction

The introduction should explain the purpose of your paper, define the research question hypothesis, and describe the circumstances under which the research was conducted. Your purpose statement will normally be a paragraph in which you explain your reasons for conducting your research. You may want to say something like the following:

> The purpose of this paper is to define Howard University student attitudes toward federal student aid programs. In particular, this study seeks to understand how students view the criteria for aid eligibility and the efficiency of application procedures. Further, the survey is expected to indicate the amount of knowledge students have about the federal student aid process. The primary reason for conducting this study is that the results will provide a basis for identifying problems in the aid application and disbursement process, and facilitate discussion among administrative officers and students about solutions to problems that are identified.

Next, the introduction should state the research question and the research hypotheses. The research question in the preceding example might be "Is student knowledge of federal student aid related to student attitudes about the effectiveness of the aid programs?" A hypothesis might be "Student ratings of the effectiveness of federal student aid programs are positively correlated with student knowledge of the programs."

Literature Review

A literature review is written to demonstrate that you are familiar with the professional literature relevant to the survey and to summarize that literature for the reader. Your literature review for a public opinion survey paper should address two types of information: the subject and the methodology of the survey.

The subject of the survey, for example, may be a state's proposed secondary education reforms. In this case, the purpose of your literature review section would be to briefly inform your readers about (1) the history, content, and political implications of the proposed reforms and (2) the current status of the proposed reforms. In providing this information you will cite appropriate documents, such as bills submitted to the legislature.

The purpose of the methodology section of your literature review will be to cite the literature that supports the methodology of your study. If you follow the directions in this manual or your course textbook to write this paper, briefly state the procedures and statistical calculations you use in the study and the source of your information (this manual or your text) about these procedures.

Methodology

The methodology section of your paper describes how you conducted your study. It should first briefly describe the format and content of the questionnaire. For example, how many questions were asked? What kinds of questions (open, closed, Likert scale, Guttmann scale) were asked, and why were these formats selected? What identifiers were selected? Why? What topics within the subject matter were given emphasis? Why? Here you should also briefly address the statistical procedures used in data analysis. Why were they selected? What information are they intended to provide?

Results

The results section of your paper should list the findings of your study. Here you report the results of your statistical calculations. You may want to construct a table that summarizes the numbers of responses to each question on the questionnaire. Next, using your statistical results, answer your research question; that is, tell your reader if your research question was answered by your results and, if so, what the answers are.

Discussion

In your discussion section, draw out the implications of your findings. What is the meaning of the results of your study? What conclusions can you draw? What questions remain unanswered? At the end of this section, provide the reader with suggestions for further research that are derived from your research findings.

Reference Page

Your reference page and source citations in the text should be completed according to the directions in Chapter 4.

Appendixes

See Chapter 3 for further directions on placing appendixes at the end of your text. Appendixes for a public opinion survey paper should include

- A copy of the questionnaire used in the study.
- Tables of survey data not sufficiently important to be included in the text but helpful for reference.
- Summaries of survey data from national polls on the same subject, if such polls are available and discussed in your text.

NOTE. Students and instructors should note that the applications of the mean and standard deviation suggested in this chapter are controversial because they are applied to ordinal data. In practice, however, such applications are common.

Glossary of Political Science Terms

Accountability   The concept that an elected official is legally, morally, and politically responsible to the voters for his or her actions

Affirmative action   The correcting of discrimination, usually racial in motivation, through government policy

Amendment   A formal action taken by the legislature to change an existing law or bill

Amicus curiae brief   A "friend of the court" brief, filed by a third party to a lawsuit who is presenting additional information to the court in the hopes of influencing the court's decision

Anarchy   Political chaos; as a political movement, the belief that voluntary cooperation among members of a society is better than any form of organized government, because government generally favors one group over others

Antifederalist   One who opposed ratification of the United States Constitution in 1787

Appeal   The process of asking a higher court to consider a verdict rendered by a lower court

Apportionment   The system under which seats in the legislative houses are apportioned among the states

Appropriation   The act of designating funds in the legislature for particular agencies and programs

Aristocracy   A system of government in which power is held by a small ruling class whose status is determined by such factors as wealth, social position, and military power

Authoritarianism   A belief that absolute power should be placed in the hands of one person or a small group

Authority   The power to make, interpret, and enforce laws

Bandwagon effect   The practice of government officials' attaching themselves to a piece of legislation or a political movement because of its popularity

Bicameral legislature   A legislature that is divided into two houses

Brief   A compilation of facts, arguments, and points of law concerning a specific law case, prepared by an attorney and submitted to the court

Bureaucracy   Any large, complex administrative system, but used most often to refer to government in general

Calendar   The agenda listing the business to be taken up by a legislative body

Capitalism   An economic system in which most of the means of production and distribution are privately owned and operated for profit

Caucus   A closed meeting of party officials for the purpose of selecting candidates for government office

Censure   A method by which a legislative body may discipline one of its members

Census   The counting, every ten years, of the total population of the United States, for such purposes as the apportionment of legislators and the determination of direct taxes

Centralization   The concept of focusing power in a national government instead of in state or local governments

Checks and balances   A method of government power distribution in which each major branch of the government has some control over the actions of the other major branches

Circuit court   A superior court that hears civil and criminal cases, and whose judges serve in courts in several jurisdictions or counties, thus going on the "circuit"

Civil rights   The rights of a citizen that guarantee protection against discriminatory behavior by the government or private owners of public facilities

Civil servants   Government employees who are not in the military

Claims court   A court that hears various kinds of claims brought by citizens against the government

Closed primary   A primary election in which only party members may vote

Cloture (closure)   A rule allowing a three-fifths vote of the Senate to end a filibuster

Coattail effect   The tendency of a candidate or officeholder to draw votes for other candidates of his or her party

Collectivism   An economic system in which the land and the means of production and distribution are owned by the people who operate them

Commerce clause   A clause in Article 1, section 8, of the U.S. Constitution, giving Congress the power to regulate trade among the states and with foreign nations

Communism   A collectivist social system in which all land and means of production are theoretically in the hands of the people and are shared equally by all individuals

Concurrent powers   Powers shared by state and national governments, including the power to tax and the power to maintain a system of courts

Confederacy   A political system characterized by a weak national government that assumes only those powers granted it by strong state governments

Conservatives   Citizens who resist major changes in their culture and their society; political conservatives tend to favor less government intervention in the social and economic life of the nation

Constituent   An individual who resides in a government official's electoral district

Constitutionalism   A belief in a system of government limited and controlled by a constitution, or contract, drawn up and agreed to by its citizens

Contract theory   An explanation of the relationship of the government to the governed in terms of contractual obligation by consenting parties

Court of appeals   One of twelve national courts in the United States set up to hear appeals from district courts

Dark horse   A candidate for political office who has little chance of winning

Demagogue   A political leader who obtains popularity through emotional appeals to the prejudices and fears of the voters

Democracy   A system of government in which the people govern either directly or through elected representatives

Deregulation   The process of reducing government regulatory involvement in private business

District court   The most basic federal court, where federal cases generally are first heard

Divine right   The belief that a ruler maintains power through a mandate from a Supreme Being

Due process   The right accorded to American citizens to expect fair and equitable treatment in the processes and procedures of law

Electoral college   Electors who meet in their respective state capitals to elect the president and vice president of the United States

Elite theory   The concept that, in any political system, power is always controlled by a small group of people

Faction   A group of people sharing certain beliefs who seek to act together to affect policy

Fascism   A right-wing totalitarian political system in which complete power is held by a dictator who keeps rigid control of society and promotes a belligerent nationalism

Favorite son   A presidential candidate, usually with no chance of winning the party nomination, whose name is placed in nomination at the national convention by the person's home state, usually either to honor that individual or to allow the state's delegation to delay committing their votes to a viable candidate

Federal   A type of government in which power is shared by state and national governments

Filibuster   The Senate process of interrupting meaningful debate on a bill with prolonged, irrelevant speeches aimed at "talking the bill to death"

Franking privilege   The ability of a member of Congress to substitute his or her facsimile signature for a postage stamp and thereby send mail free of charge

Gag rule   A rule limiting the amount of time that can be spent debating a bill or resolution in the legislature

Gerrymandering   Redesigning the boundaries of a legislative district so that the political party controlling the state legislature can maintain control

Grand jury   A group of twelve to twenty-three citizens selected to hear evidence against persons accused of a serious crime in order to determine whether or not a formal charge should be issued

Grants-in-aid   Funding given to state and local governments for them to achieve goals set by the national government

Habeas corpus   A court order requiring that an individual in custody be presented in court with the cause of his or her detention

Ideology   The combined beliefs and doctrines of a group of people that reveal the value system of their culture

Impeachment   The process by which the lower house of a legislature may accuse a high official, such as the president or a Supreme Court justice, of a crime, after which the official is tried by the upper house

Implied powers   Powers held by the federal government that are not specified in the U.S. Constitution but are implied by other, enumerated powers

Incumbent   A political official currently in office

Independent   A voter not registered as a member of a political party

Indictment   A formal accusation, brought by a grand jury, charging a person with a crime

Individualism   The belief in the importance of the needs and rights of the individual over those of the group

Inherent powers   Powers not specified in the U.S. Constitution that are claimed by the president, especially in foreign relations

Initiative   A process by which individuals or interested groups may draw up proposed legislation and bring it to the attention of the legislature through a petition signed by a certain percentage of registered voters

Interest group   An organization of like-minded individuals seeking to influence the making of government policy, often by sponsoring a political action committee (PAC)

Iron triangle   The interrelationship of government agencies, congressional committees, and political action groups, as they influence policy

Item veto   The power of governors in most states to veto selected items from a bill and to approve others

Laissez-faire   A "hands-off" policy rejecting government involvement in the economic system of the state

Left wing   An outlook favoring liberal political and economic programs aimed at benefiting the masses

Legitimacy   The quality of being accepted as authentic; in politics, the people's acceptance of a form of government

Libel   A written statement aimed at discrediting an individual's reputation. *See also* Slander

Liberals   Citizens who favor changes in the system of government to benefit the common people

Libertarians   Advocates of freedom from government action

Lobbyists   People who seek to influence legislation for the benefit of themselves or their clients—usually interest groups—by applying pressure of various kinds to members of Congress

Logrolling   A process by which two or more legislators agree to support each other's bills, which usually concern public works projects

Majority rule   The concept, common in a democracy, that the majority has the right to govern

Monarchy   A political system in which power is held by a hereditary aristocracy, headed by a king or queen

Naturalization   The process by which an alien becomes an American citizen

Natural law   The concept, popularized by eighteenth-century philosophers, that human conduct is governed by immutable laws that are similar to the laws of the physical universe and can, like physical laws, be discovered

Nepotism   The policy of granting political favors, such as government contracts or jobs, to family members

New Left   A liberal political movement begun in the 1960s, largely due to the civil rights movement and the Vietnam War, that brought about widespread reevaluation of political beliefs

Oligarchy   A political system in which power is held by a small group whose membership is determined by wealth or social position

Open primary   A primary election in which voters need not disclose their party affiliation to cast a ballot

Patronage   The power of government officeholders to dole out jobs, contracts, and other favors in return for political support

Pigeonhole   The action of a congressional committee that, by failing to report a bill out for general consideration, assures its demise

Platform   The set of principles and goals on which a political party or group bases its appeal to the public

Pluralism   The concept that cultural, ethnic, and political diversity plays a major part in the development of government policy

Plurality   The number of votes by which a candidate wins election if that number does not exceed 50 percent of the total votes cast; a plurality need not be a large number of votes, as long as it is a higher number than that claimed by any other candidate

Pocket veto   A method by which the president may kill a bill simply by failing to sign it within ten days following the end of a legislative session

Police power   The power, reserved to legislatures, to establish order and implement government policy

Political action committees (PACs)   Officially registered fund-raising committees that attempt to influence legislation, usually through campaign contributions to members of Congress

Political correctness   A measure of how closely speech, attitude, or policy conforms to certain affirmative action standards. The term is pejorative when used by conservatives warning of liberal attempts at controlling the public's modes of expression and thought processes

Political machine   A political party organization so well established as to wield considerable power

Political party   An organization of officeholders, political candidates, and workers, all of whom share a particular set of beliefs and work together to gain political power through the electoral process

Poll   A survey undertaken to ascertain the opinions of a section of the public

Poll sample   A selection, usually random, of the larger population of individuals polled

Populism   A political philosophy that aims at representing the needs of the rural and poor populations in America rather than the interests of the upper classes and big business

Pork barrel legislation   A congressional bill passed to benefit one specific congressional district, with the aim of promoting the reelection of representatives from that district

Precedent   A court decision that sets a standard for handling later, similar cases

Primary election   An election, held prior to the general election, in which voters nominate party candidates for office

Quorum   The minimum number of members of a legislative body that must be present to conduct business

Ratification   The process by which state legislatures approve or reject proposed agreements between states and proposed amendments to the U.S. Constitution

Reactionary   One who opposes liberal change, favoring instead a return to policies of the past

Recall   A process by which an elected official can be turned out of office through a popular vote

Recidivism   A tendency for criminal offenders to return to criminal habits

Referendum   Method by which voters in certain states can register their approval or dissatisfaction with a bill proposed in their state legislature

Republic   A government that derives its power from the consent of the people, who control policy by electing government officeholders

Reserved powers   Powers of the U.S. Constitution reserved to the state governments

Right wing   An outlook favoring conservative or reactionary political and economic programs

Separation of powers   A method of stabilizing a government by dividing its power among different branches or levels of government

Short ballot   A ballot listing candidates for only a few offices, as opposed to a long ballot, which lists candidates for a great number of offices

Single-issue group   A lobby group attempting to influence legislation concerning only one cause or issue, such as gun control or funding for education

Single-member district   An electoral district from which voters elect only a single representative

Slander   An oral statement intended to damage an individual's reputation. *See also* Libel

Socialism   A political system establishing public ownership and control of the means of production

Sovereignty   The concept that the state is self-governing and free from external control

Split ticket   A situation in which a voter casts ballots for candidates from different political parties

Spoils system   The practice of rewarding supporters and friends with government jobs

Stalking horse   A candidate whose primary function is to set up a constituency and a campaign base for another candidate, deemed stronger by the party, who will be announced later

Statute   A law passed by Congress or a state legislature

Straight ticket   The practice of voting for all candidates on a ballot solely on the basis of their party affiliation

Theocracy   A political system whose leaders assume that their power to govern comes from a Supreme Being who guides the actions of the government

Third party   A political party different from the two traditional parties and typically formed to protest their ineffectualness

Totalitarianism   A political system characterized by state control of cultural institutions and all forms of industry and means of production

Unicameralism   A legislature with only one house or chamber

Unitary   Referring to a political system in which all power resides in the national government, which in turn delegates limited power to local governments

Veto   The process by which the president may send a bill back to Congress instead of signing it into law

Welfare state   A state in which the government is characterized by governmental redistribution of income

Index

Abbreviations, 123–24
Abortion. *See Roe v. Wade*
Abstracts, 75, 311
Acronyms, 94–95
Ad hominem fallacy, 150
Adjectives, proper, capitalizing, 54
Administrative case studies
  anonymity and, 279
  contents of, 277
  defined, 273
  features of, 274
  Forest Rangers, The (Kaufman), 272–73
  interviews and, 276, 277
  limitations of, 275
  overview of writing, 276
  purpose of, 275
  selecting a topic for, 276–77
  text of, 278–80
  types of, 274
Affirming the consequent fallacy, 146
Afterwords, 125
Alexander, Susan, 282
Almanac of American Politics, The (Barone and Ujifusa), 168
Almanac of Federal PACs (Zuckerman), 181
Almond, Gabriel, 242, 243
American Extremists (George and Wilcox), 208–10
American Lobbyists Directory (Wilson), 181
American Political Dictionary, The (Plano and Greenburg), 169
American Political Science Association (APSA), 9
  home page, 191–92
  subsections of, 16–17
American Political Science Review, The, 9
  on acronyms in author-date citations, 95
  documentation style, 86
American Revolution, John Locke's writings and, 6
Amicus curiae briefs
  described, 282
  general considerations and format for, 284–85
  Internet resources for, 286–87
  obtaining copies of, 288
  reference resources for, 285–86
  scope and purpose of, 284
  statements of permission, 284

  summary argument from *Roe v. Wade,* 282–83
  writing, 287–89
Amnesty International, 170
Analogies, 142
Analysis of the state, 246–47
Analytical book reviews, 200–201
Analytical case studies, 274. *See also* Administrative case studies
Analytical frameworks
  analysis of the state, 246–47
  decision-making analysis, 248–52
  structural-functional analysis, 242–46
  systems analysis, 241–42
Annual Obituary, The (Mooney), 169
Anonymity, in administrative case studies, 279
Antecedents, pronouns and, 63, 64. *See also* Denying the antecedent fallacy
Antecedent variables, 20, 21
Apostrophes, 52–53
Appeal to ignorance fallacy, 151
Appeal to loyalty fallacy, 153
Appeal to pity fallacy, 152
Appeal to the crowd fallacy, 153
Appeal to the stick fallacy, 153
Appeal to unknowable statistics, 150
Appellants, 294
Appellees, 294
Appendixes, 84
  in policy analysis papers, 271
  in position papers, 235
  in public opinion survey papers, 312
APSA. *See* American Political Science Association
APSA author-date documentation system. *See* Bibliographies, APSA system; Citations, APSA author-date system
Arguments
  cogency and, 136
  components of, 133–34
  critical thinking and, 131–32
  examining forms of, 137–38
  fallacies in, 145–54
  logical forms in, 138–14
  nature of, 132
  Socratic dialectic, 132–33
  types of, 134
  validity and, 134–36

Citing Electronic Sources in APSA style.

The most recent *Style Manual for Political Science* (APSA 1993) does not offer models for citing CD-ROMs or on-line materials, and the information on citing electronic sources found in the 4th edition of the *CMS* is inadequate. Therefore, this addendum to this manual offers the following models comprised of elements taken from the APSA *Style Manual* and modified to accommodate information necessary to help students clearly cite electronic source material.

A Source on CD-ROM or disk

To cite a source on a CD-ROM or disk, follow the APSA *Style Manual* format as closely as possible, and then add the following material when appropriate:

An electronic work with a separate print publication

Following the standard APSA-style citation, add the date of publication of the electronic source, the type of medium, and the vender location and name, if known.

Book

> Jones, Randolph. 1995. *Petroleum Policy in the Gulf: How the Fire Started.* St. Louis: Washington Press. In *The Persian Gulf Crisis.* 1998. CD-ROM. Boston: Gattica.

Periodical article

> Schmetz, Ronald. 1998. "Carrot-Dangling and Glad-Handing: Confessions of an Administrative Hack." *Higher Education Policy* 7:201-223. *Daisy Compendium of Policy Blunders.* 1999. Disk. Reno: Daisy E-Sources.

Electronic reference work

> "Rainbow Coalition." *Atlas CD-ROM Encyclopedia.* 3rd ed. 1999 ed. *Gigabyte Multimedia Group.* 1999 ed. CD-ROM. Detroit: Gigabyte.

Online Sources

For online sources, first, identify the type of online source you are citing (book, article, etc.). Then, use the standard APSA citation for that type of source, followed by the date on which the researcher accessed the source and the electronic address, as in the following:

Online book

> Bibb, Dodger. 1998. *How to Administer Anything.* Natchez: Weasel Press. 9 July 1999 <http://www.snafu.com/BS/INDX.html>.

Online journal

> Dowdy, Caron. 1999. "The Suffering of Others: Counting Beans in a Bureaucracy." *Political Science Tomorrow* 2:14-37. 12 April 1999 <http://www.newrgme.com/lstls06.html>.

Online newspaper

> Jenkins, Stella. 1999. "Local Government Faces Changes." *Enid Democrat Online,* 18 October 1999. 2 November 1999 <http://www.enidpap.com/special264.htm>.

Remember that the second date (2 November 1999) is the date on which you accessed the source.

Other source

If the online material is not in a standard format (book, article, etc.), but is in another format (home page, advertisement, etc.), follow the APSA style format as closely as possible, providing information on the author, title and date of the source as well as the date on which the source was accessed and the internet address:

> Robbins, Luther. 1999. "Luther Robbins' Home Page," 13 May 1999. 2 November 1999 <http://www.lutherrobbins. com/>.

If a lengthy electronic address must be broken at the end of a line, do so only after a backslash (/).